JOTTINGS
from the
TRANS-SIBERIAN RAILWAY

Martin Kyrle

Photographs in Siberia and Mongolia
Michael Roberts

By the same author:

Martin Kyrle's Little Green Nightbook

Martin Kyrle's Little Blue Nightbook

The Liberals in Hampshire – a Part(l)y History
Part 1 Southampton 1958-65: object lessons

The Liberals in Hampshire – a Part(l)y History
Part 2: Chandler's Ford 1965-72

At the international Winchester Writers' Conference in 2013 a shortened version entered anonymously (as per house rules) for the Local History competition was awarded a 'Highly commended'.

In preparation:

The Liberals in Hampshire – a Part(l)y History
Part 3 – Eastleigh 1972-80: the thorn in the side bursts into flower

Martin Kyrle's Little Orange Nightbook

Jottings from Russia and the Baltic States

ISBN 978-0-9575220-7-7

Printed by Sarsen Press
22 Hyde Street Winchester SO23 7DR

CONTENTS

Words marked with a star (*) are listed in The Guide to Pronunciation on page 285.
Conversations in italics were in Russian.

PROLOGUE

Martin Kyrle* and Michael Roberts met in the 1950's during their student days at the University of Southampton, living in the same Hall of Residence and becoming friends. Later they chose to rent a house together while Martin, having graduated with Honours in History, undertook his Post-Graduate Certificate in Education. Mike completed his degree in General Arts.

A year later, rucksacks on their backs, mostly hitchhiking, they travelled the length of Norway and came home through Lapland, Finland and Sweden. The following year Mike was best man at Martin's wedding.

Martin stayed in Hampshire while Mike moved around the country, finally settling in Monmouth. Both travelled extensively, particularly after both had taken early retirement from teaching. Mike had always yearned to visit Russia and to travel on the Trans-Siberian Railway but the opportunity had never come his way.

By a strange quirk of fate, both were widowed within a few years of each other. Martin's wife, Margaret, had played a major role in public life as a borough councillor in Eastleigh, school and college governor and as a magistrate in Southampton. Two weeks after her funeral in September 2011 the Council honoured her achievements with a public celebration of her life. Mike attended the celebration and afterwards joined Martin at his home for some dinner.

The scene was set.

The authors. Mike (left) and Martin.

ACKNOWLEDGEMENTS

In planning our extended journey across Siberia and through Mongolia to China, we realised from the outset that it would not be possible to stop at every town or visit every interesting location. We had to make choices. Having decided in principle what we wanted to see or experience and how long we wanted to stay at each venue, we then consulted the Independent Holiday Shop in Winchester, where Alison Walker, with the assistance of Regent Holidays, specialists in travel in Eastern Europe and Russia, booked all our accommodation, guides and travel tickets and advised us how to obtain visas for all three countries.

The success of our journey, which mostly ran according to plan, would not have been possible without this professional help.

We also acknowledge with gratitude the support, professional judgement and immense patience over an extended period that Barbara Large MBE invested to edit this manuscript, my long-standing friend Dr Tony Hill, proprietor of Sarsen Press, for his continued support and advice in ensuring that the finished article finally saw the light of day, Tim Griffiths for designing the cover and Judith Blake for lay-out and design.

TRAVELLING TO SIBERIA

AN IDEA IS BORN

Savouring his coffee, Mike leaned back in his chair. 'I've been thinking about next year', he said, in a slow, measured way.

I murmured something akin to *yerrr*, wondering what was coming.

'The Trans-Siberian Railway.'

The sheer preposterousness of what he'd said took a few minutes to register.

'You're on,' I said. I thought immediately of our trip round North Cape half a century ago. 'We went to outlandish places as young bachelors. We'll do it again as old widowers.'

'I've always wanted to visit Russia but never dared,' he went on. 'I can barely read Cyrillic script. I might get totally lost and out of my depth through not being able to understand notices, let alone verbal instructions.'

'Such as which platform for the train?'

'Precisely. Now you're a widower, you're free to go with me. This is my opportunity! You're my oldest friend.'

I interrupted, 'Not so much of the old! I'm sure what you really mean is *longest-standing?*'

'You know very well what I mean! In the distant past we travelled independently to out-of-the-way places like Lapland. For a journey to Siberia, you'd be my ideal companion. You're one of that generation who did national service and enrolled on the intensive course in Russian.'

I nodded in agreement.

'Why – you even used to teach it!'

'I'm long retired from teaching Russian. I've barely had occasion to speak it in twenty years.'

'With a bit of brushing-up it would come back, at least enough to rely on if we found ourselves marooned in a tricky situation in deepest Siberia.'

'Yeah. Nothing like imminent disaster to drag long-forgotten vocabulary back from the recesses,' I said, thumping my forehead with the butt of my left hand.

Mike continued. 'Here's a thought, though. Should two old blokes like us embark on an extended trip across Siberia on our own, choosing our own stopping-off points?

Shouldn't we just take a package tour?'

'Not on your nelly,' I countered. 'We'd be stuck with what the tour operators think we ought to see, not what actually interests us.'

'And they couldn't be relied upon to find me the best places to photograph.'

'Precisely. We're both seasoned travellers with our own agenda in our heads. All we need to do is agree a *modus operandi*. To start with, how long a trip have you in mind?'

'A month, six weeks?'

'Can you get away for that length of time? You live alone. Who'd look after your house?'

'No problem. My cleaner would come in as usual. As you know, my youngest boy lives across town with his wife and my granddaughter. They'd keep an eye on the house. Deal with such things as picking up the post. How about you?'

'Margaret and I used to go abroad several times a year. Number One Son Humphrey who lived with us always coped. Since his Mum died, he's been looking after his dear old Dad.'

Mike wasn't quite convinced.

'So you reckon no problems?'

'Nothing untoward. I have friends around who will help Humphrey. Or he'd ring Number Two Son, his brother, Rupert. His biggest problem would be getting rid of all our eggs.'

'Yes, I forgot. You keep chickens. What'll happen to them?'

'Watt'll happen to them…Very good!'

Mike looked puzzled.

'What's very good?'

'Chickens have wattles. You know, the dangly bits under their beaks. People unfamiliar with domestic fowl don't always know that.'

'I didn't, but I do know some fowl language.'

'As if I didn't know!'

I went on: 'Before we set off I'll have to dispose of them just to set Humphrey's mind at rest.'

'You mean the Boston Strangler's Night Out?'

'Maybe. Or possibly I'll donate them to a friend. When I get back, I'll buy some replacement stock. I have to do that every year or two years in any case.'

Mike nodded, partly out of relief. Domestic situations sorted, we could now decide when to leave.

Put simply, we could fly to Moscow and take the Trans-Siberian for its entire length all the way to Vladivostok* without getting off.

'I've heard of tour operators offering a package with *cordon bleu* wining and dining to boot.'

'Yes, but from our perspective, utterly boring and denying us what we want most of all: contact with the country, its people and its history.'

'What happens when we get to the end of the line at Vladivostok?'

'We could take a ferry to Japan and fly home from Tokyo. Business class for a flight of that length. Come back in style. What do you say?'

'Well, that's a possibility. Got any other angles?'

'As a variation more in keeping with our interests, we could disembark at various towns along the way to visit the local museums, historic buildings or other attractions.'

'If we choose that option, it raises an obvious question: which ones?'

'I agree. That's the first decision we have to make. After all, the view out of the train window isn't likely to be very inspiring. Hour after hour and perhaps right round the clock of either endless birch forest or endless rolling *steppe*.'

'Mike, I think we'll need to break the monotony. I know a local travel agent. In consultation with her, I'll plan our own tailor-made itinerary, choose which towns to visit and decide how much time we need in each to take in the sights.'

'You'll send me your proposed itinerary before finalising anything?'

'Natch. I'll also build in some rest days to take account of our ages. We're not twenty-something hitchhikers any more. We're men in our late seventies. We may be vigorous and fighting fit for our ages, but birth certificates show incontrovertible dates. I'm reminded of that every time I look at my passport! Someone once wisely observed: Death is nature's way of telling you to slow up.'

Mike looked at me guardedly.

'We did our roughing-it back in our twenties, staying in youth hostels. When they weren't available, sleeping in barns or doorways or even under trees or at the side of a road out in the open. Not any more. Not at my age!'

'How are we going to travel? I mean, what class have you in mind?'

'First.'

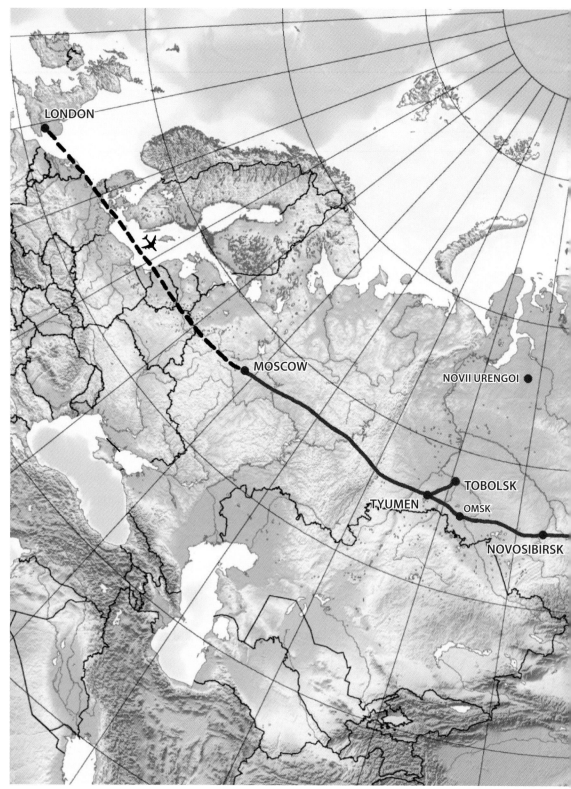

The Trans-Siberian Railway runs from Moscow to Vladivostok and the Trans-Mongolian line from Ulan Ude to Beijing. The authors travelled on the sections shown in red.

KRASNOYARSK

LAKE BAIKAL

ULAN UDE

IRKUTSK

CHITA

VLADIVOSTOK

ULAN BATOR

BEIJING

That was a relief.

He went on, 'What's more, I think we should pay for a whole compartment of four seats so that for the many hours we'll be spending on each segment of the journey, we'll have the comfort and privacy of the entire space to ourselves.'

'If we book all the separate stages on the Trans-Siberian train in advance, we'll board our first train from Moscow with the complete batch of tickets for the rest of our journey. I'll also consult my agent about times between stopping-off points. Each time we get on the train, we need to know how many hours it'll be before we get off.'

'What about guides?'

'I think we should organise one for each place we stay. They can meet us off the train and take us to our hotel. That'll save us from being prey to taxi touts and having to have ready cash. We can build it in as part of our total package.'

'The benefit of having an English-speaking guide at our disposal will be that they will know the short cuts, they'll have the car and driver ready when we need them. We won't need to carry a lot of money because all our expenses for hotels, travel, guides and admission fees will have been paid up front.'

'Including tips?'

'I assume they're getting paid an adequate rate. We won't feel any obligation to top it up in cash. I take it for granted that when we stop for coffee or a meal, we pay the bill, including for our guide. That's a tip of a sort. In restaurants we'll usually be able to pay using a credit card, which means if we want to leave a tip, we can simply add it onto the bill.

A further reason for engaging a guide is that they'll have already bought the tickets. They will be well informed about the things they want to show us. We won't have to go round some exhibit or museum trying simultaneously to read a guide book while looking at the building or artefact or view-point or maybe tomb or headstone. All we'll need to do is look at it and listen to the guide's explanation or description. You can concentrate on taking photos.

What's more, they can answer questions on the spot. We won't have to try reading it up when we get back to our hotel room.'

'Sounds a good idea.'

'Right, let's leave it there.'

'You talk to your travel agent friend. Then give me a ring.'

'You're the geography specialist. Have you given any thought as to the best time of year to do all this?'

'September. Earlier it'll likely be too hot for us, especially if we're having to hump luggage around. Any later, temperatures start to drop. As we're not used to the cold we'd be uncomfortable and probably lack the appropriate clothing. On top of that, because tourists are rare in the autumn and winter, most museums close down.'

'That makes sense. I don't really want the trouble and expense of kitting myself out with the full monty of fur coat, hat, gloves and boots just to protect myself from the elements for two weeks and then never need any of them again.'

Mike nodded agreement.

I drew a deep breath and drew the discussion to a conclusion.

'When I've got the bare bones of a plan mapped out, we'll get together and put the flesh on it. Your place or mine?'

'Mine. Come and spend a weekend in Monmouth. We can chart our course – literally! While you're with me I can show you some of the tourist attractions in South Wales. Ever been down a coal mine?'

'No.'

'Well, if I act as your specialist guide in South Wales, that'll give you some idea of what I expect when you're my specialist built-in expert when we get to Russia.'

A DIVERSION IS PROPOSED

From one of the books he'd bought, Mike had printed out a simple map of Siberia on an A4 sheet of paper. It showed only national borders, major rivers, the line of the Trans-Siberian Railway and a sprinkling of towns.

'Our major stopping-off point in Siberia has to be Lake Baikal*. That's two-thirds of the way across. When we get to the other side, we're only a couple of hundred miles from Mongolia. To most people, that's an even more exotic destination than Siberia! Seems a pity to pass so close to such a country and not visit it when were never likely to get anywhere near it again. How about making a detour?'

'How long would that take? We can't just get to the border, get our passports stamped and turn round and go back.'

'Well, we could but it would be decidedly naff doing a round trip of 800kms just for a stamp in a passport.'

'Where in Russia does the rail link across Mongolia start?'

'According to the map, we leave the Trans-Siberian Railway and change to the Trans-Mongolian Railway at a place called Ulan Ude*, if that's how they pronounce it.'

'Never 'eard of it.' I dropped the 'h' deliberately. 'How long from there to Ulan Bator*?'

'I'll find out. Judging from the map, at least a day. As we have to cross an international border, you can bet your life there'll be all sorts of buggering about at the frontier. I reckon more like a day and a half.'

'How long do we need to stay in Mongolia to see enough to claim that we know something about the place? We need to go somewhere specific to make the diversion worthwhile.'

Looking intensely at the map, Mike continued.

'That means Ulan Bator itself. Along the line of the railway, there's nowhere else big enough to be worth spending any time. Almost certainly nothing of interest to a tourist.'

'We don't want to have to admit afterwards that all we did was cross Mongolia on a train and spend a morning on a whistle-stop tour of the capital in the back of a car having buildings pointed out to us.'

'No, we don't. Exactly my point. We'd never live it down. We know we'll never be there again, so we have to treat it as a once-in-a-lifetime opportunity.'

'It looks like we'll need to allow best part of a week, and then retrace our steps to Russia, pick up the Trans-Siberian Railway again and press on to Vladivostok.'

We studied the map again. Mike pointed to Lake Baikal.

'Ulan Ude lies to the east of Lake Baikal,' I observed. 'It's 5500kms from Moscow, and the capital of the Buryat* Republic.'

'It's quite a learning curve we're facing. Buryat Republic? We're talking about changing trains in a place which until this moment we didn't even know existed!'

'Speak for yourself. The Buryats are one of the indigenous peoples of Siberia. Like most of the other native tribes they have their own autonomous republic, though I'm not sure I could have placed it with any certainty on the map.'

'The point is, from there to the end of the main line at Vladivostok is another

3500kms. It's exact total length according to this map is 9289kms. We're talking enormous distances, with many more hours stuck on the train.'

'I don't think living out of suitcases and changing hotels every couple of days interspersed with train journeys lasting up to 40-plus hours is something our aged bodies could withstand for more than a month.'

'I'm afraid you're right.'

'And, Martin, added to the stress of interrupted travel and interrupted sleep patterns, we also have to consider that sometimes we're going to have to get on or off trains at godforsaken hours in the middle of the night.'

'We're going to have to make choices. We can't do it all.'

'It's getting very complicated. Damned sight easier to take that package tour.'

'But a lot less fun! Remember all those years ago how pleased with ourselves we were when we saw North Cape, knowing we'd got there under our own steam, not as part of some coach party?'

'There's another problem at our age. We have to maintain our personal health for the entire duration of the trip. I'm on permanent age-related medication. I take six pills a day, four in the morning and two in the evening. You must have a similar regime.'

'Yes, we both need to consult our doctors. We need some specialist advice in case there are particular localised risks in Siberia.'

'Yes, there will be, but not as many as you might expect. After all, we're not going camping in the forests full of nasty insects or poisonous reptiles. We're going to travel first class on a train in the south of the country and stay in proper hotels mostly in modern cities.'

'But Siberia is pretty remote.'

'Parts of it are. About as remote as you can get. But we're not going to those parts. We're sticking to the main line. In the towns where we stop we'll never be far from medical help if we need it. It's just sensible when going so far from home to check that all our injections are in order and up-to-date. Do you know when you last had an anti-tetanus jab?'

'No.'

'Me neither. See the quack and find out. I'll do the same, if only to make absolutely certain that my travel insurance remains valid. I shall have to explain to the doc why I want him to prescribe me six weeks' supply of pills.'

'And prepare a dossier in Russian, explaining what they are and that they're prescribed by your own doctor for personal use. We don't want to give some jobsworth on the frontier an excuse to run us in for drug smuggling!'

'Ultimately our decisions with regard to the duration of our trip are governed by the fact that Russian visas are valid for 31 days from entering the country. And they don't permit re-entry unless applied for in advance.'

'How do you know?'

'I found out when I went to Russia last year.'

'On that twinning visit you told me about?'

'Precisely. My second point is this: once we've decided to take out a week to visit Mongolia, we'll have to factor in the immense expanse of a country which is the size of Western Europe and the time it'll take to cross it.'

'Are we going to need visas?'

'China and Russia both require visas, 'cos I've been there before. I'd take bets that Mongolia will be the same.'

'Application forms for visas are very detailed and complicated. Getting these takes time. Getting all three within the time available might even mean travelling to London and going in person to each embassy.'

'I'll ask my travel agent.'

The following week I tackled her. She told me that getting visas for customers wasn't part of their service and advised us to use a specialist agency. Set against the cost of their fees was the fact that they were familiar with each country's particular requirements for filling in application forms. They could guarantee to obtain them in time.

'From Ulan Ude to Ulan Bator is a train journey of 23 hours.'

'And then we fly home?'

'Not from there. There are no direct flights from Mongolia to UK. The nearest airport with direct flights to London is Beijing. We'll have to take the train from Ulan Bator, and that takes another 32 hours. A further complication is that there's only one train a week, on a Thursday.'

'You mean we're faced with an immovable *rendez-vous*, the once-a-week train from Ulan Bator to Beijing? Our entire schedule of visiting towns in Siberia will have to be worked out counting backwards from that?'

'Hole-in-one.'

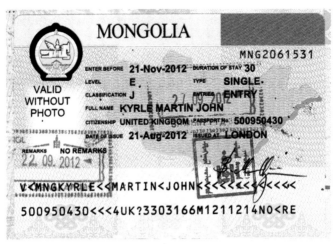

Mongolian visa.

That was it. We had reached a conclusion.

'Plan A: the Trans-Siberian Railway all the way from Moscow to Vladivostok, is shelved, and replaced by Plan B: Moscow to Ulan Ude and then divert to Mongolia, spend four or five days there and fly home from China.'

'Look's that way. We've weighed up all the pros and cons and made a decision.'

'Now the flights,' Mike said, moving on. 'I can arrange discounted flights, completely reliable. It'll cut our fares by up to 75%.'

'You *what?*' I did a double-take. Then I remembered that Mike took regular flights to Australia and understood the aviation market far better than I did. For this level of discount, you don't have second thoughts about working your other travel dates around the specific flights that the airline offers you.

Mike didn't book our flights through our travel agency, but did it himself. To take advantage of our discounts we'd have to travel to Moscow on Thursday 30th August and leave Beijing on Monday 1st October.

'That means,' I said, looking at the calendar in my pocket diary, 'to go by train to Beijing we'll have to travel on the previous Thursday, 27th September, and kick our heels in China over the weekend until our scheduled flight home.'

'If we agree that our minimum time visiting Mongolia is five days that'll mean leaving Ulan Ude on Saturday 22nd September. We're going to have a window of approximately three weeks on the Trans-Siberian Railway.'

'What I must do,' I said, 'is read the guide books and decide what visits to make and for how long, within those three weeks. Stopping at every sizeable town is clearly impossible. I'll have to do some hard thinking and by a process of elimination ensure that we see the most interesting sights while also allowing for breathing spaces in between.'

'Fine by me. You're the expert. We have almost identical tastes as regards what we want to do and see. Go ahead. At the end of all this, are you going to write another book?'

'Of course. Only this time it'll be beautifully illustrated, not just happy snaps of the sort Margaret used to take with her pocket Kodak when we were in France or Holland. It'll be a combined effort: my text and your pictures. I know you've taken up the serious study of photography since Anne died. What sort of camera have you got?'

'It's a Canon 40D with a Canon 24mm-105mm lens attached.'

'Means nothing to me. I guess other people will know what that means in terms of quality of photos.'

'Yeah, not everyone's as technophobic as you. Didn't Margaret once say to someone that in your eyes the wheel was a dangerous modern invention? I'll bring along my folding tripod, too. You never know when it might be just the thing I need to line up a sunset or catch the moment a ferry enters harbour. That's why I've got a folding one which I can carry around when I haven't got my car.'

'Sounds like we have a plan. Onward and upward! By the way, when we get to Moscow I'll have to send an e-mail to Kimry.'

'You what?'

'Kimry. It's a town on the Volga about 125kms north-west of Moscow. It's twinned with our German twin town, Kornwestheim, which gives it a tentative connection with us, a sort of twinning once removed. In April 2011 their mayor invited our Twinning Association to send a delegation. As a member of the party who took up that invitation I visited the town and then helped to entertain them when they paid us a return visit the following March.

My concern is that if they later discover that I'd come to Moscow and hadn't told them, bearing in mind that in their eyes Kimry's not that far away, they might be upset or offended. The least I can do is inform them and ask if anyone from the town would like to meet us in Moscow, enjoy a day out together and perhaps be our guests for lunch at some interesting location chosen by them.'

A PRELIMINARY SKIRMISH IS AGREED

'We've always known that our trip would start in Moscow, but you've never been there. In years to come no one would understand how yes, you've been to Moscow but no, you haven't seen the Kremlin.'

'True. Yes, I'd like to see the main tourist attractions while we're there, just in case I never get another chance.'

'Looks like our trip to Siberia will have to be preceded by a few days in the capital while I show you the principal sights. I'll ask our travel agent to book us into a Moscow hotel for a few days. We can then do Red Square and have our photos taken outside St Basil's Cathedral, like all the tourists! Once we've filled in that hole in your travel diary, she can send us off across Siberia.'

Park in Moscow outside the Kremlin.

THE JOURNEY BEGINS

'To Moscow!' – as Napoleon once said. And, as is well known, lived to regret it.

'Our flight's booked for Thursday 30th August at 08h50. The airport will want us to check in two hours prior to departure. That means getting there just before seven. To be sure of getting there by that time will mean leaving home in the middle of the night, while also taking a chance that the road'll be clear and that there are no accidents or traffic hold-ups.'

'I think it makes sense to book into a hotel near Heathrow for the night prior to departure,' I said. 'We can arrange an early alarm call and use the special bus to make sure we get to the check-in desk on time. As you live in Monmouth and I'm in Eastleigh, it makes sense if you collect me. We only have to leave one car at the hotel.'

Mike arrived mid-afternoon. 'Have you packed everything?' He was worrying about me already! 'Six weeks' supply of pills?'

'Yeah. Doctor was very accommodating. And very interested in the trip. He bought one of my previous books and enjoyed it. Says he's looking forward to reading all about our journey when I get back.'

'Ha,' laughed Mike. 'Lining up the customers already, and you haven't even written it yet!'

'In marketing terms, I think it's known as 'forward planning'. More to answer your point, he said there are no particular health risks attached to going to Siberia *per se*. It depends entirely which part you're going to and what you're going to do when you get there.

'It would be a different matter if we were going trekking or climbing, or to remote areas where they don't have hospitals. He gave me a couple of extra injections, against typhus and hepatitis A, just to be on the safe side, mainly because of my age.

I see you're taking two cases. I've got all my stuff into one.'

'Can you lift it shoulder-high, if we have to stow it on a luggage rack above our beds on the train? Are you sure there'll always be enough room for a case of that size? That's why I opted for two standard size ones.'

'Hmmm. See your point. Too late now. Just have to hope for the best.'

'I've also brought my spare pair of glasses in case anything dire happens to the ones I normally wear. I'd be stuck because I can't read without them. I've also brought the special ones I use for reading a computer screen so that if I want to use your laptop I won't have to keep squinting through my bi-focals.'

'Eminently practical.'

'You know me. Did you expect anything less? Compared to hitchhiking across Lapland, this is going to be a doddle. First class, and all that. With everything booked in advance.'

'And do we always have a first class compartment to take?'

'Not always, but we've reserved the top quality of whatever's available. All our tickets are booked and paid for whether they're for trains or long-distance taxis or admission to museums. A guide's lined up to meet us every time we get off the train. The tickets themselves are issued by the agency's office in Moscow. Our guide there will hand them over.'

'Can you guarantee the guides will all be there, waiting?'

'No, of course I can't. All I'm saying is that everything which we could plan and book in advance, we have. Just have to hope it all falls into place.'

'And if things go wrong, then I'm relying on you to do the talking!'

'Fingers crossed. You'll be reassured to know that I've been mugging up some of my old Russian books and tapes. I reckon I'll be able to cope if the necessity arises.'

The journey to the hotel was uneventful. We checked in and made our way to our room. Yes, we were sharing. Partly this was to avoid unnecessary expense, but also because as we were about to spend many days and nights together in a compartment on the railway, it would be a bit odd to be squeamish about sharing a hotel room.

I'd brought my ear plugs in case my room-mate snored.

'What time do you reckon we should have an alarm call? They want us at the airport just before seven. If we leave about six – alarm call at o-five-thirty?

'Right.'

'We won't bother with breakfast. We'll have something when we've checked in. It'll also help pass the time. That reminds me, I must remember to get a paper.'

'Or even two. Might be difficult to find an English newspaper in Moscow. Even harder to find the one you read!'

'Point taken. Anyway, half-past five is a couple of hours before either of us usually get up in the morning!'

'You may recall my earlier point about counting backwards from the Thursday train from Ulan Bator to Beijing and having to make all the preceding times and dates fit all the way across Siberia? Even before we start, we're having to do the same exercise in counting backwards.'

The hotel bus deposited us well on time at the taxi parking area where the cabs left at intervals to take passengers to their individual flights.

'I smell trouble. Our driver keeps getting ready to go and then aborting departure to scour the car park for more possible clients.'

'What's he up to now? We got on this damned people-mover half an hour ago, and he *still* hasn't left!'

'He's faffing about trying to fill up the empty seats. Maybe he gets paid per person and makes more money the fuller it is.'

We wasted fully half an hour sitting in the vehicle before the driver finally got the message that we, the passengers he already had on board, had planes to catch and would he please do his job: drive us to the bloody airport. Like *NOW!*

He got the message.

We did arrive well in time, but to some extent, unnecessarily flustered.

'Getting from our hotel to Heathrow hasn't gone too well. An augury of things to come?'

'Hopefully not, when we're five thousand miles from home.'

Heathrow was absolutely jam-packed.

'It's full of people all eyes-down trying to find their way to their check-ins and relying on signage to direct them. If you're not a regular traveller who knows the ropes, it's all a bit daunting.'

'Now, where's the business class lounge? Can't see any signs.'

We had to make enquiries several times before eventually we found it.

'Gentlemen, please help yourselves to refreshments: tea, coffee, biscuits?'

'Thank you, yes. Two black coffees.'

'These biscuits are in packets,' I whispered to Mike. 'What say we snaffle a few against possible future emergencies?'

'You mean, in case we're on the train and we've missed a meal?'

'Yes. And some sugar packets, too. They may only serve coffee on the train with one spoonful per person. I take two. Saves me having to ask every time, and running the risk of being refused because they have a policy of 'one person, one packet'. The concept of customer service isn't quite so well established in Russia as it is in the West.'

It proved a well-founded stratagem a week or so later, when, on a train with no restaurant car, we ran out of food. At least we had a few biscuits.

Have I got everything I need for a month?

Boarding the aircraft we turned left instead of right. Everyone who's flown on a scheduled flight will know what that means! For those who don't, it means you're not travelling with the *hoi polloi* but with the toffs!

We were ushered into the luxurious lounge with its soft lighting and adjustable full-length beds and allocated adjoining berths. Travelling business class for the first time was a revelation of how the other half have been living all my life.

Mike wasn't fazed. He regularly visits his eldest son in Australia and on long-haul flights always travels business class.

About an hour into the flight the stewardess approached me. 'A glass of champagne with orange juice chaser, Sir?'

Really? Just like any week-day mid-morning back at the ranch. Maybe I should give some thought to upgrading my life-style....

I thought to myself, 'I could get used to this!'

Accustomed to travelling steerage, the extra comfort and the space to lie flat and sleep properly as opposed to leaning back in an upright chair nodding off for little more than a cat-nap was, after all's said and done, most welcome at my age. I roughed it enough on the by-ways of Europe as a young man, sleeping in youth hostel dormitories or even out in the open in a sleeping bag on a groundsheet.

'They were great days,' I said to Mike, 'but now that I'm approaching eighty I no longer fancy roughing it.'

Day 1: MOSCOW

We arrived in Domodedovo*, Moscow's international airport, at mid-afternoon.

'This is the real beginning of our trip. We're supposed to be being met by a guide. Let's hope she's there.'

'What if she's not?'

'God knows. Got the name of the hotel. I suppose we'd just have to take a taxi.'

A lady of middling years was holding up a card with our names in large letters. I went up to her.

'Hello!' I said. 'We're the 'Kyrle' and 'Roberts' on your card.'

'Your taxi's waiting. This way.'

From clearing customs and passport control to being in a taxi *en route* for our hotel took barely ten minutes. Our feet hardly touched the ground. We were denied any chance to explore the airport or do any quick shopping. I presumed that she had other passengers to meet. As her sole function was to send us on our way, that's what she did.

The first inkling that our month's trip wasn't going to be without incident was immediately apparent: our four-hour flight from Heathrow was followed by three-and-a-half hours in successive traffic jams as our taxi conveyed us in fits and starts from the airport on the outskirts of Moscow to our hotel near the centre, a distance of only some 17kms.

'Talk about gridlock!' I said to Mike. 'What it costs the authorities in terms of wasted fuel, wasted time and air pollution hardly bears thinking about. '

'*You're* thinking about it!'

'Hardly the point. I've heard that Muscovites complain about it all the time, but nothing gets done.'

'Maybe nothing can.'

'I've no doubt Ivan the Terrible, Peter the Great or Stalin would have sorted it all out in a week, give or take a few executions.'

'Sort of 'Do this *now!* Chop! chop'!'

'In a manner of speaking. How's about 'Do this like a shot' only spelled out in two sentences: 'Do this. Like a shot?' Mind you, Russia today may be far from being a model democracy but it's no longer a totalitarian state. Any proposed solutions would have to be economically viable and have at least some modicum of public acceptance.'

'Our driver seems to have had the foresight to grease the sides of his vehicle. He keeps changing lanes all the time…'

'So do all the other drivers', I barked. '… and squeezing into spaces where, to us back seat drivers, there clearly isn't room.'

The driver dropped us off.

'It's almost four hours since we left the airport!'

'Well, we're here now. At last we can settle in, freshen up and find some dinner. It's been a *very* long day.'

We note that Hotel Assambleya Nikitskaya* is located on a street corner. Its entrance lobby has internal doors so that in winter the outside cold air doesn't blow in. We lug our bags down the three steps to the reception area with its desk on the right.

The receptionist, a smart young man in his early twenties and wearing a badge giving his name as 'Lev'*, greeted us.

'Good day. Can I have your names, please?'

'Kyrle and Roberts. We're booked in for five days.'

Our hotel in Moscow.

He gave us our room number and the key.

'Breakfast is served at the breakfast bar.' He indicated the bar, on the opposite side of the lobby. 'It's served on a 'help yourself' basis. There's unlimited coffee on demand. We don't have a restaurant, but we have an 'arrangement' with one. If you tell them you're guests here, they'll give you a 10% discount.'

We moved into the bar area and took stock.

'Tables look a bit on the small side. Only really room for two people.'

'I suppose this is a hotel which doesn't reckon to be much used by families with small children.'

Between us and the bar was a lounge area furnished with a couple of armchairs and sofas.

'You have a lift?' Mike asked. 'At the end of a pretty exhausting day starting with getting up at five-thirty I'm not looking forward to having to carry my case upstairs.'

'Of course, Sir. Just round the corner by the breakfast bar. You're on the second floor.'

The lift was rather larger than I'd expected.

'Bags of room!'

'Just as well. We've got bags.'

'Ha! bloody ha!'

'Here at last!'

We opened the door and manoeuvred ourselves inside with our cases. A surprise awaited us.

'Aye, aye. There's only one bed!'

'Yes, but look at the size of it! More than full size double, more like a triple. Just be careful not to roll over too far. You might get more than you bargained for…'

Part of the room had a sloping ceiling with a blind to keep out daylight. On the door was a notice advising against leaving the skylight open as rain might blow in, with an added warning that in winter snow deposited higher up the roof might slide down and end up on the floor.

The bathroom was well-appointed, with a range of complimentary toiletries. The lavatory was set in an alcove at the back. The shower consisted of a hose and sprinkler over the bath.

'We need to decide where to put our cases. There isn't much floor space. This is going to be home for five nights.'

'I think you put yours up in the corner on your side of the bed. You've got two small ones. They'll just fit in there.'

'And yours?'

'It's too big to go in the corner. I guess it'll have to be against the wall opposite the end of the bed.

My first priority,' Mike went on, 'is to get you to put my drops in my left ear. It should have been done some hours ago, but we could hardly stop the taxi and ask for five minutes' privacy.'

'That would certainly have stretched my Russian! With the added imperative that had the driver misunderstood we might have ended up getting arrested for offending public decency.'

After the required five minutes lying still to allow the drops to penetrate, it was time to find some dinner.

The shift at reception had obviously changed. Instead of Lev, two girls were in place, wearing badges announcing them as Alyonna* and Ksenia*.

'What's the name of the restaurant where you have an arrangement?' I asked.

Alyonna gave me the name.

We set off. A full kilometre later, walking directly into a setting sun and most of the time completely blinded by it, we had still failed to locate it.

'Any farther and we'll have left Moscow. Where the hell is it?'

'Let's to go back to the hotel and seek clarification.'

We retraced our steps and had just reached the hotel when…

'Bugger me – it's right next door!'

'We must have missed it because the name isn't on the entrance door or doorway, it's on the restaurant window.'

'We've had half-an-hour's appetite-inducing walk all for nothing!'

'Let's hope we don't have too many more long, pointless walks.'

It was the end of a *very* long day, but the effective start of our project.

On Day One of our stay in Moscow our guide was scheduled to meet us for our first excursion, a guided tour of the Kremlin. To allow for the fatigue of the day's journey, we'd arranged for this to be a late start: 10 o'clock.

Friday, 31st August
Guided tour of the Kremlin and Armoury Museum

Our guide was waiting for us at the reception desk at the appointed time.

'Hello. My name is Olga*. I'm your guide.' She was an attractive young woman, smartly dressed and rather pretty.

'I'm Martin. This is Mike. You can call us by our first names. I'd better warn you, he'll be stopping all the time to take photos.' I made an exaggerated gesture with my forefinger in Mike's direction. 'That's why he's come.'

'Have you been to Moscow before?'

Mike shook his head. 'This is my first time.'

'I have, yes. The first time was over fifty years ago. I attended the World Festival of Youth and Students in 1957 when I was at university. Last year I came to Kimry on a twinning visit and our hosts met us at Domodedovo but entertained us in Moscow for a day to see the main sights before taking us off to the town. Do you know Kimry?'

'I know where it is, but I've never been there. What's your connection? You said a twinning visit. You mean the town you're from in England is twinned with it?'

With Olga, our guide in Moscow.

'No. We have a twin town in Germany, and Kimry's twinned with *them*. Their mayor would like to make it a three-way twinning, but our council won't do it because of the cost implications. The Twinning Association is separate from the town council. We're developing a relationship with them independently and exchanging visits.'

'Tell me again where it is,' Mike chipped in.

'It's 125 kms north-west of Moscow, on the Volga.'

I turned back to Olga. 'How did you become a guide? I've always been interested to know why people do the jobs they do. Is it chance, or choice?'

'I did the training course and took specialist exams to become a Moscow tourist guide, and that included learning English.'

'We're at your disposal! Let's go!'

After spending most of yesterday sitting in an airport lounge, sitting or sleeping on a plane and then sitting in a taxi, it was a relief to get some exercise and get the old legs moving again. The Kremlin was only a ten minute walk.

Olga began to explain. 'The Kremlin in Moscow is the finest example, but by no means unique.'

I chipped in. 'First among equals', or as the Romans so eloquently put it: *primus inter pares.*'

'You mean there are others?' asked Mike.

'All historic Russian towns had a kremlin. In Russian, *kreml* simply means a fortified post. Historic towns in Britain often have a castle, just as in France you'll find a château or the ruins of one. Our equivalent of Moscow's Kremlin is the Tower of London but there are other medieval fortresses elsewhere in the country.'

'All as big as this one?'

'No, this is by far the biggest but that's because in the Middle Ages it was the Tsar's residence and the seat of government. It's also built entirely of stone and brick, whereas many in smaller towns were built of wood and haven't survived.'

'The climate?'

'Yes, or destruction in war or revolution. But some are comparatively well preserved. It's the same in Russia as it is back home.'

Within the fortress walls the collection of buildings reflected the architectural tastes at different epochs since its initial construction. In front of us was a concentration of several very ornate churches with the familiar onion-shaped domes and highly decorated mosaic and brick features dating from the centuries of Tsarist rule up to 1917.

The modern buildings are more austere, such as the one which, during the Communist era, housed the Supreme Soviet until its demise in 1991 and the functional present-day Senate building which houses the President's office.

Having Olga as a guide made all the difference. She took us directly to where we could best admire the most interesting panoramas, whether historic buildings or those now accommodating the Russian Government, enabling Mike to line up good shots. We didn't waste the time that we would have wasted if we'd been trying to find our way on our own. Olga knew exactly where to take us.

'Let me show you the famous *Tsar kolokol*,' she said. 'It's one of the main tourist attractions. The great bell was commissioned by the Tsaritsa Anna, niece of Peter the Great. She reigned from 1730-1740.'

The Church of the Nativity dates from 1393.

Olga explained that work began in 1734.

'By 1737 decoration had been completed and it was hoisted above the casting pit to cool. Unfortunately, a fire broke out which burnt through the wooden supports holding the bell. Attempts to put out the fire with water caused differential cooling. When the damaged supports gave way, the bell fell back into the pit and a piece broke off.

The bell is 6m high and 6.6m in diameter and weighs just over 200 tons. The broken piece alone weighs 11 tons. The decoration shows Jesus, the Virgin Mary, John the Baptist and various Russian rulers and their patron saints. Tourists don't usually spend time looking for such detail. They want to get on with their visit and move to the next site.'

She continued, 'The next item in the tour is the Armoury but as we don't have much time I'll take you to the most important exhibits.'

We walked past the rest almost without a side-long glance. We had an hour to spend in the museum, not all day.

'What I most want you to see are the suits of armour. They show the differences between your armour and the plate armour favoured in Western Europe in the final stages of development before full suits went out of use', I said. 'With the introduction

The 'Tsar bell' weighs 200 tons and the broken piece weighs 11 tons.

of gunpowder, full suits of armour ceased to offer protection against the new weapons of choice: firearms.'

'The helmets are particularly different,' Mike observed. 'They remind me rather of oriental ones I've seen in books about Chinese armour or the ones worn by samurai warriors in medieval Japan.'

We moved rapidly to the next hall.

'Here is a collection of coaches. Some were presents from foreign kings and were never actually used because they were too big.'

Mike stopped in front of the biggest exhibit, an enormous covered sledge with glass windows.

'You can say that again!'

'Yes, it's probably the biggest, but in fact that one *was* used. In 1741 the Empress Elizabeth needed to get from St Petersburg to Moscow to support a *coup* by supporters aiming to put her on the throne. A journey which normally would take eight or nine days she managed to cover in just three by having her carriage pulled by 23 horses.'

'That was quite an achievement, but my admiration lies with the coachmen!'

'Time for a spot of lunch,' said Mike, with a tone of authority in his voice. 'We've been walking non-stop for four hours. We're beginning to feel the strain. And a bit peckish.'

'Olga, where do you suggest we go to get something to eat?'

'There's a handy Italian-style café over there,' she said, pointing across the square. 'You choose what you want, put it on your plate, take it to the cashier and pay. It's very quick and easy. You don't have to worry about what something's called in Russian.'

'Will you join us? We'd like to treat you to lunch.'

'No, thanks.' She didn't elaborate.

My guess was that she had other visitors to shepherd around later in the day and wanted a break after a long and tiring session with us.

'We just go in, walk round, choose what we want, pay for it and find a table to sit at? It's as easy as that?'

'Yes. You'll manage fine on your own. Anyway, you can speak Russian, can't you?'

'Well, after a fashion, I'm not confident I'll know what everything's called.'

'You won't need to. It's all laid out on tables. You help yourself.'

Olga's assurances were correct. We chose dishes more or less at random, not always being sure what they'd taste like but we were willing to experiment. Mike took several photos of the mounds of food on display. Other diners eyed him with some suspicion. Was he some sort of plain clothes hygiene inspector? I guess they were partly reassured when he addressed me in English.

We took our trays to a table, sat down and found, with some relief, that on the whole we'd chosen wisely.

Mike finished his beer. 'I'm ready for a nap now.'

'Me, too. I haven't recovered from our flight yesterday yet.'

We walked back to the hotel and turned in for a decent sleep. We both needed it!

That evening, we set off to find some dinner.

The restaurant where we'd dined the previous night was closed to the public for a wedding party, which was in full swing when we passed the window.

'What now?'

'Find another one, of course. Doesn't matter much which. It's all going to be new to us.'

'Well, since you mention it, here's one practically next door, so why not here?'

I read the name on the door. 'Mmm, 'Bela Rusya.' Presumably, cuisine from Belarus.'

'Which is where, exactly?'

'White Russia as opposed to Red Russia, which historically meant Muscovy, in other words, this bit we're in now. It's the land lying between Muscovy and Poland.'

Immediately we stepped inside, we could hear live music. Folk tunes were being played on a violin and a guitar.

'Combined with traditional food, this'll suit us just fine.'

'I'll experiment with the ethnic beer,' said Mike. 'You?'

'I don't like beer. I'll stick with apple juice.'

The menu was in English as well as Russian but that didn't help much when the names were not descriptions of ingredients but what the dishes were called in Belorussian.

I explained to Mike: 'A Russian tourist goes into a restaurant in London. Imagine the following conversation with the waitress:

'Please explain what is 'bubble and squeak'? And this 'toad-in-the-hole'. In England, you eat *toads?*'

Fortunately the illustrations showed us whether it was soup, meat or fish. We opted for *solyanka*, a rich soup of sausage, cured meat, carrots, cabbage and capers, served with a garnish of chopped dill and sour cream and accompanied by a hunk of crusty bread.

This dish turned out to be a staple which appeared later on the menu on the train. It proved a valuable fall-back because at least we knew what it was.

'Service is a bit slow,' observed Mike. 'And the waitress seems to wear a permanent frown.'

'Maybe she's not keen on foreigners?'

Saturday 1st September
Free

Before we set off for the day, I sent an e-mail to Kimry from Mike's laptop, suggesting a river trip, with lunch on board or at a pleasant restaurant, which we would host.

'They'll know how to organise it,' I assured Mike, 'and we'll enjoy a new slant on Moscow by seeing the Kremlin and other prominent sights in central Moscow from the river. It'll also help pass the time, without being too physically demanding.'

'That'll be the day after tomorrow. How are we going to spend our free day today?'

'Arbat.'

'What's that?'

'It's one of the oldest streets in central Moscow. One of the few to survive the enthusiastic demolition and redevelopment programmes during the Communist era.'

'How far is it?'

'I reckon it's walking distance.'

'So we can head off on our own?'

'Provided we have a map. Ask reception if they can oblige.'

The weather was fine and sunny. Ideal for what we were planning for the day.

Arbat.

We walked the entire length of Arbat, looking at the street scene or at buildings of interest.

'Bit of a let-down, this. Seems to be mostly souvenir shops, eating establishments under various guises and stalls selling second-hand books.'

'Not forgetting the artists and cartoonists doing portraits 'while-u-wait', or rather 'while-u-sit.'

'So where are the cobbled alleyways and the medieval houses with overhanging upper storeys?'

A souvenir shop in Arbat.

'Russia never had them. In medieval times they still built in wood, apart from cathedrals and monasteries plus one of two *kremls*. In the Middle Ages when the growth of trade in Western Europe gave rise to a class of rich merchants and even richer nobles establishing towns and filling them with fine houses and palaces and patronising learning and the arts, Russia was vast, land-locked, backward and impoverished.'

'And pretty much isolated from the rest of Europe?'

'Yes. Moscow itself was merely the fortified stronghold of the Grand Princes of Muscovy who ruled over just this one province, although in the course of time they came to rule all of the rest. The Renaissance never happened here, any more than the Reformation did.'

'We buy old books'. 'I buy scientific literature'.

'Not really that much of interest to see, then? Rather a disappointment.'

'Even if they had had our sort of medieval development, it wouldn't have survived the constant invasions. In the thirteenth century it was the Tatars from Central Asia. You know, Genghis Khan's lot. Then the Poles during the so-called 'Time of Troubles' at the beginning of the seventeenth century. Then the French under Napoleon invaded in 1812.'

'You mean *War and Peace* and all that? Didn't the Russians set Moscow on fire to deny the invaders shelter as winter set in?'

'Then it was the turn of the Nazis during World War Two. In addition, there was the so-called 'modernisation' during the period of Communist rule. But at least there's some variety, from modern tower blocks to quasi-traditional style.'

At the far end we reached the Ministry of Foreign Affairs, a vast Soviet-era building which Mike saw as presenting something of a photographic challenge.

'How do I get it all in?'

'If we cross the road via that subway, there's a little park. You'll have room there to line up your tripod in various positions until you're satisfied.'

It only took him five minutes.

On the way back to the hotel we decided to find somewhere for lunch.

'If we go up a side street, it's likely to be both quieter and a bit cheaper.'

'OK. Which one?'

'How should I know? Let's just take the next side road and trust to luck.'

We turned right, into a street which at first didn't look too promising. But forty yards along it, there was, to our relief, a restaurant.

'Here's one. Seems to be serving Russian food, not some ethnic cuisine.'

'We'll give it a try.'

Inside, there was a central staircase which divided halfway up the flight, leading to a mezzanine upper floor.

'Up there?'

'No. Here in this corner.'

The café off Arbat where we had lunch.

When it came to paying the bill, we got a nasty shock. I produced my credit card. The proprietor turned up his nose.

'I'm sorry. We don't take credit cards. Only cash.'

I was incredulous!

I went back to our table and stuttered to Mike in disbelief, 'This is central Moscow, well inside the tourist area, yet they don't take credit cards! How much cash have you got on you?'

By emptying our pockets, we just managed to scrape together enough roubles.

'Well, we got out of there by the skin of our teeth', breathed Mike with a heartfelt sigh of relief. 'Better find a cash point and get hold of some more money. Where do you suggest next? We've got the rest of the afternoon.'

'The other attraction to visit in central Moscow is Gorki Park.'

Relying on the map, it looked as though it was a long walk. So it proved. It took us a full hour to reach it. We noticed along the way a number of foreign embassies. We were particularly intrigued not only to find that Luxembourg had an embassy, but also that the compound was absolutely enormous.

'Bearing in mind just how small Luxembourg is, they could probably clear the entire duchy of slums and re-house the people in their Moscow embassy.'

'Do they have any slums in Luxembourg?'

'I didn't see any when I visited, but then I didn't go out into the suburbs,' I replied.

Another even more incongruous plaque caught Mike's eye. He pointed out to me what he'd spotted.

'What's it say – *Embassy of the Kingdom of Cambodia*'? Didn't know they still had a king.'

'Well, that's what it says on the gate. There,' I pointed, 'under the national coat of arms.'

'Yeah. But why does it say it in *English* when this is Moscow?'

'Pass.'

We walked across the bridge over the River Moskva to Gorki Park. At the entrance, security guards were checking bags, though not mine for some reason.

'You must have an honest face!'

'Or maybe they know foreign tourists don't carry prohibited items into the Park. Such as booze, perhaps.'

'Or their own picnic. Doing the kiosks out of business.'

'Now you'll see what I saw when I was here for the World Festival of Youth and Students: people enjoying themselves. For those who want to play table tennis the table's provided, just bring your own bats and ball. Chess players: chess boards set up in stone, bring your own pieces.'

'What are all those people in white clothing and chalk make-up doing?'

'Nothing. That's the point, they're mime artistes. You'll see them in various poses. Look,' I said, pointing one out. 'There's a woman dressed as a tennis player. She stays

'Bring your own bats and balls.' Tables provided in Gorki Park.

stock still, then every now and then shifts position to a different pose to avoid getting cramp, such as changing her stance from serving to retrieving a back-hand.'

'How do those living statues make a living? Very few people seem to be leaving them any money. Even those who use them as back-drops for family photos.'

'Perhaps the few who do leave some money are very generous.'

We walked around, listened briefly to a rather good jazz pianist on a bandstand and observed people posing for photos alongside it or sitting around on benches or on the grass listening.

'Time to get back. I don't really fancy the long walk. What about a taxi?'

The first cabbie we accosted wanted 1000 roubles, about £20.

I turned sideways to murmur in Mike's ear.

'Seems a bit steep, for a couple of miles at the most.'

'Maybe it's the going rate in Moscow,' he murmured back. 'We've no way of knowing.'

A mime artist in Gorki Park.

He spurned our offer of four hundred. 'Take it or leave it' was the clear implication.

'You too, mate', I thought, but resisted the temptation to challenge him and simply turned away.

Turning to Mike, I said out loud, 'We'll walk back over the bridge to where we noticed a metro station. See if we can use that.'

'Great idea. Should save us a few bob.'

'Let's hope so. But I've never been on the Moscow metro other than with a Russian companion. Doing it unaided is going to present a bit of a challenge.'

'Any idea what line we'll need?'

'Not the proverbial foggiest. I don't even know what the procedure is for buying a ticket. Is the system totally automated or do you buy a ticket from a clerk?'

'And we don't know which station we want or even what it's called.'

'No, but we've got the map. If we compare it with the metro map, we should be able to work out where the nearest station is to the hotel. You're the geographer. Why do you think I brought you?'

As it turned out, the list of stations was displayed on a huge board. Comparing the station names with those marked on our map, we worked out that we only had to travel two stops. I found it difficult to hear what the booking clerk was saying through her little window, but after a fair amount of '*I'm sorry, please say that again a bit louder*' I ended up with two tickets at 28r. each.

'Rather better value than one thousand for a taxi, Mike!'

'Now you know why I brought *you*.'

Home, rest, brush-up and then dinner.

The restaurant offering discount to guests at our hotel was again closed, so back to Bela Rusya.

This time the music came from an accordion and a small instrument something akin to a ukulele.

The players were a middle-aged couple in national costume, playing folk songs on demand for a table of middle-aged men who knew the words and wanted to join in with the performers. Everyone was having a wonderful time!

'Is that a balalaika?', Mike asked.

'No. The sound-box is the wrong shape.'

We chose a table in a different position to where we'd sat the previous night, but if we thought we'd thereby escape the morose waitress, we had another think coming!

'It's the same one we had last night!' Mike whispered in mock horror. Think she might be in a better mood?'

The answer was hardly reassuring.

We ordered. Ten minutes passed as we sat twiddling our thumbs. The waitress came back and asked Mike to repeat his order. She'd apparently forgotten!

The situation wasn't made any easier by the language barrier, the din and Mike's hearing aid on the blink, to boot.

The middle-aged men who were joining in the folk songs stood up to leave, but before doing so they all came over and engaged us in conversation in whatever bits of English they could muster, their way of making us feel welcome. It was an unexpected gesture, as we had been sitting some distance away. We'd been enjoying the music and their singing. They'd obviously noticed us joining in the applause.

As smoking in restaurants is still permitted, I decided to finish my post-prandial cigar. We ended up being the last customers. When I wished our waitress goodnight in Russian, for the first time in our two visits she smiled.

Sunday 2nd September
Sergiev Posad*

'Today we're going to visit the central administrative complex of the Russian Orthodox Church. As a comparison, imagine the C of E combining Canterbury Cathedral and Lambeth Palace on one site.'

'You've been there before, haven't you?'

'Yes, but that was back in 1957 when it was called Zagorsk.'

'So what happened?'

'Well, Vladimir* Zagorsky was a leading Bolshevik during the Revolution. In the Communist era when such people died, it was the custom to honour them by naming a town after them. He died about 1930, I think, which is when it was given his name.

Half a century later enthusiasm for communism began to wane. Towns which had lost their historic names began to petition for their reinstatement. Particularly this one, as it's not only the headquarters of the Orthodox Church, it's also the official residence of the Head of the Church, the Patriarch of All Russia.'

'How big is it?'

'It's bigger than my suggested Canterbury/Lambeth combination because there's a cluster of other ecclesiastical buildings of historical importance, as well as a seminary.

It was originally named in honour of St Sergius of Radonezh*, who was a celebrated monk who founded forty or so monasteries in the fourteenth century. Its old name was restored back in 1991.'

In 1957 I'd travelled there by train. I assumed that on this occasion, we'd do the same.

Olga arrived at reception. She found us sitting in the lounge area reading our English newspapers.

'Our car's outside.'

I was pleasantly surprised. We were going to travel in comfort. Just as well, as it took an hour.

'The authorities have now constructed a designated vantage point where visitors can stand to view the whole complex,' said Olga. 'Our driver will drop us off here, then he'll park the car. He won't be joining us on the tour.'

We found ourselves standing with a crowd of other tourists, but mainly Russians, as it was a Sunday. On a hillock on the far side of a shallow valley, the complex of medieval ecclesiastical buildings lay before us, protected behind the original walls.

Mike's face was a picture! 'What a size!' he said, amazed by the extent and variety of what he was seeing.

'You'll note,' I said, 'that they're located inside a solid defensive wall, just like Canterbury Cathedral and for the same reason. In the lawless Middle Ages monasteries and wealthy churches needed protection from the mob. In Russia monasteries doubled as fortresses.'

At first glance, we were dazzled by dozens of truly magnificent onion domes all shining brightly in the sun. The vista was as utterly awe-inspiring as the Church had intended it to be when it was erected five centuries ago.

'I've got our tickets,' said Olga. 'I've booked us time with an English-speaking specialist guide. Her name is Irina*. She'll be able to explain the significance of particular icons and what particular buildings are used for. Mike will need a special permit to take photographs. She'll help him buy it.'

Irina must do all this umpteen times a day. I marvel at her ability to stay focused.

Olga explained that one of the distinguishing features of the interior of an Orthodox church is the proliferation of icons forming the iconostasis, the screen separating the body of the church from the sacristy.

She continued: 'Icons are pictures of saints. To the right of the sacristy door is the one after whom the church is named. They are often very lavishly decorated, as is so much of the church, both interior and exterior. They are there because Orthodox Christians believe in the intercession of saints.'

'Like Roman Catholics,' Mike butted in.

A panorama of the Lavra Monastery at Sergiev Posad.

'I think that in many respects once you've seen the inside of one Orthodox church you've seen them all', I murmured. No matter how old, or otherwise, an icon is, it's still an icon. In common with all those pictures and statues we find in other parts of Europe of the Virgin Mary, Jesus and the prophets and apostles, the fact is that no one knows what any of these people looked like so all representations are based on the artists' imaginations and the style predominant at his time.'

As we walked through the main entrance, a vast archway, Olga explained that in the monastery at Sergiev Posad some 260 monks are in residence. In addition, about 1000 students in the seminary are studying for the priesthood.

It was the first day of term. The new intake, the 'freshers', were all lined up on the steps of one of the cathedrals for their group photograph, watched by a crowd of tourists, amongst them many proud parents and siblings.

'Training for the priesthood takes five years,' Olga informed us. 'As well as religious studies, they learn foreign languages. Entry qualifications are high.

In the Orthodox Church priests marry. The parish priest is supposed to be the 'father' of his parish and his wife the 'mother'. Monks, of course, don't.'

Part of the iconostasis.

There seemed to be no shortage of candidates. There was also no shortage of people of all ages crossing themselves and bowing. In the refectory, a service was in progress. People were queuing to kiss the glass covering an icon.

This prompted a thought about the hygiene implications. Maybe the absence of epidemics demonstrates the power of prayer. But it remained just a thought.

'Ah! The tomb of Boris Godunov* and his family. I'm a long-standing admirer and I've always wanted to see it.'

'Remind me who he was.'

'He was Regent during the reign of Fyodor I*, the son of Ivan* IV, that's Ivan the Terrible. He was feeble-minded. When he died in 1598 without an heir, Boris was proclaimed Tsar. For his times he was very progressive in his outlook and encouraged education and international trade. As he came from comparatively humble beginnings, he had many enemies amongst the older noble families who were jealous of his rise to power.'

'So he was assassinated?'

'No. He died in 1605 of natural causes. Unfortunately his son who succeeded him, Fyodor II, died a few months later. The country descended into chaos as rival factions fought amongst themselves over who should be the next tsar. One lot even invited the Poles to invade in support of their candidate. That's why it's called 'the Time of Troubles'. It ended in 1613 when Mikhail Romanov* was elected Tsar, and

The tomb of Tsar Boris Godunov and his family.

A mural above an archway.

New seminarians pose for their group photograph.

the Romanov family held the throne for the next three hundred years.'

'I suppose you want a photo?'

'Indeed, I do. I want my photo taken alongside the tomb as a mark of my esteem. OK?'

Mike waited for a moment when no other tourists were in shot.

Olga seemed impressed by her visitor's unexpected specialist knowledge of her country's history. I have to confess that even though I am in many ways a specialist in that subject nonetheless it was gratifying to be able to impress a professional guide!

From the details of power struggles in Russia at the beginning of the seventeenth century, Olga brought us back to present-day reality.

'Would you like to try some of our special round honey cake?'

'Where?'

'We'll pop into the snack bar.'

'I'll also take a glass of *kvass.*'

Mike interposed. 'What's that?'

'It's made from fermented rye bread. I quite enjoyed it in Red Square back in '57.'

'Get on with it. We'll head back to the car, which means running the gauntlet of hundreds of stallholders selling souvenirs. I could only describe it as tourist tat.'

'Well, there's tat and tat. I want just one pictorial souvenir to remind me in perpetuity of the fact that I've been here. I'll settle for a small plaque showing the monastic buildings. If I do this at every place we stay or visit for the next month I'll have a full mantelpiece. If any visitor ever asks me what they all are, I'll be able to bore for England!'

Mike made a face. He knew I wasn't kidding!

At that point it started to rain. All the stallholders began frantically to cover up their goods with plastic sheeting. We reached the car just as it set in for the day.

Back at the hotel mid-afternoon, it was time to part.

'We shan't see you again, Olga. This is goodbye. Thanks for doing a splendid job.'

She smiled. 'Thank you.'

We both shook hands with her and went into the hotel.

As we were both pretty knackered after another four hours constantly walking, we decided to spend the remainder of the day resting.

'This evening, why don't we try that Japanese-style restaurant a couple of doors away?'

When we arrived, Mike made a surprising observation: 'We appear to be the only patrons, which seems odd for a Sunday night.'

'I think I'll try their octopus starter. It had better be worth it. It's 800r. My main course of duck only costs six hundred. I suppose it's easier to find ducks in the vicinity of Moscow than octopuses. Or should that be 'octopi'? I'm never quite sure.'

'Nor me. The price is because you're paying for the transport costs.'

'Care to join me in a toast?' Fresh kvass on sale to thirsty visitors.

Monday 3rd September
Free

Anticipating a favourable response from our friends in Kimry, I was most gratified when an e-mail arrived on Mike's laptop from Marina, the mayor's official interpreter.

Mike read it out. 'I've booked us on a boat trip along the river to the Kremlin and back. I'll be with you at midday. Tatiana's coming, too.'

'Who?' asked Mike, not, of course, knowing anything about Kimry or its civic staff.

'She was our official guide when our twinning delegation visited last year. She doesn't speak any English but when she came to Eastleigh last spring I made a point of bringing her back to my place so that she could see what an ordinary English house was like. She took loads of photos, including a timed one of the two of us sitting in armchairs in my conservatory drinking coffee. I took her on a tour of my garden to show her what sorts of fruit and vegetables I grew and to see my chickens. She took photos of them, too.'

'I've booked us on the river trip, with lunch/dinner on board,' continued Marina's e-mail. 'All you have to do is fill in the time until then. I'll be with you about midday, but Tatiana will be with you a bit earlier as she's stayed in Moscow overnight.'

Tatiana arrived. I introduced her to Mike. Almost immediately, Marina turned up and we were able to plan the rest of the day.

'Would you like us to take you to see Arbat?'

'No, sorry. We did that on our own yesterday.'

'Alright. Let's just walk to the metro. We only need to go the couple of stops, then we get off and walk the rest of the way along the bank of the river to the jetty where the boat's moored.'

The boat, bearing the company name Radisson, was very large, and presumably was regularly hired for wedding and anniversary parties or for hosting business receptions. The waitress in attendance at the end of the gangplank examined

Tatiana, Martin and Marina.

Marina's tickets and conducted us to the dining area. On this trip the tables were mostly laid for couples, but for us, a table had been set for four right in the bow with the best view in any direction.

I took stock. 'There's an access door onto the deck in the bow, where diners can pop out for a smoke. I'm sure Tatiana will do that. She's quite partial to a fag. And you'll be able to go out and get better shots and angles.'

'Not many other passengers,' Mike observed.

'That's because of the time of day. Most people are at work.'

'That lot over there,' said Mike, indicating with a movement of his head but avoiding looking directly at them, 'look like they're being entertained at the expense of the firm.'

'Alright for some.'

Mike, Marina and Martin at table on the pleasure boat on the River Moskva.

The river is not tidal. We hardly noticed when the boat slipped its moorings. Because of its size, there was scarcely any perceptible motion. We proceeded majestically, allowing plenty of time to absorb the scenery and for Marina to explain to us the names of particular buildings.

Mike, meanwhile, was constantly taking advantage of our proximity to the door onto the bow to nip outside to avoid having to take photos through the glass in the windows and getting reflections on them.

'What's this huge sculpture coming up ahead?', he asked.

'It's honouring Peter the Great's founding of the Russian Navy 300 years ago. It's created some controversy because the good burghers of St Petersburg say it ought to be there because that's where Peter's navy was based when he founded it. Moscow had nothing to do with it. Besides, Moscow's a thousand miles from the sea!'

'We're sailing round the back of the Kremlin! We'll be able to see the entire complex from an unusual angle.'

This weather's perfect,' I said. 'I'll even have to put on my sunglasses! And what's more, it's perfect for your photography.'

'For our lunch,' said Mike, adding it all up, 'we've had wine, two bottles of water, four glasses of fruit juice, four main courses, two desserts and four coffees, and the bill for four of us comes to 6800r. I reckon that's about £140 in our money.'

'I'll put those details in my book. Readers will be able to decide whether they agree that that's a pretty good deal for a two-hour dinner while floating through the middle of a capital city. Can you run through the details for me while I write some notes?'

'The ladies had chicken *'diablo'* with baked potatoes (650r.), you had a confit of duck in bilberry sauce (600r.) and I had medallions of beef in a mushroom sauce (750r.), with red wine. I think it was Chianti. It was 320r. a glass.'

We took the metro back and arrived at the hotel by 18h30. Once again we were tired. There'd been a lot of walking.

Portrait of a happy man! The author enjoying a smoke.

Mike poses as we approach the sculpture honouring Peter the Great who founded the Russian Navy.

'Thank you for a most interesting day. We've seen Moscow from a new angle, enjoyed a long, slow meal and, of course, your company!'

I think Marina blushed.

'Thank you for taking the trouble to come all this way. I know you now have a two-and-a-half hour bus journey back to Kimry.'

Marina didn't mention it, but I knew that she'd already done the journey to get here this morning. Such are the demands when fostering international friendship!

As they prepared to leave, Tatiana rummaged in her bag.

'I'd like you to have these cakes and bars of chocolate as a parting gift for your forthcoming travels.'

'That's very kind of you. Please take my greetings back to Kimry to the mayor and others there who remember me.'

'We will.' We hugged each other goodbye. They left to get their bus.

'We're off to Tobolsk tomorrow,' Mike reminded me. 'This is the longest continuous stay in one place that we're going to have for the next month, when we'll be more or less continuously on the move either unpacking or packing. I think we need to think carefully about how we pack.'

I thought through our immediate priorities, listing them aloud to ensure I hadn't missed anything.

'I need to check that we have the right tickets and that for each of us our medication is in order. I'm taking four pills each morning and two more at night. Three times a day I have to put drops in your left ear.'

'Yes, I picked up an infection a couple of weeks ago. It was so severe at the time that I was afraid I might have to call the whole thing off, as the song goes.'

'Glad your doctor got it sorted. As you have to lie still for ten minutes after each treatment to give the drops time to penetrate, it means that whatever we're doing and wherever we are we'll have to factor in the need to find an opportunity for you to lie down full length and for me to do the medical orderly bit.'

'Never thought of you as Dr Zhivago.'

'He'd turn in his grave, if he had one.'

Day 8: TOBOLSK*
Tuesday 4th September
Overnight train to Tobolsk

Raining! Streaming down and rattling on our skylight. By the time we'd had breakfast and I'd done Mike's ear it was easing off and the sun had come out. In fact, it had become quite warm.

'We want to make the most of our last few hours in Moscow before heading off to catch the train at 15h00. What do you recommend? You're the one who's been here before.'

'There's just enough time to walk to Red Square, where I can show you the Lenin Mausoleum.'

'Remember those young blokes on our plane dressed as soldiers in the Napoleonic Wars. What was all that about?'

'Going to take part in some sort of re-enactment, I expect. Moscow's celebrating the 865th anniversary of the founding of the city in 1147, but it's also the bi-centenary of the Battle of Borodino* between the armies of Tsar Alexander I and Napoleon in 1812.'

'Who won?'

'Napoleon won the battle but at a heavy cost. It was the turning point in his fortunes not just here in Russia but on the rest of the continent. It was all downhill after that, culminating in his defeat at Waterloo in 1815.'

For this reason, when we reached Red Square, we found that it had been converted into a temporary showground with two areas surrounded by stands. Reading the posters, one was for a demonstration of horsemanship by the Kremlin Equestrian School. The other was for an international festival of military music being staged later in the week. Most of the square was cordoned off to allow for tiered seating to be erected.

'Pity we'll be long gone before they perform.'

'C'est la vie. As they *don't* say in Russia.'

We couldn't savour the usual broad views of either Red Square, Krasnaya Ploshchad* or St Basil's Cathedral, because of all the temporary stands. There was also a cantonment of tents, where presumably the two young re-enactors on our plane would be bivouacked.

However, the mausoleum was open.

'Not much of a queue. Looks like we'll have the place almost to ourselves.'

'What's admission cost?'

'Nothing. There's no charge. Not even for foreigners.'

Backpacks, rucksacks and other large items, however, were charged 40 roubles. Mike wasn't even permitted to take his camera, as a sign in Russian and English clearly set out: 'No bags or cameras in the mausoleum.'

'If we get searched and they find my penknife, they might confiscate it. Let me stow it in your bag as a precaution.'

We were repeatedly searched.

'Mike,' I said, 'I'm glad they didn't find me in possession of my knife. Not sure my Russian is up to explaining that it's nothing sinister, Officer, I always carry it. No, it's not a weapon, it's for cutting up fruit or cleaning my finger nails.

'How many more times are we going to be frisked? Don't they trust the first one to do it properly?'

'I wonder at what it's costing to pay all the military personnel on duty. I'm sure they could be more usefully employed elsewhere.'

'It's very dark inside. Can you see OK?'

Mike felt obliged to help me negotiate the steps down into the viewing area where Lenin was lying in state. When I saw him fifty-five years ago, Stalin was lying beside him. Times change!

'Doesn't he look small! And he has tiny ears! He could almost be a doll!'

The thought occurred to me that if Mike had said that when the object of his observations was still alive there might have been consequences.

Back outside, Mike was admiring a splendid equestrian statue, which gave him quite a surprise when he read who it was.

'It's Marshal Zhukov*!'

'He commanded the Soviet armies which captured Berlin in the final stages of the war.'

'Why is he shown on a horse? He certainly wouldn't have ridden one into battle in WW2.'

'He began his career as a cavalry commander in the 1920's.'

It was nearly noon. Mike was feeling hungry.

'Lunch again at that same self-service Italian-style cafe we went to before?'

'It could hardly be handier, directly outside the Kremlin wall. What's more, we get a good view of the eternal flame honouring the Unknown Warrior from World War Two. Or, as the Russians call it, the Great Patriotic War.'

Inside there was a massive table displaying every conceivable variety of salad and meat.

'How's that for a pie and pizza counter! How does the system work?'

'You choose your main course, pie and whatever. They serve it on a plate, then you go to that table and help yourself to whatever else takes your fancy to go with it.'

'The salads appear to be uniformly priced, except for corn-on-the-cob which is priced individually.'

'Doesn't bother me. I don't like corn-on-the-cob. I don't care how they price it because I won't be choosing it.'

The equestrian statue of Marshal Zhukov.

Some diners seemed to be piling up their plates. They got their comeuppance at the check-out, where their plates were weighed. They were charged according to weight. A canny system!

Our choices were similar: an excellent cheese pie, roast potatoes and mixed salads.

Then back to the hotel, check the room to make sure we haven't left anything behind, bring our luggage down in the lift and wait for our taxi.

He's scheduled to arrive at three o'clock. He's early.

'Shall we go now, as he's here?'

'No. If we leave earlier than necessary we'll have even longer to hang about at the station.'

'Well, what's still to be done?'

'Have we settled the hotel bill? I know it's mainly for laundry.'

'Go and do it, then. I'll wait here with the bags.'

'How rude! That's no way to speak of the girls on reception!'

Mike understood the joke, but it was perhaps just as well that they didn't hear us. They might have got the wrong idea about English humour, assuming that they were familiar with slang, such as 'bags' being a derogatory term for women.

We arrived at Yaroslavski Station by 15h20, and were met by the agency's rep who was clearly expecting our taxi. Whether he recognised the number plate or the driver wasn't clear. He was a middle-aged man with grey hair and introduced himself as Anatole. He was quite surprised when I addressed him as 'Tolya', which is the familiar form of his name in Russian and what friends would actually call him. His task was to collect us from our taxi and walk us to the platform and show us how to find our train when it came up on the departures board.

'My English is a bit limited,' he confided. 'My first foreign language is German.'

'Just give me the instructions in Russian. Then repeat them in German to my friend. He understands it better than me. I'm sure we'll understand fine.'

Tolya seemed quite relieved on hearing this. 'Your train won't come up on the departures board until four o'clock. When it does, it won't show the name 'Tobolsk' because that's not its final destination. It'll show 'Novii Urengoi'*.

A Trans-Siberian train is shunted into Yaroslavsky Station.

A Trans-Siberian train is ready to take us across the Urals to Tobolsk.

As I'd never heard of that town, I had difficulty taking the name in. But without Tolya's services, locating the train to Tobolsk when it's shown on the departures board under a totally different name would undoubtedly have posed a problem for a visitor. Even more so, if that visitor was unable to read Cyrillic.

Having satisfied himself that we knew what to look for on the board and would be able to find the train when it arrived, Tolya made his excuses and left.

'What now?' asked Mike.

'Time to kill. As we're standing outside the station cafeteria, we might as well go in for a drink. If you want a second reason, it's beginning to rain.'

Indeed, despite the weather being unexpectedly warm, a gentle drizzle was beginning to fall.

The cafeteria was crowded, with a lot of passengers in a similar predicament to us: where do you put your luggage while sitting at the table? If you put it on a chair, then that may stop someone else being able to find a seat. If you stand it in the aisle alongside your chair, then you cause an obstruction.

At four o'clock I went outside to see if our train was showing on the departures board and to check the platform number. Tolya's information had been absolutely spot on.

'Here comes the train. Time to head off to find our carriage. The number is shown on the ticket. Even though the compartment and seat numbers are shown as well, we know the attendant will show us to our seats.'

Siberia – here we come!'

Oh! no we don't!

We walked along the platform until we reached the carriage bearing our number but the door was firmly shut. No one was being allowed on, despite the rain. The platform was open to the elements. I wondered if passengers were treated like this in midwinter.

'All aboard!' Off to Siberia at last!

Finally the carriage attendant – the *provodnitsa** – arrived, opened the door and checked our tickets and passports. She seemed a bit apprehensive at having two foreigners, perhaps because not many of them head for Tobolsk.

Her responsibility is to lock the doors when the train is moving. I hoped there wouldn't be any accidents requiring emergency evacuation! She also controls access to the toilets, which again she locks about ten minutes before the train reaches a stop, which can be for as long as forty minutes.

At the end of the corridor outside her cabin is a samovar, which provides a constant supply of hot water for passengers to make their own drinks. The *provodnitsa* keeps it topped up with cold water.

At regular intervals she vacuumed the corridor and each compartment. One soon learned to recognise the Russian for 'Can you lift your feet up, please.'

At 16h49 the train pulled away a minute early and proceeded at a leisurely pace.

Mike had been reading a booklet about the Trans-Siberian Railway, full of gloom and doom about the dangers of theft on trains. It also warns that as the restaurant cars are franchised out to private enterprise, the quality of available refreshment is unreliable. It may be real food properly cooked or

This charming lady looked after us on the first leg of our excursion.

nothing more than the equivalent of crisps, coffee and soft drinks. As soon as we were settled into our compartment, I set off down the train to do a *recce* and take in the lie of the land.

'We're in luck, Mike! There's a proper restaurant car, with at least three kinds of soup and half-a-dozen meat dishes on the menu, plus three fish dishes, including trout, and various concoctions using chicken. The waitress even offered to bring the card to our compartment and serve us there.'

'For free?'

'No, there's a 15% surcharge.'

'Let's accept the offer. We haven't yet adjusted our mind-set to what's going to be the longest train journey either of us has ever made in our entire lives. Let's face it, we're going to be on this train for almost 40 hours.'

'OK. We'll go to the restaurant car for our coffee afterwards. It's 100 roubles for an espresso. Sugar's extra – ten roubles.'

Seems every little helps.

After two hours and fifty minutes there was a scheduled stop at Vladimir for 20 minutes. The platform was thronged with itinerant vendors selling all manner of foodstuffs: rolls, soft drinks and even dried fish.

The samovar is in the corridor opposite the attendant's cabin.

It was apparent that many Russians don't buy food on the trains but bring their own and make up any shortfall by buying from the hawkers who patrol the platform at scheduled stops. Seems to work. There was no announcement when the train moved off again. Just as well none of the passengers were still stretching their legs or buying top-ups.

Bed-time.

'I see they've made our bunks up on top. Er, how do we get up there?'

'There's a hand-hold.'

'Yes, but it's out of reach.'

'Which means there must be a ladder.'

'Lunch is served!' Eating our first restaurant meal but in our compartment.

'Where? On the cross-Channel ferries it's alongside the clothes hooks. There's no sign of any ladder anywhere in here.'

Indeed, close examination of the door frame revealed a ladder of sorts consisting of three rungs, ingeniously folded into the wall, which opened out once you'd worked out the mechanism to release it.

No one forewarned us about this contraption. That includes our specialist agency.

It seems the travel agents and railway authorities both assume that you've been on a Russian train before and know how it's equipped.

Having clambered up, I remarked to Mike: 'Fun while it lasted. Trial and error. Check how many fingers you've got left when you've finished. '

As is the case with bunks on the cross-Channel ferries with which I am all too well acquainted, the rungs of the access ladder were murder on bare feet. It was advisable to wear shoes. Then you have the complicated manoeuvre of hoisting yourself up vertically, twisting to lie full length on the bunk horizontally and at the same time remembering to keep your head down to avoid hitting it on the ceiling.

Probably would have been easier if I wasn't six feet tall, I thought.

Having managed to lie full length on the bunk, I was relieved to find that it was very comfortable, with a reading light and even a hand-hold to help me keep steady when the train got up to top speed and a handy little shelf on which to put personal objects. In my case, my watch and glasses. Plus my sandals. I was not going to stand on those rungs again barefoot if I needed to go to the toilet during the night!

Wednesday 5th September
On the train to Tobolsk

'This compartment's actually quite comfortable, but I'm very glad to have it all to ourselves. We seem to pretty well fill it with only the two of us. It must be very claustrophobic with four, especially if they're as big as us.'

'Buying four seats for the two of us wasn't an unacceptable extravagance after all, then?'

We slept soundly.

'It's 8 o'clock. I think I'll try out the washing arrangements at the end of the corridor, before the rush starts.'

'Morning cuppa?'

'I'll ask the attendant.'

She supplies free hot water on demand. She also makes tea or coffee for a small fee. That's the way the system works. It helps boost the attendant's wages.

'I've got my own tea, English tea in a bag!'

She was quite intrigued.

'Please, let me give you a couple to try it. You have to drink it in the English style, with milk.'

I put them in her hand. *'Oooh, thank you!'*, she said, with a broad smile. She looked at them a bit suspiciously, as if not quite sure what to make of them. I don't think she'd ever seen a tea bag before.

Russians drink their tea either with lemon or just straight, also not in a cup but in a glass, held in a special metal holder with a handle known as a *podstakannik**. This translates as 'under a little glass', which aptly describes how you use it. You put your glass of tea in it to avoid burning your fingers. I still have one which I brought back as a souvenir from the Youth Festival in 1957.

My *podstakannik*.

'Breakfast in the dining car?'

'Right. How far is it?'

'A couple of compartments towards the rear.'

We made our way and found seats facing the bar so that we could observe the comings and goings of the other passengers and perhaps see our order being prepared.

'There's no specific breakfast menu. It's just what was on offer last night.'

'Seems the Russians haven't yet embraced Western Europe's love affair with the *croissant* and *pain au chocolat* or the similar morning choices of cereals or regional breads and spreads.'

The waitress recommended a dish comprising eggs, ham, onions and tomatoes.

It arrived freshly prepared and was very tasty. I'd brought some sachets of sugar nicked from the hotel, so that was 20r. saved! Every little helps, even when you're travelling first class. . .

'It's half-past ten. Where the hell are we? Any idea?'

'Well, the station name board says Balezino, but I don't know how it's pronounced so I'll have to ask the attendant. Russians have a disconcerting tendency to put the stress on the last letter with place names ending in 'o'. A case in point is the famous Napoleonic Battle of Borodino.'

My suspicions were confirmed when I asked the *provodnitsa*. Our stopping place was pronounced with the stress on the final 'o': Balezin-*o*. Not that it really mattered We were not getting off and we'd never be here again.

But I like to get words *right*. If you're going to have to say it, even to yourself, you may as well pronounce it correctly.

'The timetable says we're stopping here for 25 minutes. Shall we stretch our legs?'

'Most certainly. I need a smoke.'

According to a sign on the platform the temperature was 12°C, which the locals must have regarded as high summer because most of them were walking around in shorts and sandals. The hawkers were out in force with tables of food and tourist tat, others were carrying baskets of dried fish or plastic bags of apples or tomatoes. One even had a cart laden with slippers and sandals in all sizes.

At about two o'clock we reached the city of Perm, 1435km from Moscow. We were scheduled to stop for 20 minutes.

'Ah, Perm,' Mike said to me, seeing the name on the station board and taking the opportunity to test out his ability to read Cyrillic script.

Unbeknown to him, our *provodinitsa* was in earshot. She couldn't control her impulse to correct him.

'*P-yair-m!*'

What can one say? That's the way the Russians pronounce it. No point in entering into a debate!

The weather, bright sunshine in a cloudless sky, was nothing like what we were expecting. Summer is summer. Siberia may have fierce winters under looming skies, but this is September, not winter.

Once on our way again, I decided that a call of nature could no longer be denied and headed for the lavatory. At the end of the corridor was an overhead illuminated sign, flashing alternately whether or not the toilet is vacant or the time and temperature on the train (+20°C). There were toilets at each end, so one of them was conveniently adjacent to the attendant's tiny cabin.

Vendors on the platform at Perm.

The bar.

Stacked between the window and the rail was a bag of papers clearly labelled in English 'Toilet Seat Cover', with pictorial instructions on where exactly to tear the paper cover to make it fit over the seat. To my considerable surprise, it worked.

When I'd finished I noticed that the roll of toilet paper was alarmingly small and realised that I had fallen foul of Kyrle's Second Law of Public Bogs: always check that there is enough paper on the loo roll. Even that there's any paper at all! My personal requirements and the very last piece of lavatory paper fortunately coincided but as Wellington said after Waterloo: it was a damned close-run thing.

The peculiar characteristics of the paper provided in the train toilets evoked my curiosity. Grey, not white, in colour, very rough in texture which possibly makes it more absorbent. More importantly, it's not perforated at regular lengths into individual pieces as our toilet rolls are in Western Europe. Instead, it's just one long roll. When you want to tear a piece off you have to grip it firmly in one hand and scrumple it up and tear it vigorously with the other. Because you can't tear it off in a straight line, you end up using more than you need and wasting a lot of paper [*v. picture on p 272*].

Perhaps it's cheaper to manufacture without perforating it in sections as we do but surely it's a false economy if passengers end up using more? In another sense it *is* perforated: it has actual holes in it due to shoddy manufacture! I leave you to consider the implications.

We travelled remorselessly east.

'We'll shortly be crossing the Urals, the historic and symbolic boundary between Europe and Asia.'

They extend some 2500 miles from the Arctic to the *steppe* and rise to heights of up to 2000m. At their southern end where we crossed them they appeared as undistinguished hills which we barely noticed.

The sunshine remained with us. By now it was 16h55 Moscow time. The sun felt very warm, coming through the train windows.

Looking out at the passing scene, Mike observed: 'The railway line is usually moving through an avenue of trees, mostly silver birch. In this strong sunlight, we're getting persistent flashes of light as the trunks interrupt the sun's rays. Not good for someone inclined to epilepsy.

Do you think this is a planned arrangement or did it just happen? Were the engineers deliberately shielding the line by creating a line of trees to prevent heavy snow drifting and blocking the track or was the line built through trees and just left as is?

Much of the time, mind you, we're passing through forest. At other times it's quite clear. The so-called protective line is only a few trees deep.'

In the distance, we picked out fields and buildings.

'Have you noticed the farm buildings?'

'Er, yes. What about them?'

'Well, there's hardly any use of brick. They're usually wood, with iron roofs.'

'Matter of using what's available, I suppose. Bricks have to be made and brought in. That would cost because they're heavy to transport. Wood's free and there's plenty of it. I expect a lot of the iron roofing is cannibalised from redundant farm machinery.'

'Interesting to see what sort of agriculture they practise around here. Some of the fields are enormous yet they seem mostly to be of grass.'

'Winter feed for livestock?', Mike suggested.

'Yes, probably. But many of the cottage gardens have flourishing crops of vegetables and flowers.'

Only very occasionally do we spot the owner.

The line is used extensively for freight. The trains are very long and often headed by a double or triple locomotive. The major cities all have extensive marshalling

A village viewed from the train window.

yards and at every station there were lines of wagons hitched up ready to go once our passenger train had passed.

'Where's our next stop?'

'Yekaterinburg*. It sort of marks the southern end of the Urals. According to our timetable, it's exactly 1814kms from Moscow.'

'You know it's where the Tsar and his family were shot in 1918?'

'Yep, even I know that. In a cellar, wasn't it? All very hush-hush.'

'Yes. The White Army – the counter-revolutionaries – was doing well at the time. The Reds were afraid that if things carried on like that Nicholas would become their figurehead. If they got rid of him, his supporters would give up. Pity about the rest of the family, though.'

'What we need to remember,' said Mike, 'is that the time zone changes at regular intervals. The working time on the train itself remains Moscow time, regardless of what the real time locally may be.'

'Can you confirm the time?' I asked our *provodnitsa*. *'I need to adjust my watch.'*

'We're two hours ahead of Moscow.'

'What time do we arrive in Tobolsk tomorrow?'

Our *provodnitsa* had taken a bit of a shine to us, possibly because we were the only foreigners on the train. Perhaps my earlier token present of a couple of English tea bags had put her in a favourable mood. Maybe, too, she felt an element of relief.

She probably anticipated a language problem, but as it turned out, one of her two foreign charges could manage in Russian.

'Eight-thirty. I'll wake you at eight o'clock. That'll give you half-an-hour to get ready.'

'Fine. Thank you.'

I returned to our compartment to relay this information to Mike. His response was immediate.

'We won't bother with breakfast. We'll have that once we reach our hotel.'

At six-thirty in anticipation of, at last, starting on our tour proper, we were all packed and ready when our kindly *provodnitsa* duly knocked on our door.

'Eight o'clock!'

She slid the door of our compartment open, preparatory, I presume, to shaking us if we were still both asleep. She was mildly surprised to find that we were up and packed.

'Thanks, we're all ready.'

A wonderful sunrise greeted us through the trees. We passed over a huge river, the Irtysh*. We were treated to a bird's-eye view of the town of Tobolsk as we thundered past. The station, for some reason, is located ten kilometres beyond the town.

Thursday 6th September
Arrive in Tobolsk. Free

We were quite weary because although we'd slept while we'd been on the train it had been interrupted sleep. We'd had to get up fairly early in order to be packed and ready to detrain on arrival. This wasn't the terminus. The train only made a normal stop.

We pulled into the station on schedule at 08h29, to be met by…

No one.

'Aren't we supposed to be being met?'

'Yes, 'course we are. Maybe they've been held up somewhere.'

'In a place this size? At this hour?'

It was quite a small station and 10kms from the town. Very quickly the few other passengers alighting had gone off by taxi or by private car to their homes, if they were locals, or if not, to a business engagement.

'There's a girl with a placard saying 'Tob Tur' in Cyrillic. I suppose she's waiting for someone who's booked an excursion with a local travel agency called Tobolsk Tours.'

So we thought.

We stood around for ten minutes or so, waiting for someone to arrive in a cloud of dust, rush over and apologise for being late. When the cloud of dust failed to appear, I went over to the girl with the placard.

'Excuse me, do you know the people you're waiting for?'

'No. It's two men from England. I don't have their names.'

'Well, we're the only foreigners to have got off the train. It must be us. But why are you carrying a placard with 'Tob Tur' on it? Is that Tobolsk Tours? We don't know anything about them. We're travelling through an agency based in UK.'

With the benefit of hindsight, it's obvious that our London agency had arranged for a local agency styling itself 'Tobolsk Tours' to provide our guides during our stay and to meet us from the train. They hadn't thought of telling *us*. We were expecting to be met by someone carrying a card with our names on it, as had been the case at the airport in Moscow and at the station where we boarded the train we'd just arrived on.

It was fortunate that the railway station at Tobolsk was in a semi-rural location, not one thronged with people. Had it been, we might never have ventured to question the girl with the placard.

'Our taxi's waiting,' she called out. 'This is our driver, Rashid*.'

'That's a good Russian name,' I thought to myself. Rashid was a swarthy, thick-set, middle-aged chap of decidedly Tatar appearance. As he was clearly not an ethnic Russian, it was perfectly consistent that he hadn't got a Russian name.

Rashid was determined to show willing.

'Welcome to Tobolsk!' he barked, smiling broadly and showing a row of uneven teeth.

That was his only contribution to our conversation, but it made us feel welcome because he'd obviously made a supreme effort to *be* welcoming. A nice thought.

'What's your name?' I asked our guide.

'Natasha.'

'Where did you learn your English?'

'I trained as a primary school teacher. I teach English.'

With Natasha, our guide in Tobolsk.

'You're not a full-time guide?'

'No. We don't have enough tourists for it to be a full-time job.'

Soon we arrived at our hotel, the Hotel Sibir*, a rather old-fashioned establishment but with some modern additions. The bedroom was furnished with pre-revolutionary heavy wooden furniture but had a shower in a bathroom with an intimidating array of nozzles.

'Isn't 'Sibir' the Russian name for Siberia?' asked Mike.

'Yes, I replied. 'Not exactly imaginative.'

We were immediately aware that in one aspect we'd struck gold.

'Here, look! We're right on the main square and there's the *kremlin* and cathedral on the other side! We couldn't have hoped for a better location. What we've come all this way to see is right on our doorstep!'

The cathedral looked new or at least newly renovated. Its onion domes were painted in blue with gold stars or entirely in gold. They caught the morning sun and shone against the sky, which was mostly bright blue but with occasional passing clouds.

'They're absolutely magnificent! Look's like I made the right choice in coming to see the cathedral complex in Tobolsk rather than those in other towns along the Trans-Siberian line.'

However, we both felt exhausted after 40 hours on a train.

'I want nothing more urgently than to get some breakfast. It's now 09h15.'

'I need to get into a proper bed and sleep undisturbed by the continued juddering of a train and those frequent and inexplicable stops between stations. They're one of the reasons it took us 40 hours to get here.'

'But some breakfast first. I fancy a tasty snack. Then up to our room to catch up on some shut-eye.'

We woke up in time for lunch.

'The *kremlin* we've come to see is across the square. Why wait for the guided tour tomorrow? Nothing to stop us just wandering across and seeing if we can get in.'

'Yes. The sun's shining. The conditions are ideal for me to take photos. We've nothing else to do as this is a free day. I'll have all the time in the world to take shots. Who knows, perhaps tomorrow it'll be raining.'

The cathedral of St Sophia in Tobolsk.

Panorama of the cathedral of St Sophia behind the walls and towers of the kremlin.

'Yeah, sure. Grab the opportunity while it's here.'

Tobolsk has an interesting history. It was officially founded in 1587 when the tsars decided to set about colonising Siberia. It then became the centre of trade with China. As such it was the capital of Siberia at a time when most of it hadn't even been explored by Russians, let alone settled. A century later masons were sent from Moscow to construct the cathedral of St Sophia and the stone *kremlin,* the only such edifice in Siberia, to defend it.

It became the seat of the first governor of the province, Prince Matvei Gagarin*, appointed by Peter the Great in 1708. As Siberia was gradually opened up and cities were founded farther east and nearer to trade routes, it gradually declined in importance. When the planners of the Trans-Siberian Railway chose the southern route through Tyumen*, 250kms south, by-passing Tobolsk, the town was left high and dry. The railway connection wasn't constructed until 1972.

The main part of the modern city is built on the high ground behind the *kremlin.* Here are located the oil and chemical industries and the residential areas where most of its residents live.

'This *kremlin* is the oldest in Siberia. Just our luck, Mike, that we come here while it's undergoing extensive restoration.'

'Yes, scaffolding everywhere. We can pick out its dimensions but I'll have trouble getting decent photos.'

Fortunately, restoration of the cathedral had recently been completed. It dominates a bluff rising about 100m above the original Old Town lying between it and the River Irtysh. We were able to wander unchallenged around the cathedral

The walls and towers of the kremlin in Tobolsk, the only stone kremlin in Siberia.

A watchtower in the kremlin, fully restored.

Watching out for an approaching enemy army.

The ramparts of the kremlin (interior view).

precincts, and climb a flight of uneven steps, with no handrail, up to a walkway inside the parapet to see for ourselves its commanding position, dominating the flat, low-lying landscape stretching as far as the eye can see.

A pleasant promenade has been laid out around the outside of the ramparts and we spent a sunny afternoon idly enjoying the views of ramshackle houses far below, watching a boy in his back garden playing with his dog and a man sawing planks to build a new wooden staircase outside his house. Even though we were 100m above him and he was a couple of hundred metres away nearer the river, we could hear every blow from his hammer. A noisy cockerel added to the domestic sounds, which carried on the air.

'See the ferries? Look very tiny from here.'

'Seem to be two of them. One for vehicles and one for foot passengers and each with its own separate landing stage.'

'Don't appear to be working to any sort of timetable. Just crossing to and fro almost non-stop.'

A new wall had been built around the seminary alongside the cathedral. By sheer chance we came across a bas-relief honouring Gagarin – the Governor, not the astronaut. No dates or other details were shown, perhaps because in 1721 Tsar Peter the Great hanged him for corruption!

'Dinner?'

'Let's settle for the hotel. I don't fancy buggering about looking for anything better. Even if there *was* anything better, it would be some distance away and we'd have to walk.'

The bas relief commemorating Prince Matvei Gagarin, the first Governor of Siberia (1708-14 and 1716-19). He was imprisoned by Peter the Great in 1719 and hanged for corruption in 1721.

This was the road up which tea from China finally reached Russia: the kremlin in Tobolsk. The incline and road surface are unchanged, though the town lost its connection with the tea trade in the eighteenth century.

A domestic scene below the bluff. The green area behind is a pond covered in algae.

'Shall we order some wine? Reckon we've earned it after all this travelling.'

'Good idea.'

I summoned the waiter.

'Can we have two glasses of wine, please?'

'A bottle of wine, sir. Of course.'

'No, not a bottle. We only want two glasses.'

'We only sell wine by the bottle.'

'Oh.'

I turned to Mike.

What, then? Do we go without, or buy a whole bottle? We're here tomorrow. We should be able to get through it.'

'OK. We'll give it a go. It's a long time since I had wine on my cornflakes.'

We ended up with a *vin de table* Spanish white from Valencia, the sort known in my household as *Château Plonque.* But it wasn't being sold at plonk prices: 1000r. (£20)! We'd be more careful next time.

Our room had a vestibule and a bathroom complete with bidet. I recalled when Margaret and I found ourselves in a hotel room with one of these, we always used to call it a 'bidditt', in mocking pretence that as uncouth provincials we were not familiar with such a facility and didn't know what it was for let alone how to pronounce it.

Quelle luxe!

'Here, look at this shower! Looks like it's been designed by the same engineer who created the Tardis. It's got a whole range of complicated controls.'

'If you press the wrong one, you'll probably get projected into space.'

'There's a set of instructions here,' said Mike, pointing to a sheet of paper stuck to the bathroom wall and protected by cling-film.

I examined it closely.

'Very useful. It explains in minute detail exactly which knob does what and to whom. The problem is, it's in Russian and there's no translated version for the benefit of non-Russian-speaking guests.'

This is supposed to be an international hotel, not some fly-blown hostelry out in the sticks.

I gave up as I didn't have the technical vocabulary and went back to experimenting with the controls in the shower.

Eventually I discovered how to get it to play music while I conducted my ablutions, *quelle* more *luxe!*, but not how to tease the monster into providing me with hot water to make it likely that I will indulge in such an undertaking.

'Here, Mike. You have a go.'

By sheer chance he found that the way to get hot as opposed to cold water from the showerhead was not to try, ineffectually, turning it to the left or right, or even up or down, but to *tilt the knob*. Who'd have thought of that in a month of Sundays? Simple, once you know. Maybe I should have tried out the 'bidditt'. No time like the present for a new experience to add to the mix of life's rich pattern.

Friday 7th September
Guided tour of Tobolsk, then drive to Tyumen to join the Trans-Siberian Railway to Novosibirsk*

Our guide, Natasha, arrived five minutes late with another, 40-ish, lady who turned out to be the proper Tobolsk guide. Unfortunately, she spoke only Russian, with Natasha struggling to translate.

Our car from yesterday and Rashid, our Tatar driver, arrived but instead of heading for the *kremlin* as per the original plan we were taken in the opposite direction to the cemetery where we were shown the tombs of various Decembrists, in particular the most important of them, that of Count Muravyov*.

The guide didn't explain the historical importance or otherwise of the Decembrists. To an ordinary tourist the significance of the tomb would be entirely lost. Mike only had the vaguest idea who the Decembrists were. In contrast, as a specialist, I was able to explain to Mike their significance.

'The Decembrists were so called because of the month in which their revolt took place. They were aristocrats who'd been to Paris in the aftermath of the Napoleonic Wars and had seen Western society. They wanted to see Russia catch up with the West, which Peter the Great had attempted to do a century before.

When Tsar Alexander I died in December 1825 they attempted a coup in order to force his successor, his brother, Nicholas, to modify the autocracy or even rule as a constitutional monarch. They failed completely, and five of them were hanged – the last public executions in Russia's Imperial history. Thousands were sent into exile in

Siberia. Some were merely required to live out their days there, far from their estates or the Court at St Petersburg. Muravyov is a case in point. Others were sentenced to hard labour in the mines and sent to Chita* and Nerchinsk in the Far East to work in chains. When their sentences were completed their punishment wasn't over, as they were ordered to remain in Siberia as exiles.'

'Did Nicholas ever relent and offer pardons?', asked Mike.

'No, but when he died in 1855 his successor, Alexander II, granted amnesty.'

'So some came back to Court?'

'Yes, some did. Others remained where they were due to old age, lack of money or merely that after living so long in Siberia they were happier to stay there with their friends, families and familiar surroundings rather than up sticks and try to pick up the pieces of their former lives after three decades away. Those who'd been sent into exile in Tobolsk started a school for women and showed the local inhabitants how to treat cholera and also how to avoid it by boiling their water before drinking.'

The point here is that our guide wasn't doing a very good job, taking it for granted that a foreign visitor would be knowledgeable about Russian history in the 1820's. It transpired later that the last tourists she'd had were an Italian couple six months before. I wonder what they made of being shown Count Muravyov's grave and being told he was a Decembrist. For all they knew, that referred to the month in which he was born!

It then got worse. Our guide showed us the tomb of Dmitri Mendeleev*, a notable nineteenth century chemist who is credited with inventing the periodic table of elements who was born near Tobolsk although he spent most of his life in St Petersburg. OK, local boy makes good, even if he did most of the making elsewhere.

She then started talking about a writer named Yershov*, whose sole work of literary importance was a fairy-tale entitled *The Humpbacked Horse*, published in 1834 while he was still a philosophy student at St Petersburg University. He corresponded with Pushkin, who commended him for the quality of his poetry and fairy tales. As Pushkin is regarded as the father of Russian literature, it says a lot for Yershov's youthful talent as a poet and writer that he received such compliments. The fact remains that nothing he ever wrote afterwards left any discernible mark. Few people have ever heard of him, including me, even though in my younger days I studied Russian literature and taught it to A level. We'd come to Tobolsk to see its *kremlin* and cathedral. I didn't take kindly to spending precious time being dragged

The memorial to Yershov, depicting him with scenes from his most famous work: 'The Humpbacked Horse'.

around a cemetery looking at the graves of people I'd never heard of.

As we drove off in the direction of the Old Town, Mike spotted some interesting street sculptures.

'Can we stop, please. I'd like to have a closer look and take some photos.'

Rashid obliged.

'They're very finely executed. What are they?'

'They illustrate scenes from *The Humpbacked Horse.*'

'I'm glad to see them at the side of a road where passers-by can see them, not stuck in some theme park.'

After Mike had satisfied himself with his photo-taking, we drove off and parked outside a huge brick church.

'This,' explained our local guide, 'is a Catholic Church built in the late nineteenth century by Polish exiles. It's now pretty much redundant because there aren't many Catholics left in Tobolsk and the resident priest has long since gone. There's one in Novosibirsk. He occasionally comes to minister to the few we have left.'

I can't imagine it's very often, as it's a round trip of nearly 2000kms / 1200 miles.

Why we spent ten minutes parked outside this church, I have no idea. It wasn't a particularly elegant building. I've seen plenty like it in England. Not even of much historic importance, merely a reminder that following the unsuccessful Polish uprising in1863 against Tsarist rule, many revolutionaries were sent into exile. Enough of them ended up in Tobolsk for them to build themselves a church where they could continue to worship in their own way. How interesting is that to your average tourist?

Next stop was a mosque, heavily restored. Then down a bumpy road to the car ferry. Are we going to go on it, across the Irtysh, have a bit of a river trip?

No, we're not. We're going to park, get out and wander across the shingle down to the water's edge and be asked if we want to dabble our fingers in the river. Gee, whizz! The ecstasy consequent upon such a prospect leaves me palpitating with indifference.

In the modern, higher town, flats built in the Soviet era sit alongside newer, more expensive, apartments. Further out is an area of industrial development, which is the basis of Tobolsk's economy.

In the lower town are an assortment of wooden houses, some little more than huts, others quite large and many dilapidated, while others are in the process of being restored.

'Lots to photograph here,' said Mike.

He particularly admired a number of picturesquely derelict ones. Sadly even though the guide stopped for a long chat with one of the owners, we didn't get an invitation to take a look inside. Of greater interest was the house where for several months in 1917-8 Nicholas II and his family were lodged immediately after the Bolshevik Revolution.

At last we were driven up to the *kremlin* and given a chance to see inside the cathedral. Following a programme by successive post-Soviet presidents to restore historic buildings, it has been largely rebuilt. It's much like any other cathedral, with icons and relics of holy men. Despite the Soviet authorities' official policy of hostility towards the Orthodox Church following the revolution in 1917, a substantial percentage of the population remained religious. There is a politico-social motivation to this restoration work, as well as encouraging tourism.

'Come here and look at this!'

Mike is the first to notice the display in the porch of photos showing how it was as late as 1967. Weeds four feet high grew outside the main door and the roof had caved in. An absolute fortune must have been spent on restoration. There can be no doubt that the results are spectacular. All the icons are, of course, modern, that is, painted in the last twenty or thirty years and of no historical interest. We proceeded to the ramparts to admire the view which we'd discovered for ourselves the previous day.

I looked at my watch and saw that it was now a quarter past two and we'd been walking or occasionally driving for nearly four-and-a-half hours non-stop, without lunch or even a coffee break. The guide was still in full flow and showing no signs of letting up. Natasha was struggling to keep up with the translation. Enough is enough. It was time to put my foot down.

'I've had enough now. I want to go back to the hotel to have a rest and have something to eat.'

The guide was not pleased but there wasn't much she could do if the tourist who's paying her said he no longer wished to continue the tour.

We walked back across the square to our hotel and found that as it was now half-past two, the restaurant had closed. I suggested (!) to our guide that she had a word with the kitchen staff and asked them to provide us with something to eat. After all, the fact that we'd got back after closing time was entirely her fault.

As far as I was concerned, a bowl of soup and some bread would do fine.

The car ferry on the River Irtysh.

*The householder is unable to afford repairs and refurbishment,
but continues to live in his house.*

The mansion where Tsar Nicholas II and his family spent the winter of 1917-18.

'The main restaurant is being laid up for a wedding party later,' Natasha informed us. 'They want to put you in a private room.'

'Fine by us.'

Some salad and bread appeared on the table, then a bowl of borscht.

'Will some rice and mince do?'

'Yes, sure. Anything.'

They brought it immediately, which meant that it was standing on the table getting cold while we consumed the borscht. By the time we were ready to eat it, it was cold and inedible. I left mine on the table untouched. Cold mince and cold rice? Ugh!

While all this was happening, the guide went off without a word. In fact, we never saw her again.

'Natasha, will you have some lunch with us?'

'No, thank you. I'm not hungry.'

She sat watching us eat. When we'd finished she said, brightly, 'Now we can go to the museum.'

'Sorry. I'm too tired. I'm going to our room for a nap.'

'Goodbye, then,' said Natasha. 'I'll be back at 9 o'clock to see you off in the car to Tyumen to catch the Trans-Siberian train.'

Iconostasis in the Cathedral of St Sophia.

The iconostasis in the Cathedral of St Sophia.

Inside the Cathedral of St Sophia.

I think she was a bit embarrassed because her instructions were to take us to the museum and her agency might want to know why this hadn't happened. If she said, 'They refused to come. They insisted on going up to their room for a nap', she might have some explaining to do.

We never did see the museum, which is the former prison, even though it was part of the tour for which we'd paid. Its main claim to fame is that for a time Dostoevsky was held there.

One should always learn from experience. From this frog-march round Tobolsk led by a guide clearly imbued by the ethos of the Gestapo (*Vee haf vays of making sure you see everything!*) has evolved Kyrle's Second Law of Tourist Guides: if the tour starts in the morning, before setting off, ask when are we stopping for coffee and what time is lunch?

One should make it perfectly clear that no matter what sort of schedule the guide has written down on her dossier from her agency, she is going to have to allow time to rest and to eat lunch at lunchtime, not halfway through the afternoon. 'What time do we have lunch?' is not a question open to refusal. If the tour is scheduled to continue between the hours of twelve and one, then between those hours we're stopping for lunch. The guide can decide where. After all, she knows the area. She can choose the café or restaurant. We'll pay. But not stopping is not an option, no matter what instructions she's had from her office.

In my own case, if a guide can't deduce when she first meets me that, at my age, I am unlikely to be able to go on for four hours without a break, or doesn't think it necessary to enquire, then there's been something wrong with her training. We were clearly greatly prized by the Tourist Board, as Tobolsk is not *en route* to anywhere else. Tourists are few and far between. Those who come have made a deliberate choice to make the journey. Natasha told us that the last time she'd spoken English to tourists was for the Italian couple six months previously. The time before that had been two years ago.

Time for dinner before we depart. It can't be in the restaurant because of the wedding party, which is now in full swing. The music is deafening. I wonder about the aural safety of the guests. For that matter, I worry about the staff who have no option but to endure it. They promise us service in a side room when we decide we're ready to eat.

After dinner the previous evening we'd wandered out to see the cathedral again.

It was floodlit, and Mike wanted to take some shots. They were most successful and he'd been busy downloading them onto his laptop so that he could show me the best ones and delete those that he regarded as sub-standard.

I decided to go out onto the square to see what I could find at the souvenir kiosks, looking for something small to remind me of my visit to Tobolsk. I noticed another stall selling a variety of pies and other snacks. Buying some of these might be a good idea as we were due for another long train journey, fifteen or so hours from Tyumen to Novosibirsk. I went back to seek Mike's opinion. By the time we returned it was ten past six and the stallholder had packed up for the night and gone home.

The wedding party was still going full blast. Lots of young people dressed up to the nines were coming out to the hotel lobby to chat, as they couldn't make themselves heard in the restaurant. Others stepped outside for a smoke. In the privacy of our side room, the noise was just bearable. We heard a compère organising games for children. In that din? They should be prosecuted for child cruelty.

We finished off last night's bottle of wine just to get it out of the way. I didn't want to carry it when I already had a litre bottle of fizzy orange juice in my shoulder-bag, in readiness for a long train journey. Tatiana's parting gift of cakes and chocolate plus assorted biscuits I'd pocketed in the first class lounge at Heathrow Airport added to the weight I had to carry.

Natasha arrived to see us off with Rashid. We observed him desperately trying to fix the lights on the car which was to take us to Tyumen. Not a comforting augury, as it was 250kms and we'd be travelling at night on roads with no illumination. In Russia, once you leave a built-up area the roads are not lit.

It was a very long and pitch-black journey and without the comfort of seat belts. Rashid wasn't wearing his and although we had them attached to our seats, no buckles had been provided to which to fasten them. There may be laws governing road safety but they seem to be honoured only in the breach.

'We got this wrong,' I muttered to Mike, as we sped through the inky darkness. 'We're travelling through countryside we'll never cross again and we can't see any of it. I'm sure out there there are rivers and valleys and forests and fields and farms and villages, and we're missing the lot.'

'Yes, but we had no choice. The train leaves at ten to three in the morning.'

'Yes, I know. But on reflection, we should have arranged to travel in daylight and spend a night in a hotel in Tyumen.'

Two views of the Cathedral of St Sophia, beautifully flood-lit after dark.

'But that would have had a knock-on effect on the rest of our trip. You know that as well as I do'.

'Too late now. Something else to put down to experience.'

Rashid was very keen to be friendly. Having apparently attended college in Kazan* where he'd picked up a little German, he was anxious to try this out on Mike. Here is the scenario: two Englishmen in Russia in a taxi on the far side of the Urals, being driven through an ink-black night by a Tatar talking to them in broken German. You couldn't make it up.

We stopped a couple of times for Rashid to top up his nicotine level and made one comfort stop at our request. It was almost midnight when we reached the station at Tyumen, meaning we had two-and-a-half hours to kick our heels. Although the train departed at 02h50 local time, it was 00h50 according to the train, which operated, of course, on Moscow time. Rashid took us to the station café and we had coffee and snacks, waiting for the departures board to show us which platform for the Trans-Siberian. How Rashid spotted the platform number I'll never know, as I couldn't make it out, but spot it he did.

He then helped us with our luggage: Mike with his one big case, me with my two rather smaller ones and my shoulder-bag with our travel documents and supplies of food and drink.

Thanks, Rashid, I said to myself, for helping us beyond the call of duty. You could have just dumped us at the station and buggered off home. Instead, you stayed with us until nearly three in the morning and when I proffered a small tip you told me it wasn't necessary and tried to decline it.

'Rashid, thank you for waiting with us and seeing us onto the train. We'd like you to have a drink on us when you get home.'

I pressed a 500r. note into his hand.

At least I prevailed on that score, and I can't think of any taxi driver who better deserved a tenner.

NOVOSIBIRSK

Saturday 8th September
On the train to Novosibirsk

On the platform we found our carriage. We showed our tickets and passports to the attendant. She muttered something unintelligible. It appeared that she didn't like the fact that our seat numbers weren't shown and went off to find her supervisor. She arrived all dressed up like a Brigadier-General in the Railway Militia in a crisp white blouse and shoulder boards. She was charming and obliging and resolved our seating problem, whatever it was.

We examined our compartment. For some reason unexplained by science, when Mike and I go into a railway compartment, he instinctively takes the right-hand side and I the left.

Problem: there were two mattresses and two covers but no linen.

'That's because there's been a minor foul-up. We're not expected.'

'So goodbye to our plans to get our heads down straightaway, without waiting until the train sets off.'

'Well, if we can't turn in, let's sort ourselves out. This is going to be our home for the next sixteen hours. Where do we stow our luggage?'

I tugged at my seat.

'It lifts up.'

'Maybe it does, but the opening's too small for any of our cases. If we want to make use of it, we'd have to unpack everything.'

'You're right. But as we've bought four seats, we can use two as seats and we can plonk our cases on the other two and use them as mobile chests-of-drawers. I've got our food and drink in my shoulder bag for easy access. That can sit on top of my case.'

As with the train we had taken from Moscow to Tobolsk, the table under the window didn't fold down but was fixed. The carpet runner, on the other hand, wasn't. Put the slightest pressure on it, other than straight down, and it slid away and you lost your balance and fell over. Highly disconcerting.

We had the same arrangement as before with regard to opening up a fold-away ladder to get onto the top bunk. Instead of the little netting shelf to put my glasses on, there was a locker with a hinged flap on a very strong spring. It fulfilled the required function but was not as simple. We were anxious to get some sleep as soon as possible. It was now half-past three in the morning.

The lay-out of the carriage was the same as on the train from Moscow to Tobolsk: toilets at each end and overhead flashing signs showing the inside temperature and the time. Moscow time, that is, not the real time in the towns and villages we were passing through in the dead of night. The lights alternated to show whether or not the toilet was occupied. At one end was the attendant's cabin. After our experiences enduring forty-two hours on a train three days previously, it felt quite like home!

'Let's eat some of that cake Tatiana gave us in Moscow. It's not going to improve being carted around. Besides, I have to carry it. It makes sense to eat it and then buy something else to replace it.

I've also got a whole carton of tea bags from my kitchen and some sachets of sugar pocketed at restaurants and the packets of instant coffee we acquired at the airport. With the hot water provided *gratis* by the attendant, we can have quite a cosy picnic.'

The design of the platform in Omsk is typical of the Soviet era.

This stayed the worms as far as breakfast was concerned. Later in the day an obvious question arose.

'Lunch?'

'I see the menu's in both Russian and English.'

'At last we really *are* on a Trans-Siberian train which regularly carries foreigners and attempts to cater for them, in both senses!'

'The scenery is just as monotonous as it was on the way to Tobolsk. Then it was everlasting birch trees. Now it's mildly undulating.'

'Still a lot of trees, but now and then we get a long vista of flat, rolling fields. Have you noticed that there's never any sign of movement or activity or any sign of animals, either wild or domestic?'

We passed various halts, too small for us to stop. In most cases they were too small even to warrant a name. Presumably anyone wanting to alight is on a local train and either lives there or is visiting family or friends. They'd recognise where they are without the need for a name.

Even with sizeable towns there was usually only one sign, either over the main door or above it at the very top of the station building.

If it was written in fancy decorative script, it could be quite challenging to read it in the time it took the train to pass through the station. This made it more difficult to follow the map to know exactly where we were. Most people travelling in Germany have the same problem when a station opts to put up its name in the version of Gothic script adopted during the Nazi era. Picturesque it may be but it's very difficult to read, unless you're a specialist.

'Have you noticed that often there's a hard track running alongside the railway line, occasionally being used by a car?'

'Perhaps in rural areas this may be a cheap way of providing some sort of road.'

The journey passed uneventfully. We arrived in Novosibirsk on time but an hour earlier than we'd expected as I hadn't thought to check whether we'd lost yet another hour while moving eastwards.

We had.

The local time was 18h40.

Luckily we were all packed and ready to go. As the train terminated here, we weren't under any pressure to get off quickly.

This underlines another important point for travellers on the Trans-Siberian

Railway: not all trains start in Moscow or go the whole way to Vladivostok. Some of them terminate *en route*, as our train was now doing here, at Novosibirsk. Others start from other towns and go as far as, for example, Irkutsk and stop there.

As in Tobolsk, we are met at the station by…

No one.

No one with a card, no one coming up to two foreign visitors with lots of luggage and introducing themselves. What's gone wrong with our agency, to leave us stranded for the second time in a row? We stood in the middle of the Arrivals Hall, very obviously newly arrived and expecting to be met. Nothing happened.

'I'll go outside to look in the car park. You stay here and guard the luggage.'

Again, nothing.

Back to the platform. Still no one.

When I got back to Mike, a young man with our names on a card was explaining.

'My name is Nikita*. I was told my clients were travelling in wagon number 10 but you were put in wagon number 2. I've been waiting for you at the wrong end of the platform.'

'O.K. No lasting damage. At least you're here now. By the way, what do you do when you're not meeting visitors off a train?'

'I'm a scientist at the university. I make a bit of extra cash working for the agency.'

By the time we arrived at The River Park Hotel, it was 19h30. The right time for dinner, for which we were more than ready as we'd been travelling since the middle of the night.

We entered our room on the twelfth floor to find to our surprise that it had a lobby, with our bathroom on the left and cupboard space on the right. The bedroom itself was oblong. A large chest of drawers was positioned more or less facing the door. The beds were in opposite corners, as far away as possible from each other.

At dinner, unfortunately, we hit the same snag as previously in Tobolsk: another damned wedding party. The music was being played at absolutely unbelievable volume. I was surprised that the chandeliers weren't shearing from their mountings, yet there were people actually inside dancing in this inferno. Back home, Health & Safety would have sent in the heavies without a second prompting.

A waiter showed us a small separate dining room, next to the main one.

Impossible. Too noisy. Couldn't eat a meal in such a din.

A waitress shouted above the deafening music: *'There's a café-bar on the third floor.'*

We decamped up there.

The hotel was modern and lavishly equipped. We were ensconced on the ninth floor, with a balcony providing us with a panoramic view of the River Ob and three bridges, carrying respectively a road, the railway and the metro.

The café-bar had four bar stools and table seating for about twenty more people on chairs or divans. The barman merely served, having apparently a solitary chef chained to a gas stove in a kitchenette behind him who prepared all the orders.

'Service is a bit slow.'

'Positively snail-like.'

'I see nothing positive about it. It's *negatively* snail-like.'

'Have it your way.'

'I guess it's OK if you're not particularly hungry or you have all the time in the world to sit with your tenth beer, sharpening your knife against your fork to pass the time while waiting for some grub to appear on a plate.'

'Much as I enjoy the privilege, I still can't get used to the fact that I'm allowed to smoke in the bar even though there are other guests here eating.'

'Enjoy it while you can. They're bound to catch up sooner or later.'

Unfortunately, this freedom to indulge is of no value to me as I only smoke cigars, and in general *after* a meal, not before. Laws and regulations there may be, but they appear to be much honoured in the breach, as they were when we travelled from Tobolsk to Tyumen in Rashid's car with no seat belts fitted.

Sunday 9th September
Guided tour of Novosibirsk

Nikita was waiting for us in the hotel lobby with a companion.

'This is your guide.'

Another Olga! Very short in stature, but she was very organised and a professional. She immediately handed me her business card.

We began with the usual question: 'Where did you learn your English?'

'At university I studied English and German and spent some time in Bavaria as an *au pair*.'

'I guess there's more demand for English?', I ventured, glancing at her business card. As is the custom in business circles, her details were in Russian on one side and in English on the other.

'Do you have any family?'

'Two small children. My husband's an engineer. Currently he's working on a contract in Norilsk on the Arctic coast. Winter's already set in there, unlike here in the south.'

The temperature was indeed not in the least wintry. It was in the comfortable low twenties.

With Olga, our guide in Novosibirsk.

'I've been told you want to see the market.'

'No, we don't,' we both said simultaneously. 'We never said anything of the sort!'

'A market's a market,' I went on. 'Meat, fish, bread, vegetables and fruit laid out on stalls are the same the world over, allowing for climatic conditions and what grows where. Not a lot of point going round that sort of market if you're not going to buy. We're staying in hotels, not self-catering. Different when I'm in France. There I rent a *gîte* for a week and shop in the local outdoor market if I'm lucky enough to be there on the right day of the week. Otherwise I use a supermarket.'

It was now ten o'clock. I had no wish to repeat the forced march that we'd endured in Tobolsk. I decided to come straight to the point, here in the hotel lobby.

'At some time between midday and one o'clock we would like to take a break and have some lunch. Choose somewhere nice. Of course, we'll pay.'

Olga readily agreed.

'We'll go first to the city centre, where I want to show you our huge statue

The imposing statue of Lenin.

of Lenin. It's flanked by socialist realist figures of happy workers, peasants and determined soldiers, as one would expect of a statue erected during the Communist period.'

Nikita dropped us off in the square. The statue of Lenin was as imposing as Olga had promised.

'That enormous building immediately behind the statues is our opera house. It's the biggest one in Russia, outside Moscow. I can take you inside and show you the foyer, but unfortunately we won't be able to see inside the auditorium. It's closed today.'

Leaving the opera house, we walked a few yards to the rear on the right-hand side. There, a memorial garden commemorated the defeat of the White Armies in 1919.

'We'll go now to the ethnographic museum, which I know you especially want to see. It's only a short drive.'

'Indeed, we do. It's one of the reasons we've come.'

They had exhibits of the skeletons of prehistoric rhinoceroses and bears and a reconstruction of a mammoth. Other rooms were devoted to mementos from the time of the revolutionary struggle between the Red and the White armies after the end of the First World War.

We walked down a flight of stairs and through a low archway to a little lobby with lockers, to leave our rucksacks in the cloakroom. As the museum was maintained at a comfortable room temperature, I left my anorak as well.

Alongside the exhibits, I was particularly anticipating the opportunity to see the displays of costume and way of life amongst the indigenous nomadic people, principally the Evenki*, who still live in the Far North in a harsh and unforgiving environment.

We were shown exhibits of the life-style of people living in the Altai Mountains to the south, where, because of the altitude, it's fearsomely cold in winter.

Olga told us about them.

'They're friendly provided you don't attempt to disrupt their way of life, like the Chinese.'

Mike interrupted. 'And the aboriginal people of Australia.'

Mike is something of an authority on Australia, as his eldest son lives in Melbourne and he visits frequently.

Olga continued. 'Their bodies can't metabolise alcohol in the same way as Caucasians. That means that after two or three beers they're as affected as a European is after he's had ten.'

I don't know if this is true, but both Olga and Mike seemed to be in agreement.

Going back down the stairs to the cloakroom, I was so completely preoccupied watching my feet on the steps that when I straightened up to go through the archway I didn't realise that it was lower than my head height. I hit my forehead full belt on the stone wall and broke the skin approximately on the hair-line.

Thump!

Ouch!

Scalp wounds always result in copious bleeding. This injury was no exception. Blood poured down the side of my face. Mike dashed into the gents' toilet to grab a roll of paper to help mop up the flow. I staggered to the nearest place where I could sit down in case I suffered from delayed shock and passed out. But the bleeding showed no signs of abating. The toilet roll was soon exhausted, Mike gave me a handkerchief and that too was soon completely sodden. I needed medical aid, quickly.

'There's a hospital quite close,' said Olga. 'It's actually the children's hospital, but they'll be able to give you first aid.'

We collected our belongings and left as quickly as I was able to manage. Although I felt OK, I was still bleeding profusely. Something needed to be done and needed to be done quickly before I bled to death.

Nikita drove us to the hospital in about ten minutes flat and we joined the queue in the waiting room. I was so grateful that we weren't on our own but had a local guide who could explain to reception what had happened. In particular, that I wasn't some drunk who'd fallen downstairs, nor had I been in a brawl.

As I was obviously in need of immediate treatment, they put me at the front of the queue. None of the other patients seemed to mind.

'Have you got your passport?' the receptionist asked.

'No, not on me. It's in my hotel room.'

'Have you got travel insurance?'

'Yes, but again the documents are back at the hotel.'

They accepted my word that I had a valid policy.

Mike wasn't allowed in and had to wait outside. I took off my coat and shoes. The nurse sat me on a bed while she cleaned the wound, sprayed it and applied a pad.

Olga, meanwhile, was translating the doctor's questions, which mainly concerned whether or not I was feeling giddy, nauseous and had I had an anti-tetanus injection. I was happy to inform him that I felt absolutely fine apart from the fact that I was losing blood by the litre. As a result of consulting my doctor before travelling to Siberia about any precautions he thought I should take, all my injections were up to date.

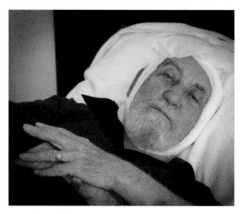

The author performs his Vincent van Gogh tribute act.

Not wishing to use any adhesive plaster because it would stick to my hair and be both painful and difficult to remove, the nurse wound about six feet of bandage round my face from scalp to under my chin to hold the pad in place. I looked like a walking Christmas pudding about to go in the pot or a character in a children's comic suffering from toothache, rather than someone with a head wound. At all events, I was not a pretty sight.

But at least the bleeding had stopped.

'I need to return to the hotel to fetch my insurance documents and passport.'

'I'll do that,' jumped in Nikita. 'I'll take them to the hospital and drop you three off for lunch at a restaurant on the way.'

We had lunch at an airy, very contemporary circular building consisting mainly of glass, which, from the upper floor, had commanding views over the city centre.

Nikita returned when we were about halfway through our meal.

'Everything's sorted with the hospital. The doctor says that tomorrow you'll have to go to another hospital to have the bandages removed and to see if any further treatment is necessary.'

'What now?', asked Olga.

'Kirov's* House. That's the main reason we've come to Novosibirsk.'

Surprisingly, the little wooden house where Sergei Kirov lived around 1908 when he was in exile has been preserved, even though it lies right in the middle of the modern city. I wasn't expecting that there'd be much to see but the fact that it's there at all was a minor miracle.

Olga concurred.

'Modern Russians aren't much interested in the more depressing periods of our post-revolutionary history,' she said. 'When it comes to the Stalinist purges and the minutiae of the Communist dictatorship in the 1920's and '30's, they'd really rather not lift the stone and look at what's underneath. It's altogether too ghastly.

I know the custodian. She says she gets very few visitors nowadays for precisely that reason. Young Russians aren't interested in Kirov. He may have been an important figure in the Communist hierarchy in the 1920's but he disappeared from the scene in 1934 when he was murdered on Stalin's orders.'

Eighty years on, I thought, frankly, who cares?

It was only a short walk to the house. We arrived to find it very, *very* firmly shut, with shutters closed and bars across the door in the form of a St Andrew's cross. I guessed the custodian had had enough for one day of twiddling her thumbs and had gone home. We'd come five thousand miles for nothing!

'There's a small park behind the house, about the size of a tennis court. It's got a statue of Kirov in the middle.'

'At least I can take some photos,' said Mike. He was relieved that at least we'd get *something* out of our otherwise abortive visit in search of Kirov.

Had we been able to go inside, would we have been particularly overwhelmed at seeing Kirov's writing desk or his bed? I doubt it. Only a specialist in Soviet history would even know who Kirov was. I know that because of his murder, he never became the leader of the Communist revolution for which he'd previously seemed destined. Stalin's purges and his devastation of the peasantry took place partly because Kirov wasn't around to stop him, which is why Stalin had him…

But that's history of the 'What if?' variety. In the real world, Kirov hardly matters now. But having come this far, I would have liked a quick peek inside his house to get a feel of what sort of life he'd led in exile.

Back at the hotel Olga pressed me about the place to go tomorrow for my check-up.

'I know a private clinic which will be much better than going through the bureaucracy of another public hospital.'

From my experiences at my time-share in Lanzarote when I had a mini-stroke, I knew my insurers wouldn't object if I was acting in good faith.

She rang the clinic.

'It's called Avicenna. I've got you an appointment for tomorrow morning at nine-forty.'

Sergei Kirov.

The wooden house where Sergei Kirov lived, preserved in the centre of the city.

ЗДЕСЬ В 1908 ГОДУ
ЖИЛ И РАБОТАЛ ПЛАМЕННЫЙ
ТРИБУН РЕВОЛЮЦИИ,
ВЫДАЮЩИЙСЯ ДЕЯТЕЛЬ КПСС
И СОВЕТСКОГО ГОСУДАРСТВА
СЕРГЕЙ МИРОНОВИЧ
К И Р О В
(КОСТРИКОВ)

Plaque explaining that in 1908 Kirov lived and worked here.

This would mean a taxi at 9 a.m. My plans for a lie-in on our free day had gone by the board. We'd have to have an alarm call at 7 o'clock to make sure we'd had breakfast before we went. By the time we returned, the restaurant would have finished serving.

This trip is a constant juggling act!

'Here's the name and address of the clinic,' said Olga, as she wrote them on a piece of paper. 'I'll ask reception to book you the taxi and tell him where he'll be taking you.'

All this time I had my head swathed in a blood-stained white bandage and was wearing my cap, even indoors, to try to be a little less conspicuous.

Thanks, Olga, for making these arrangements, I thought to myself. It's presumably not part of your brief, but you've acted as a Good Samaritan as anyone with any sense of decency would do when faced with someone, particularly a foreigner far from home and in distress. I know I'd do the same, were our positions reversed.

Nikita and Olga went off together. We were not scheduled to see Olga again. Nikita was due to take us to the station at 00h30 the day after tomorrow to catch our train to Irkutsk, assuming I'd been passed fit by the clinic.

Any idea we might have entertained about having dinner in the restaurant again went by the board as there was yet another wedding party or maybe it was a celebration of an anniversary. It made no difference: a lot of noise and it was a private 'do'. Other guests in the hotel were excluded.

We took the lift to the third floor café-bar and ran into a totally different problem: a gathering of a dozen young men had commandeered all the tables and chairs. The harassed barman told us that he could take our orders but it would be some time before we got anything to eat as he had to serve this party first. As it was slow enough last night, this wasn't an attractive prospect.

'I'll have the herring with onion and potato,' I said to the barman. I knew I would be on safe ground, as it was what I'd had the night before.

'A plate of your three smoked cheeses,' said Mike, placing his order.

A few minutes later, the barman plonked a plate of what look like nibbles in front of us: two sorts of cheese, some pieces of dried fish and some small savoury biscuits. We assumed that this went with our drinks. Mike's beer and my apple juice arrived at the same time.

As the party had taken all the chairs, we were forced to ensconce ourselves on two divans, with a low table between us. They were comfortable, which was just as well, we thought, as we're in for a long wait.

Dish after dish arrived at intervals for the party behind us.

After an hour, one of the party turned round and asked us, in English, where we were from.

'England.'

'I did a BA in Business Administration in London,' he said. 'No, I'm not a Russian. I'm an Uzbek from Samarkand. I took an MBA at university in Tashkent.'

'What are you all celebrating?'

'We're all agents and we're discussing successful deals.'

'What's your name?'

'Olim.'

We shook hands as he returned to his meal.

I've met my first Uzbek and pressed the flesh!, I thought to myself. Another box ticked!

'It's now an hour-and-a-half since we ordered,' muttered Mike, in a grim whisper. 'I'll go and order another beer.'

I accompanied him to the bar, not to place an order but to have a word with the barman.

'Forget my second course.'

It was ten o'clock, too late for me to eat a substantial meal and go to bed straight after.

At this point my starter arrived, spot on one hour and fifty minutes since I'd ordered it. It now became clear that the plate of cheese and dried fish had not been nibbles for both of us to enjoy with our drinks, but Mike's starter! He'd ordered, remember, a dish described on the menu as three smoked cheeses. One of the items on the plate was fish. Smoked it may well have been, but nonetheless, fish and not cheese. There are lies, damned lies, and, it seems, bar menus in Novosibirsk. Mind you, the fish tasted OK. It's just that it wasn't what Mike had ordered.

I think what threw us was the Russian custom of serving two people separately when they're sitting together at the same table. This results in one of them getting his food before, maybe long before, the other, so that instead of eating a convivial meal together, I was eating while Mike was watching, wondering when his meal was coming. By the time Mike's food arrived, I'd finished and it was now my turn to watch while he ate. Having dinner together turned out, under these rules, not to be a joint undertaking but a spectator sport.

This would never happen in Western Europe, where a waiter wouldn't dream of serving two people at the same table separately unless expressly requested to do so. I also noticed that Russian waiters take your plate away as soon as it's empty, instead of waiting until everyone at the table has finished. It seems they're trained differently here in Russia.

'It's taken two hours waiting for us each to get a starter!'

Mike went back to the bar.

'Coffee for both of us, please, and now! I'll wait here while you make it.'

When the barman gave us our cups, we drank up and left.

We shall certainly report back to our agents in England about a Russian hotel which lets out its restaurant to outside parties and condemns its resident guests to go hungry.

'They'll probably claim that this isn't the case. That we could have ordered room service.'

'Maybe, but would it have been any quicker? There'd be a surcharge, which is taking advantage of a predicament which the hotel management has caused. Looks to me like a case of sharp practice.'

In our room, we took a turn on the balcony for a breath of fresh air. The sun was a blaze of red and gold in a clear blue sky, slowly sinking behind the railway bridge, graced with a wisp of elongated cloud.

'Mike, this is a unique opportunity for you! If you put a photo of sunset over the River Ob into an exhibition at your camera club, it'll have a built-in title. Either 'Ob served' or 'Ob scene'.'

Ob-viously!

Once in bed, the bandage under my chin was very uncomfortable. Another reason for not being able to get to sleep was the noise from the party nine floors below. Added to that, there was a permanent funfair located some 500 yards away on the river bank, which stayed open until 2 a.m. to extract the last possible rouble from its customers.

Sunset over the River Ob.

Monday 10th September
Free

The first item on the agenda was get to the clinic on time and have this damned bandage removed.

Breakfast was quite amazing in terms of what was on offer, even a glass of champagne if you fancied one at that time in the morning. The problem was, all the allegedly hot food was cold, including the portion of scrambled egg I took from the bowl immediately after one of the cooks had replenished it. It actually *arrived* cold, even though straight from the kitchen.

Dozens of unusual dishes were laid out. Some I'd never seen in my life and had no idea what they were. Strangest of all, no porridge, which is a staple. This was, after all, Russia, home of *kasha* as in the famous quotation from Gorki's novel *Dyetstvo*, 'Childhood', about his harsh upbringing as he travelled with his family around the Volga region: '*Shchi da kasha, pishcha nasha*' ('cabbage soup and porridge is our fare'), implying that that was basically all that the wretched Volga boatmen lived on.

The taxi arrived on time to take me to Avicenna. Mike accompanied me in case a sudden need arose. It took half an hour through the Monday morning rush hour. Olga had warned me that the entrance was round the side of the clinic but clearly it wasn't. There was no sign of any side entrance nor indicative arrows. I went in through the front door, directly into the waiting room. What was all that about side doors?

The receptionist addressed me in Russian at normal speed, clearly someone who didn't take prisoners or wasn't accustomed to dealing with foreigners. As soon as I gave her my date of birth it was clear that I was on the list to be seen. After I'd left my coat in the cloakroom and donned a pair of plastic overshoes, as required by local health and safety regulations, it was just a matter of sitting with Mike and waiting my turn.

I was soon called to move to the next stage, waiting in the corridor outside the consulting rooms. Mike, meanwhile, remained in the main waiting room. Half-an-hour after the official time of my appointment the nurse called me in. Not unlike home! She cut off the bandage while the duty doctor read the paper that I'd brought from the children's hospital, explaining what the treatment had been and why. The doctor was a pleasant young man who spoke a little English, which he enjoyed trying out with a native Englishman, probably for the first time in his life. We got along fine.

He tested my eyes with a small hand-held torch and examined my tongue. He was satisfied that the wound was healing. As I hadn't experienced any side effects, such as vomiting or headache, he told me no further hospital treatment was necessary. He then applied a bright green liquid to the wound and said to me:

'You'll have to go to a chemist and buy a bottle of this. It's called 'Green'. Then apply it once a day, standing in front of a mirror.'

'I have a friend with me. He can do that,' I replied. *'Can you write down the prescription on a piece of paper which I can give to the pharmacist?'*

As this was a private clinic, I was also expecting a serious fee. But no. We shook hands and he told me that as it was such a small matter there'd be no charge. I also noted with surprise that no one had asked to see my insurance documents and my passport, which I'd brought in the certain expectation that I'd be asked to produce them.

I deposited my overshoes in the bin by the door. Off we went in our taxi to the nearest pharmacy to get a bottle of 'Green'. It cost 9r. 90k (about 20p). On return to the hotel I was amazed that the total bill for the taxi was only 930r. (about £19), which included waiting an hour or so outside the clinic, making a detour to find the pharmacy and waiting while I was served.

Back at the hotel, I could only think of one thing. I wanted a proper shower and to wash my hair! I realised I'd have to take care not to irritate the area around the wound.

However, opening the bottle revealed a snag.

There was no dropper, no brush. How was I expected to apply it? The doctor had used a cotton bud, but he hadn't warned me to buy some at the chemist's along with the medication.

Mike offered to come to my aid.

'I'll make a roll with a piece of toilet paper.'

He did, but it made a horrible mess and green liquid got into my hair, leaving a vivid stain on my forehead.

'I look as though I'm radioactive! It's such a violent colour. Must consider a career change at the end of this trip: go to the States and get a walk-on part in *Star Trek* as some sort of alien. Maybe having a green streak in my hair will be seen here in Siberia as a fashion statement. 'Have you seen that Westerner with the green streaks in his hair? That's real *cool*!'

Then Mike made a discovery: There was a whole packet of cotton buds in the bathroom. Our hotel supplied them as standard. Enough for the remaining days of my treatment and then some.

 A right turn-up for the books.

Three days later, after regular application, Mike had good news.

'Your scalp has healed. There's no need to use it anymore. That 'Green' must be mighty powerful stuff!'

When I got back home, I showed the bottle to my doctor to ask if he knew its formula. He had no idea. I still keep it in a drawer in case I ever cut myself badly enough to warrant painting myself green again.

Having a free day was intended to give us a chance to have a rest and catch our breath, but also the chance to possibly explore on our own. The hotel was splendidly equipped, well designed and was knee-deep in staff, but suffered one serious disadvantage: it was nowhere near the city centre or any local shops.

We could, I suppose, take a taxi, but to where, precisely? We'd seen the main attractions, and if we simply said 'Take us to the shops' which shops would they be, and how would we get back?

'There may not be a taxi rank near the shops,' Mike suggested.

'We're total strangers in a city with 1½ million inhabitants where we're only staying for two days. We haven't time to familiarise ourselves with its lay-out or public transport system. I really don't feel up to trying out the metro. We don't know the names of any of the stations, how far it might be to the centre or how you go about getting a ticket.

It would be worth finding out were we staying longer, but hell! – we're leaving tonight!'

In such circumstances, learning to navigate solo around Novosibirsk was a skill with an early sell-by date. We wouldn't be coming back. For a tourist there's nothing to come back *for*, reconciled as I am to never seeing the inside of Kirov's house.

But the experience gave rise to Kyrle's First Law of Hotel Locations.

'The weather's fine. We can walk somewhere.'

'Yes, but it's about 28°C. Down to the river bank will be far enough.'

There were several cafés, but they only sold soft drinks and crisps and also had very loud music. Not what we needed. We ambled through a rather pleasant park, but with nowhere to rest as there weren't any seats.

We climbed up a long flight of steps to the main road. I stopped a passer-by.

'Excuse me, is there a restaurant anywhere nearby?'

He pointed one out. It turned out to be one of those where you can see what you're buying and kitchen staff serve out portions on request so that you can even get served merely by pointing.

'We'll join the queue, 'follow my neighbour' and see how it works.'

We enjoyed a pleasant snack but, most of all, the opportunity to sit down after wandering around in the boiling sun.

'Let's climb the stairway up to the bridge and walk part-way across the Ob and enjoy the view. I can take a series of pictures,' said Mike.

'Doesn't sound very exciting,' I responded, 'but standing on a bridge over the River Ob is a bit exotic for someone from England. After all, it *is* the fourth longest river in the world. Someone from Novosibirsk would probably feel the same way about walking across the Thames and admiring the view from Waterloo Bridge. But

Road bridge over the River Ob. On the left is the metro bridge.

it's about half a mile wide and a hot day. I reckon that once I've seen the view from halfway across, that'll do me.'

Back to the hotel for a rest and to do our packing. We enjoyed a cup of tea, courtesy of my supply of tea bags. I played a game of solitaire on Mike's laptop. When I'd tired of that, I e-mailed younger son, Rupert, to tell him 'Dad's now out of hospital' just to worry him, as I hadn't told him that I'd even been in! Then a nap. It was going to be a long night.

'As we're not vacating our room by the regulation check-out time of midday, we have to pay an extra 2500r. We have to pay by 21h30 and be out of the room by midnight, or there'll be another 3000r. on top.'

'Sounds like a right rip-off!'

'Nikita isn't due until 00h30. Let's take our luggage down to the reception area and park ourselves on a sofa.'

Luckily I still had English newspapers picked up at Heathrow Airport, which were enough to tide me over. No signs of any foreign papers anywhere, not even in Moscow, let alone halfway across Siberia.

IRKUTSK*

Tuesday 11th September
On the train to Irkutsk

Our train was waiting, as it started from here. On one of its wagons was a board which said 'Novosibirsk – Vladivostok'. In Cyrillic, of course.

'I must get a shot of that,' said Mike. 'I reckon this is the first time I've actually seen the name 'Vladivostok' on a train. It's a bit on the exotic side.'

'I remember flying into Beijing twenty years ago from Hong Kong with Margaret, and being similarly affected by seeing 'Ulan Bator' on the airport departures board. For us from Western Europe, this rubbed in just how far away we were from home.'

Our compartment was quite different from the previous two and really *was* first class, like something out of *La Belle Epoque*, all mirrors and polished wooden panelling. We'd asked our agents to book us first class on the train. Sometimes there *was* no first class and we'd had to make do with the best that was available.

For the first time we had a proper compartment for two people as opposed to four. It would be a pleasure to be able to sleep on the bottom bunk as there wasn't a top one. If I needed a pee in the night, I wouldn't have to wriggle around while lying horizontal, putting on my sandals in order to manage the ladder without lacerating my feet on the rungs.

'Novosibirsk – Vladivostok'.

Our compartment for two.

The space above the door extended out over the width of the corridor.

'There's enough room for our bags and your computer case.'

'These pillows are square and enormous! We don't need two each.'

'Let's stow the spares in the lockers under the beds. This compartment is going to be home for the next day-and-a-half. Let's start off by making it as comfortable as possible.'

Showing the luggage space extending over the corridor.

We woke up to find the view from the window wasn't much altered but we were able to see wider vistas as the land had levelled off and the unending forest had given way to scattered clumps of woodland.

'This, I suppose, is the *steppe* as opposed to the forest,' I observed to Mike.

I went off to get some hot water for morning tea to start the day. The water also enabled me to wash down my medication. Coffee later, then some chocolate and cake.

Lunch.

We were alone in the dining car and had time to relax while relishing the attempts by someone clearly without any English to translate the menu by looking words up in a dictionary and when there were two translations to choose from, plumping for one of them.

What on earth is the dish on the menu described in English as 'the language of beef'? The Russian word he's looked up in the dictionary is *yazik**, which translates into English as either 'language' or 'tongue', meaning either 'tongue', in the sense of the language you speak, or the actual tongue in your mouth, which in the case of some farm animals can be eaten as a delicacy; ox tongue, for example. 'The language of beef' was actually tongue of beef, or as we would call it, ox tongue. A fairly routine dish, but mis-translated it brightened up our day no end.

The menu promised us 'Hot shak with bird'. At this point a Russian dolly-bird with assisted blonde hair half-way down her back and wearing shorts up to her navel sashayed through the compartment.

'That,' Mike opined, 'must be the bird. Now where do I get the hot shak?'

But I digress.

'Well, it's obviously a hot dish; that is, they cook it to order. The Russian for *hors d'oeuvres* or snacks is *zakuski**, but they also sometimes adopt the English word 'snack' and transliterate it into Cyrillic as 'CHAK'. If you transliterate back into English, the Cyrillic 'C' becomes Latin 'S' and the Cyrillic 'H' should become our 'N', resulting in 'SNAK'. He's transliterated the first letter but forgot to transliterate the second one and left it. Not knowing any English, he read the Russian 'H' which has the sound 'n' in Russian as an 'N' and didn't realise that in English we read the letter 'H' as an aspirate.'

Do keep up.

As for the bird, I turned to the Russian version at the front of the menu. What it actually said, in Cyrillic, of course, was 'Julienne of bird'. On the next line a lengthy explanation indicated that the bird in question was chicken with assorted vegetables. The dish was, in fact, chicken julienne.

We ordered it. It came some time later, as it was cooked to order, in four little silver pots with long handles, two on each plate, beautifully presented and absolutely delicious.

Full marks for the food. *Nul points* for the translation.

'Hot shak with bird', otherwise known as chicken julienne.

Other variants were 'Beef bailed in mustard', which I presumed was just a spelling mistake, and 'Boiled language with vegetables', which we worked out for ourselves. 'Meat in a princely way', 'Hot in Russia' and 'Sea gift for a gourmet' were all more or less accurate translations of the Russian, but sounded odd and didn't make any sense, because whereas the Russian version in the menu was followed by a description of the ingredients, this was missing from the English version. We were left guessing.

Approaching Krasnoyarsk* the landscape changed. Hills. The countryside for the next few hundred miles was the same as Southern England were it not for the style of the houses in the villages we passed and, of course, the much greater distances between them.

Village houses were all detached, single-storey and built mainly of wood, with painted shutters and ornamental fretwork surrounds to the windows. Their plots were separated by picket fences with a standard elongated wooden diamond between each post and painted in uniform colours of green and cream.

Single storey village house.

We arrived at Krasnoyarsk at midday, and had a twenty minute scheduled stop. Just enough time to stretch our legs on the platform. Mike was out with his camera, looking for anything interesting. He spotted the engine of another train on the next platform and set off gleefully.

'My forebears were railwaymen. It's in the blood!'

Working their way along our train were a couple of wheel-tappers, an occupation which I thought had disappeared in England years ago. One of them wandered over to Mike to admire his camera and said he had a similar one. The two of them started an *aficionados'* discussion of the intricacies of cameras and the refinements of various lenses, angles, close-ups and all the rest – in English! Moreover, this wheel-tapper had a good accent. Eventually he excused himself and walked away, saying that he needed to get back to work.

Assuming we still have any wheel-tappers left in England, I wonder how many of them could engage a Russian tourist on a station platform in an expert discussion of photographic techniques in their own language?

The wheel-tapper at work.

Moving off, the countryside was now attractive, with hills which occasionally had steep-sided slopes. The fields were enormous, with stooks of drying wheat scattered higgledy-piggledy, not in straight rows as farmers do it in England. I know, because as a boy I used to work in the fields at harvest time stooking; that is, thrusting my fingers into a sheaf in order to pick one up in each hand and ram the heads together to make a stook consisting of six or seven sheaves. Damned hard work in the broiling sun it was, for 1s 3d an hour (about 6½p in today's money). My forearms were covered in specks of blood from being pricked by the sharp ends of the straw. A rural childhood was tough at times.

Wednesday 12th September
Arrive in Irkutsk. Free

We arrived on time, though what time that was I had been unable to discover. We were now five hours ahead of Moscow, that is, nine hours ahead of UK. It's important to know that, if you're sending e-mails and expecting answers. It's midday here. In the UK they're still having breakfast and are not yet in the office.

Along the platform, down the stairs, through the underpass, up the stairs and into the Arrivals Hall, which was overflowing with people.

Most of them were standing on the top step looking at the electronic arrivals/

departures board which is conveniently placed directly above the tunnel which is the entrance and exit from the underpass. This ensured that arriving passengers coming up the stairs and encumbered by their luggage had their way completely blocked by a stationary, immovable phalanx of people who are not looking at them and not moving aside to let them through but gazing directly over their heads, gawping at the arrivals/departures board.

The main railway station in Irkutsk is not an example of good design.

'Someone should be here to meet us, with a placard with our names on it.'

There wasn't.

We stood where we thought we'd be the most conspicuous but no one approached us. A number of people were displaying placards. When we made enquiries, none of them was waiting for us. After half-an-hour we resigned ourselves to the probability that whoever was supposed to meet us was not now going to show up. We'd have to get to our hotel by ourselves.

We were accosted by a driver purporting to be a taxi. Whether or not he was, I really couldn't be bothered to check. We'd just got off a train after thirty hours, we were tired and hungry and had not been met as arranged. Anyone willing to take us to our hotel would do. He produced a card with the fare scrawled on it – 500r. He repeated it in English and pressed us to actually *say* the words 'OK'. He wanted us to agree his price and to acknowledge that we knew how much it would be and that we'd got the cash. He'd done this before!

With hindsight, he wasn't a licensed taxi driver at all but a bloke with a car making a bit on the side, and probably charging us twice as much as a proper taxi would as well as undermining legitimate cabbies, getting cash-in-hand and not declaring it to the income tax authorities. He was relying on his targets being too tired to care, tourists who turned up at the station exhausted after a long journey and who didn't speak any Russian.

Good economics, from his point of view. A fast buck, cash in hand, and tax-free. Bad, from the point of view of Irkutsk's reputation for making visitors feel welcome.

'Why don't they employ someone to patrol the waiting area,' I asked Mike. 'When they see passengers who've just arrived and are obviously lost, or, in our case, marooned, their job would be to offer assistance. Perhaps get them a genuine taxi who will charge the proper fare?'

'It would provide some local language students with a couple of hours work a day. At the same time, it would do wonders for the city's image.'

It was only a short drive to our hotel. I paid the driver his extortionate rate without demur, as I'm going to make a claim on my agents when I get back and seek compensation. Ultimately it won't be coming out of my pocket. I can even e-mail my own agency in Winchester later today and they'll start chasing up the local agency here for compensation and an explanation. I want to know *why* whoever it was who was supposed to meet us, didn't show up.

Breakfast, a shower and some sleep in a bed. Thirty hours on a train drains you.

The hotel had an enormous foyer with a very high ceiling. The reception desk was situated on the right, lifts were in the middle and to the left a wide corridor with, at intervals along its length, several boutiques selling souvenirs and leading, we later discovered, to the bar and restaurant. In stark contrast to Novosibirsk, it was only 20 minutes walk from the city's main thoroughfare of shops and restaurants, Karl Marx St., *ul. Karla Marksa*.

'Once again, we're on the ninth floor. Thank heavens for the lift!'

'Yes. Hotel Irkutsk is very modern and spacious.'

'The receptionist has given us a plan of the town,' I said. 'We should have no difficulty finding our way around.'

'Amongst the restaurants shown on the street plan in my guidebook,' I said to Mike, 'there's one named *Snezhinka*, which means 'snowflake' in Russian. Just for fun, why don't we study the map to see if we can find it? We need some lunch. We might as well have it in a restaurant which the guide book mentions. See if we concur with its assessment.'

'Fine by me, but first, let's take a walk along the promenade beside the river. What's it called?' His voice rose at the end of the sentence, as he struggled to remember.

'It's called the Angara, with the stress on the final syllable, Angar-*a,* like Vladivost-*ok*.'

It was a beautiful day. The sun was shining. Many of the city's buildings are of stone construction as opposed to wood or brick. Irkutsk was developed at the end of the nineteenth century, and looks much like any city in Western Europe, and in particular in France, which was developed during *La Belle Epoque*.

'In case you're not aware.' I said to Mike, 'Tsar Alexander III was determined to underpin Russia's claim to the Pacific coast and saw the construction of the Trans-

Irkutsk.

Siberian Railway as essential to achieving this objective. The station here was opened in 1898 and the first train from Moscow arrived in 1900. After that, Irkutsk grew in importance as the regional centre of government and the gateway to the Siberian Far East. There's a huge statue of Alexander beside the river, symbolically facing east to spur on his countrymen to settle the land and exploit its natural resources to the glory of Mother Russia.'

Walking further along the promenade, we came across another statue. Mike read the inscription.

'This is the other Gagarin. Yuri, the pioneer astronaut.'

'In Russian,' I added, 'a *gagara* is a northern diving bird, which, in English, we call a loon. Not many people know that. More people know that 'Yuri' is the Russian equivalent of 'George'.

Ten minutes later, closely following our map, we found *Snezhinka*.

'It looks very late nineteenth century France,' said Mike, eyeing the façade.

We went inside full of anticipation.

'The interior decor is another slice of *La Belle Epoque*, like our railway compartment.'

'Indeed. Aah, look. There's a generous range of dishes on offer on the menu.'

Our waitress was slim and pretty and rather diffident with us foreigners, which inspired Mike, wishing, in an undertone, that he was half a century younger. A gentleman in his late seventies with the, naturally, self-controlled, hots is not a spectacle guaranteed to improve the appetite of the friend facing him on the other side of the table. He'd love to photograph her, solely in the interests of photographic art, you understand, but can't think of a way of doing so without creating a scene or causing offence.

'We've read about a local delicacy, the *omul**.'

'It's a small fish unique to Baikal.'

'It's on the menu.'

'Surely we're duty bound to try it?'

After eating it, I observed to Mike, 'I must say it wasn't much different from any other white fish I've eaten elsewhere. Presumably it all depends on how it's cooked or what sauce is used.'

'But did you enjoy it?'

'Yes. I'll chalk it up as an experience I wouldn't have had if I had not come to Baikal. That's the only place where it lives.'

Mike leaned across the table, adopting a confidential tone of voice.

'Have you noticed that the other diners coming and going, both male or female, are almost all dressed very stylishly and very expensively, regardless of their age?'

'I'm once again pleasantly impressed by the habit of modern Russians to dress up and look the part,' I replied. 'It's such a contrast to England, where many men think dressing smartly means putting on a tie while still leaving the shirt collar undone. Women think jeans and a tee-shirt are suitable attire for a business lunch, as long as they wear extra make-up and a pair of fashionable ear-rings.'

Dinner that night, though, was another matter. Yet again, the hotel had let its restaurant out for a private function without telling its other guests and without making any alternative provision for them.

The waitress in charge was quite dismissive. 'It's a private booking.'

She didn't deign to offer any suggestions as to what we were supposed to do if we wanted to eat. Yet twenty yards back along the corridor was a café-bar, which we

Our meal, in Snezhinka, with the local fish, the omul.

passed on the way to the main restaurant. It served bar food, yet she didn't tell us it was there! We just happened to look inside on the off-chance, saw a chap sitting at a table having a bowl of soup and realised it wasn't a bar only serving drinks but that it also served food.

We found a table and examined the menu.

'I rather fancy *pyelmyeni**, those Siberian dumplings stuffed with mince, served in a bowl of broth, which I first encountered in Novosibirsk. They'll go well with my apple juice.'

'I'll opt for their salad,' said Mike. 'Then the soup. I'll give the local beer a try.'

'Best of all, with my coffee I can smoke a cigar and unwind. It's been a long day.'

After lunch coffee. Elegant crockery, even in Siberia.

Reception accosted us with a phone call from Marina, the local guide in charge of our visit whom we hadn't met, to say that the driver sent to meet us couldn't find us. She didn't explain why. We're both six feet tall, we both have beards, which make us stand out in a crowd because they're not common amongst Russian men. We had three cases and a shoulder bag. We were standing, together with our luggage, in the middle of the concourse. Not exactly what you'd call invisible.

Yet he couldn't find us! How long did he wait after the train had arrived? Did he allow sufficient time for us to disembark from the train and get from the platform to the Arrivals Hall? Where did he look, failing to find us? The ladies' lavatories?

I'm confident that the reason he couldn't find us was because he wasn't there. Maybe he could try the excuse of having gone to the wrong station or that he met the wrong train. Neither mistake would be remotely likely for a local. It's quite simple: he overslept. No excuse. It's your job. You failed to do it. I shall seek compensation. Your head on a spike remains an option.

The receptionist continued: 'Marina says she'll meet you in the hotel lobby at ten tomorrow morning for your planned visit to the restored mid-nineteenth century houses of the leading Decembrists Prince Volkonsky* and Prince Trubetskoy*, and then to the city's museum.'

I sent an e-mail to my travel agents in Winchester to say that whatever they did, it worked. I sent another to Rupert to say no need to worry any more about Dad and hospitals. Panic over, wound's healed.

Didn't mention that I was still sporting a patch of green hair.

Thursday 13th September
Guided tour of Irkutsk, including the houses of the Decembrists Prince Volkonsky and Prince Trubetskoy

We came downstairs to the lobby to meet Marina, who overnight had morphed into Lyudmila*, a charming middle-aged lady who began by addressing us in French. OK by me, but it seemed to indicate a flaw in the briefing programme.

We quickly confirmed which language we'd like her to use.

'I used to be a guide on tourist ships sailing in the Mediterranean,' she told us. 'I've travelled extensively in that part of the world. That's why I also speak French.'

The site of the original Cossack fort.

We began by driving to the site of the original Cossack fort, erected in 1660. It's now just an empty paved square, but it's the location of the city's memorial to the war dead of 1941-5, complete with an eternal flame. This flame was brought from St Petersburg after having been lit from the one burning at their much larger memorial to commemorate the victims of the Nazi siege.

Symbolic plots of earth brought from each theatre of war commemorate the main battles. Stone slabs bear the theatres' names in memory of those who fell there.

Then to the cathedral. Inside, a young priest was taking a service with a small group of people participating in some highly accomplished singing. No one took any notice of the visitors, Russians as well as foreigners, who wandered in to gaze in wonder at the ornate gold shrine of St Innokenty*, the local saint.

Innokenty was sent by Peter the Great to represent him in China, but was refused entry at the border by the Emperor, who at that time was under the influence of the Jesuits, who'd got to him first. Forced to withdraw to Irkutsk, he was appointed the first bishop of the diocese. He devoted the rest of his life to preaching the gospel to the local indigenous people, the Buryats*.

'He was only 51 when he died in 1731,' Lyudmila told us, 'and was greatly revered in his lifetime. During restoration work to the monastery some thirty years after his death, his body was disinterred and was found to be uncorrupted. When inhabitants in distant parts of the region who invoked his name reported miracles, he was raised by the church to sainthood.'

We walked towards the river and up the wide, shallow steps of a footbridge for a panoramic view of the city.

'There are lots of 'Ivan loves Olga'-style graffiti with entwined hearts scrawled in chalk on the steps,' Mike observed. 'And the iron railings at the sides of the bridge are festooned with padlocks tagged with the names of lovers who chose this method to publicly declare their eternal devotion to each other. Rather sweet, don't you think?'

Declarations of love!

'I understand they also observe this custom on the Charles Bridge in Prague,' I replied, 'though when I was there for the Christmas Market ten years ago, I must confess that I didn't notice the phenomenon.'

Locked in undying love!

Lyudmila took us back, on foot, to the nearby Znamensky* Monastery. The customary line of beggars were sitting outside. Most were old people who, we presumed, had inadequate pensions and trusted that people visiting a religious site would be generous enough to give them a few coins.

Lyudmila did.

Outside the church is the tomb of Prince Trubetskoy, whose house we were due to visit shortly. He died in 1854. Tsar Nicholas died the following year. A year later the new Tsar, Alexander II, granted an amnesty which permitted exiles to return to their estates.

We walked past another statue, commemorating Grigory Shelekhov* (1747-95), who was described by Pushkin's teacher, Derzhavin*, as 'Russia's Columbus'. In the reign of Catherine the Great he discovered Alaska, claimed it for Russia and established permanent settlements there.

Nearby was another statue. Mike asked me if I knew who it was.

'Admiral Kolchak*.'

'Who was he?'

'Leader of the White armies in the Civil War which followed the Bolshevik Revolution in 1918.'

Lyudmila was keen to explain to us why the statue was there.

'The new post-Soviet regime in Russia has adopted a deliberate policy of laying to rest once and for all the historic struggle between Reds and Whites and to move on. As a part of the process of national reconciliation, this statue was erected in 2004 as a visible symbol of the official policy of burying past conflicts.'

She pointed out the date on the plinth: 2004.

'In 1920 Kolchak was captured and shot only a few hundred metres away from where his statue now stands. It is acknowledged now that during his career in the Tsarist Navy he was decorated several times for bravery. As commander of the Black Sea Fleet during the First World War, he enjoyed considerable success against the Turks.

Admiral Kolchak, Leader of the White armies in the Civil War.

In other words, he was a hero, but from the Communist point of view he had been a hero on the wrong side. So long as the Communists were in power, he was not going to be given the recognition that his exploits merited.

Lyudmila explained. 'The new regime is in a position to recognise past injustices and make some sort of posthumous amends. Hence the statue. The people of Irkutsk have their own particular reason for remembering him positively. He founded the city's first university.'

Lyudmila pointed with her umbrella to the base of the statue. 'You'll notice that there is a bas-relief of a White Army soldier and a Red Army soldier, pointing bayonets at each other. But the points are lowered. That shows that they are confronting each other, but not actually fighting. It's highly symbolic.'

A car was waiting to take us to the Trubetskoy House. It is reputed to have belonged to him but no one's absolutely sure. Even if it's not the right house, it's a house of the right period. The contents are all contemporary; that is, mid-nineteenth century. In most cases they belonged to the Prince and his family. It's a modest construction and open to visitors all year.

Prince Volkonsky's house, though, was most certainly his and is much larger. It was originally erected in 1838 in the village of Urik, his place of exile some 70kms from Irkutsk. It was dismantled in 1846 and brought to its present site when he was given permission to reside in the town.

The Trubetskoy House.

Prince Volkonsky's house.

For many of the Decembrist exiles, the passage of time saw sentences of hard labour in the mines completed or rescinded and the terms of the original judgments modified. Later, restrictions on where exiles could live were partly lifted.

These aristocratic incomers were educated. In their new place of residence, they set about raising standards in both public and private life. In other words, they set out deliberately to bring to Siberia some of the refinements of life as they'd known it at Court in St Petersburg or on their estates in European Russia.

This led to a remarkable improvement in the lives of Siberians, as the exiles introduced advancements in agriculture, including new crops, opened the first hospitals and schools, including schools for girls, and created amongst themselves and their associates a cultivated society which enjoyed music, poetry, literature and political debate. All of these were unknown in Siberia before their arrival.

'They may have been an elite,' I said to Mike, 'but back in European Russia in those days other aristocrats were also an elite. Russian literature contains plenty of novels and plays on this theme. Chekhov's *Uncle Vanya*, *The Cherry Orchard* and *Three Sisters* are all plays about the life of the leisured classes. Siberia had never had a resident educated, cultivated elite before the arrival of the Decembrists.'

'You mean, thanks to the Decembrist exiles, Siberia now acquired one?', said Mike.

'Precisely. After dinner in Volkonsky's house, the gentlemen retired to the Prince's study to smoke, discuss politics and read newspapers, often French ones. The ladies withdrew to the Princess's salon to enjoy music, as Princess Maria Volkonskaya was an accomplished musician. They'd talk about fashion and whatever else in the 1840's and 1850's passed as suitable subjects of conversation between refined ladies.'

On display in the music salon is the world's best surviving example of a pyramidal piano.

'And it can still be played,' Lyudmila assured us.

Princess Volkonskaya also created a wintergarden, a hothouse where she grew lemons and other exotic plants. The custodians of the house have re-created this, with the same plants that she would have known. These were shown to us during our tour of the house.

Beside the doorways in the house there were dockets with explanatory cards in various languages about the contents of each room, often giving enormous detail.

We didn't have time to read them. A tourist with a professional interest would, perhaps, take much longer than we did, because we were merely seeking to get the flavour of what life in aristocratic exile was like. For example, it's interesting to see a contemporary French newspaper, but I don't think I'd actually want to read it, especially as I'd have to stand, as there were no seats for visitors in the room.

In the grounds are the wooden outbuildings where Volkonsky's servants lived. His coach house and the stables for his horses can be viewed from the outside. As they're used by the staff as offices, they are not open to the public.

Lyudmila then took us to the regional museum for a tour.

'There's a display explaining how Mikhail Gerasimov*, through his use of prehistoric skeletons, pioneered the science of reconstructing faces from skulls. His work forms the basis of modern reconstructive forensic science.'

Gerasimov (1907-70) was a Soviet scientist with a world-class reputation.

We viewed cabinets depicting tribal life among the local nomads, the Evenki, and of the Tofalars who still live in isolated communities in the taiga, the coniferous forest lying between the tundra to the north and the temperate forest to the south. There they follow their traditional way of life and speak their own language, which has no written form. They firmly resist all attempts at integration.

At the last census, only 800 of them were left. Such is their resistance to modernisation, their children usually get no more than two or three years' schooling. Their young men are considered unsuitable for military service and as a result are not subject to conscription.

Our tour finished at half-past two.

'Instead of driving us back to the hotel,' I suggested, 'why don't you drop us outside *Snezhinka* where we enjoyed lunch yesterday? We'll make our own way back.'

Lyudmila readily agreed.

Mike was keen to re-visit *Snezhinka*.

I think I knew why!

We enjoyed another very pleasant repast and another encounter with the *omul*. Mike was disappointed that the waitress he so much admired yesterday wasn't serving our table this time.

'We'll explore the rest of the area, then walk to the hotel through the streets using the city map.'

'Great,' agreed Mike. 'I can take loads of pictures of street scenes, dilapidated wooden houses, small parks and ordinary people going about their daily lives.'

Back at the hotel the restaurant was again out of bounds, hosting a very noisy party. We only wanted a light meal and would have happily gone to the café-bar but we were given no choice and no advice from hotel staff. I trust my agents will read this and take note.

Friday 14th September
Guided tour to the Taltsy Open-air Museum and Listvyanka* on Lake Baikal*

We met Lyudmila in the foyer at 10h00 and drove south-east 70kms along the Angara towards its source in Lake Baikal, to the Taltsy Open-Air Museum.

Lyudmila explained.

'The increase in the local population necessitated the construction of reservoirs and occasionally the drowning of ancient villages. The best examples of historic rural buildings were dismantled and moved to this site to be preserved.'

It occurred to me that readers familiar with the open-air museum at Singleton in West Sussex will understand the concept perfectly.

The first building to attract our attention was a reconstruction of a seventeenth century Russian wooden fort, built to protect the new administration as it attempted to enforce payment of the fur tax.

I turned to Mike. 'I can just imagine what went through the heads of indigenous Buryat hunters on being told that the Russians had arrived. From now on, they'd have to pay a tax to the Tsar for continuing to do something which they'd done from time immemorial!'

'To start with,' I continued, 'to a Buryat in the seventeenth century the question would have been, 'What's this thing called a tax? I've always hunted sables, like my father before me and his father before him. What do you mean, I've now got to pay you every time I catch one?'

No wonder the Russians found it necessary to build a fort!'

They also added a wooden church, the smallest I've ever seen.

Lyudmila pointed to a small building some distance from the entrance to the reconstructed fort.

A reconstruction of a seventeenth century Russian wooden fort.

The small wooden church.

The rural schoolroom.

'One of the exhibits here is a genuine rural school.'

It had a single schoolroom, a corridor outside where the children hung their coats and at the far end, the teacher's living quarters.

'In that respect,' I said, 'it's not so different from the first school I attended, aged five, in a tiny hamlet, where the head teacher lived upstairs but had her own private front door.'

Lyudmila was rather surprised when I said this. She then pointed to a weekly calendar, pinned up on display.

'The timetable shows that the children attended six mornings a week from the ages of 10-12 and were taught to read, write and count and received religious instruction. Bright ones could continue for two more years and learned some Russian history as well.'

Going into another reconstructed building, this time a farmhouse, Lyudmila explained how the different rooms were used.

'The warmest place to sleep was on top of the stove. This was reserved for the oldest and youngest or an honoured guest.'

This may sound alarming to anyone who is not familiar with Russian stoves.

They're far larger than ours in Western Europe. They usually have their chimney to one side or at the back. Most importantly of all, they're sheathed in tiles so that it's possible to lay bedding or just a coat or blanket on top and then to lie on it and sleep.

'The entrance lobby was left unheated,' continued our guide. 'It was kept as a space to keep food dry and out of reach of wild animals while also ensuring that it didn't go off.'

Some rooms had explanations in English, but in very strange English. The person writing them was using a dictionary, without having a real grasp of the language. However, it was a welcome attempt. I gained at least a vague idea of wedding customs more rapidly through reading about them in odd English than I would have had I been forced to read them in perfect Russian. They sounded extremely complex. I skipped most of the text because, due to the garbled English, it was too much bother to try to disentangle what they were trying to say.

'I see a lake,' said Mike, pointing. 'Let's go and take a look.'

'There are also a lot of souvenir stalls,' I chimed in. 'Do we need anything?'

'No, only a fridge magnet for your collection.'

'I suppose this round sort of tent is a typical Buryat house made of felt.'

It doubled as a shop selling slippers, gloves and handicrafts, for none of which, unfortunately, either of us had any personal need.

We were not the only visitors. Several Russian family groups and a large party of other foreign tourists were also looking around the display. Three parties of schoolchildren arrived. Some were drawing the buildings, while others were enjoying the use of a large rope, thoughtfully provided for impromptu contests of tug-o-war.

Looking at my watch, I realised that it was time for something to eat. I'd already noticed the equivalent of a tea-room.

Lyudmila took us inside. The school parties had got there first! They didn't take long, as most of the kids only wanted a bar of chocolate or some other single item, not to place a lunch order.

'What do you recommend?', I asked Lyudmila. 'We're not very *au fait* with Buryat cuisine.'

I didn't fancy another tussle with pseudo-English and another 'hot shak with bird'.

'Try *sbityen**,' she replied. 'It's a drink made from honey and herbs and served hot. And then *pozy**. They're the Buryat version of Russian *pyelmyeni* and filled with mince.'

When they were served they were twice the size of *pyelmyeni*, with a hole in the top and very filling. Exactly the sort of stodge you'd need in the winter when the temperature can drop to –40°C.

Sbityen and pozy, with a bowl of solyanka.

I discovered that unless you sprinkled the *pozy* liberally with salt, they had almost no taste.

'There doesn't appear to be much in the way of seasoning or spices in Buryat cuisine,' Mike commented, pulling a face.

'Maybe not available naturally in their environment, and them too poor to buy such luxuries?', I replied.

'We can have some more *solyanka*.' he suggested, seeing it on the menu. 'It's obviously as much a staple here as it is back in Moscow.'

'Good idea. Stick to what we know.'

Unfortunately it was served half-cold. By the time I'd finished it and started on my plate of two *pozy*, they were equally cold. Lukewarm and basically tasteless dumplings filled with cold mincemeat are not a culinary delight, no matter how much salt you sprinkle on them.

The little cemetery shows carved wooden crosses in Orthodox style used in rural Russia centuries ago. A 'sotka' was a measurement of land equal to 100m². Six 'sotka' would be about the size of 2½ tennis courts. There is an explanation in English (of a sort!) for the benefit of visitors.

Village Cemetery

The exposition "Village cemetery of the end of XIX and the beginning of XX century" was open in 1992. It consists in cemetery chapel built by analogue of the chapel from the village Sukhaya on the lake Baikal, common grave, grave mounts. The cemetery is enclosed by gap fence with wicket-gate and gates. The area of the cemetery is 6 sotka.

The small village the chapel served as the cemetery church where the funeral service over the deceased and the praying services were performing. In winter, the coldest period, the deceased was not intered in Middle Angara region. The deceased coffin was staying in the chapel up to the set thaw.

The common grave was appeared in the museum in 1956 after the graves were transferred from Talci cemetery submerged by water of Irkutsk reservoir. The grave mounts with the crosses and "gobets" (the funeral structure with the crosses) were made by analogue to the cemetery monuments of the Middle Angara region.

In 1992 the cemetery was sanctified by the bishop of Irkutsk and Angarst Vadim. The funeral service ritual was performed over the common grave.

When we'd finished lunch, I turned to Lyudmila, who'd been nibbling a sort of roll. Evidently, she was not much more taken by the prospect of lunching off cold *pozy* and tepid *solyanka* than we were.

'And now?'

'Listvyanka.'

Back in the car, it wasn't long before we reached a ribbon development between a line of low but very steep wooded hills and the bank of the River Angara down to the point where it meets Lake Baikal. This was the famed summer holiday resort of Listvyanka. The road ran between the shore and a long, continuous line of houses and shops. On the shore itself there were occasional tiny shacks where boats were advertised for hire. Groups of small children were paddling. The continuous line of shops on the landward side was occasionally broken by a small square crammed with market stalls. Because the town was so attenuated and didn't appear to have a town hall square or obvious centre, it was difficult to decide whether Listvyanka is a large village or a small town.

We went to the market and found jewellery made from a purple stone unique to Baikal, known as charoite*.

This would make an ideal present at some stage for some lady of my acquaintance, I thought, and lashed out 1800r. for a pendant. Lyudmila had guided us to this particular stall as she knew it was rather cheaper than any of the others and certainly cheaper than in the shops I subsequently visited in the village.

Listvyanka market.

Listvyanka is a popular tourist town. Dozens and dozens of stalls were all selling similar items. For the people of Irkutsk, and there are more than half a million of them, in the summer this is the nearest place they have for a family day out at the seaside.

'How can so many competing stallholders possibly make a living?', I wondered to Mike.

'I suppose they must do, or they wouldn't all be here. But it can't be *much* of a living.'

Smoked omul sold on the shore.

Looking at the boats, for lake trips or to hire, and the serene beauty of Baikal we must assume that Listvyanka gets a lot of tourists and that every one of them is going to spend some money. After all, the nearest seaside is over a thousand miles away, and to get there probably requires a Chinese visa.

Nearby, there's a very modern museum, where we found an excellent exposition of Baikal's topography, with imaginative videos on loops illustrating the area over geological time and exhibits of local fauna. It explained how a skilled hunter could find a hibernating bear and lure it out and kill it with a special knife aimed at its heart. What happened if he missed with his first thrust was left to the viewer's imagination.

'There's a small aquarium, too.'

'Ah! A real live *omul*! They don't only exist on a plate!

Exhibits of local molluscs were displayed in cases. Fish and other marine specimens were displayed in jars. Finally we came to a tank with two Baikal seals, *nerpas*, which are a freshwater species unique to the lake. Fish kept appearing on the surface of the water, being dropped by a member of staff out of sight above the tank. The seals performed graceful somersaults to catch the fish and, in the process, provided visitors with an acrobatic aqua-show.

'Now I'm going to take you to the local church,' Lyudmila said. It's about a kilometre inland. Originally it was on the lake shore, but had to be moved because it was in danger of being inundated. Some of the icons are older than the church building, because they've been brought there from elsewhere.'

As usual, there were a couple of beggars outside, an old woman and an old man who was sitting in a wheelchair. On our return Lyudmila stopped to give them some coins. I noticed that the old man had no hands but had very sunburned stumps from, one presumes, spending the summer in the open air sitting outside the church in his chair, begging.

Next day we were due to make a trip on the Circum-Baikal Railway. Lyudmila warned us that it didn't have a restaurant car. We needed to provide our own picnic. We'd need, therefore, to do some shopping. As we were due to leave the hotel at 07h00 before breakfast was served, we'd have to buy our own sustenance at a supermarket here in Listvyanka.

It was just like any supermarket in Western Europe, full of countless varieties of sausage, cheese, pastries, fruit and the usual household staples. They even arranged for fruit to be sold individually. We didn't buy any, but watched customers weighing it themselves and sticking a label on it, just as we would in the UK.

The following day we discovered our mistake in that supermarket. We'd over-bought and had food left over which we ended up having to take with us to the next places on our trip. One such item was a tube of mayonnaise. Why on earth had we let Lyudmila talk us into buying *that*? It ended up in Mike's case and was lugged all the way back to England unopened, where he told me later he didn't finish it till Christmas. She also persuaded us to buy a set of plastic cutlery which, when we opened it on the train the next day, we discovered consisted of spoons and forks but no knives.

Many of the people in Listvyanka, locals as well as visitors, were in shorts and flip-flops, since the temperature was in the mid-twenties C. The dress code here in Siberia is remarkably similar to anywhere else. The Russians, whether in Moscow or Irkutsk, look like any crowd of people in Western Europe, with none of the legions of shapeless old women in headscarves, calf-length dresses and boots so beloved of popular myth and cartoonists. It may be different in winter.

Fashionable girls wear their hair long. Style dictates high heels. In many cases *very* high heels, which is all the more surprising when pavements are not that well maintained and are often cobbled. Laying aside for a moment the ubiquitous Cyrillic script, we could easily think we were in Western Europe.

A fashionable young Siberian enjoying the sun.

There were a few beggars, usually outside churches.

In the café-bar that night we enjoyed yet more *pyelmyeni*. I overheard a thick-set, oldish chap at the bar ask in English for a beer before wandering off to sit by himself at a table. I went over and told him he was welcome to join us if he'd like some English-speaking company.

'I'm Tony. I'm from Canberra,' he said, by way of introduction. 'I went to Australia as a child when my parents opted for the '£10 Poms' scheme back in the 1950's. I've just retired from my business and I'm taking some time out to travel the world.'

'I've been to Australia many times,' responded Mike. 'My eldest son and his family live in Melbourne.'

Tony was with a group of friends who'd come via Beijing across Mongolia and he spoke very highly of Mongolian hospitality.

'This is precisely the trip we're scheduled to do in a week's time. Can we pick your brains on what to look out for?'

Tony was happy to offer some advice. He was staying in Irkutsk for a couple of days before getting the train to Moscow but would not be getting off *en route*.

We spent a very pleasant couple of hours together.

'Ships that pass in the night', observed Mike.

Saturday 15th September
Guided excursion on the Circum-Baikal Railway

We were collected at 07h00 by taxi to the station, and met our new guide, Irina, for which the familiar form is Ira, *pronounced Eera*.

'What do you do when you're not guiding visitors?'

'I'm studying for my diploma. I trained in business studies in China.'

'So you speak Chinese as well as English?'

'Yes, but I haven't used it for some years and I've forgotten a lot.

'Join the Club. I say the same about my Russian.'

Our guide, Irina.

We had a three-quarters of an hour wait for the main line train to Slyudyanka*, where we waited another hour on a different platform for the tourist train which would take us for our excursion. This is along the old line, now a dead end, which takes tourists to Port Baikal, on the opposite bank of the Angara to Listvyanka, at the point where the river flows out of the lake, the only river to do this. All the others flow in. Eventually the Angara joins the mighty Yenesei*, whose outfall is in the Arctic Ocean.

The usual mix of vendors were on the platform. Ira bought a smoked fish. Another *omul?* As a result of this, for most of the rest of the morning she sat opposite me with the fish in one hand, peeling off the skin with the other and putting the flesh into her mouth. In my view, only a Russian would buy a smoked fish and sit on a train eating it raw with her fingers in the way we would eat a packet of crisps. I can't imagine myself buying a smoked mackerel, then picking the skin off and eating it with my fingers, least of all, in public. *Chacun a son goût,* but occasionally one comes across some very odd *goûts.*

Until 1904 the railway from Irkutsk followed the river to Port Baikal, from where passengers took a ferry across the lake to Mysovaya (nowadays called Babushkin) on the eastern shore. To continue their journey, they then took another train belonging to the Trans-Baikal Railway. In summer violent storms, with waves up to 6m in height, often disrupted the ferry's timetable. In winter, the ice was too thick even for an icebreaker specially commissioned and transported from European Russia. Passengers had to cross the lake on foot or by horse-drawn coach.

After crossing one of the 200 bridges on trestles, the tourist train stops to allow passengers to explore and take photographs.

In 1893 it was decided that although the south shore of the lake is virtually all cliffs which fall sheer into the lake and the cost of building a railway would be greater per kilometre than on any other section of the entire railway, nonetheless it would have to be done.

The engineering work necessitated the construction of 33 tunnels and 200 bridges on trestles, and the relics of some of these are visible alongside the existing track. At other times it ran on an embankment only a few feet above the shoreline.

One of the 33 tunnels.

The line was completed in September 1904. The views on the stretches between the tunnels were idyllic, with the lake on its best behaviour, absolutely flat calm and shimmering in the bright sunlight. On a sunny day like this it was hard to imagine 6m waves and storms worse than they get in the Black Sea.

The calm view from our train.

Much of the rest of the carriage was occupied by a school party, who spent most of their time playing cards or standing over each others' seats talking, not taking a blind bit of notice of the wonderful scenery. They weren't badly behaved, just kids out for the day, enjoying themselves, but I couldn't see them deriving anything from their trip on the Circum-Baikal Railway that they couldn't have gained on a train trip to the nearest town and back. They were all 'socialising' like mad. You don't need to buy a premium-priced ticket on a tourist train to do that.

We stopped at irregular intervals for 20 minutes or so in the middle of nowhere in particular, usually at a vantage point for a view. Mike took photos through the window, but he preferred to stand in the intersection between the carriages where he could take shots from both sides of the train and have a greater choice of angles. Occasionally our view through the window was interrupted by a passing freight train. Russian freight trains are so long that they seem to go on forever.

On one occasion when the train stopped, Mike went off to take up his position in the intersection to grab a particularly attractive shot. Just as he was lined up, yet another freight train came past and totally blocked his view. By the time it had passed, our own train had moved off so the vantage point was missed. He returned to us in the carriage where, by good luck, we were in the nearest seat, oathing about 'bloody freight trains'.

The next time he went off to the intersection, Ira leaned across and said to me, 'I bet a freight train comes past now.'

Sure enough it did! We both burst out laughing. Ira was much more relaxed with us than any of our other guides, and genuinely had a sense of humour.

Her prediction that Mike would yet again be baulked by fate in his quest for a decent photo has now passed into my personal vocabulary. It's when I prophesy something bad and it happens and I laugh and say 'Told you so!' For example, I say you're going to drop something and you do and I laugh, this is 'having an Ira moment'. Essentially it's light-hearted banter between friends, laughing at each other's minor misfortune. Mike's only lost a possible photo-op, not his wallet. I shall long remember Ira for her unintended contribution to the expressiveness of the English language and giving it a new phrase.

Each time the train stopped, souvenir stalls appeared like fairy mushrooms selling the usual tat: *matryushka* dolls – the type you open to find a smaller one inside – jewellery, plaques to hang on the wall or fridge magnets depicting a local scene.

Sometimes there was a disused tunnel we could walk to and then walk into for a few dozen yards. I couldn't see much point.

At other times there were the remains of former rail bridges and other vestiges of engineering works and occasionally there would be a tiny settlement of two or three houses. On one occasion a local artist who lived in an isolated house nearby had some of his works laid out on the platform for inspection and sale.

At our third stop, due to the platform not being long enough for the train, we had to walk its entire length before we could get off and found that the last car had a café selling snacks and coffee. We needn't have bothered shopping yesterday and stocking up. Except, of course, that bringing our own comestibles was much cheaper.

This kindled the formation of Kyrle's First Law of Restaurant Cars, which says: get an authoritative answer to the question: does the train we're catching tomorrow / next week / on my trip next month have a restaurant car? 'I think so' or 'I don't think so' are not acceptable responses.

I want a reliable, definitive answer, either a dead-certain yes or an equally unequivocal no. Have you asked the railway company? Have you read their brochure? Yes or no. Which is it? Are you absolutely sure? If there *is* a restaurant car, then we know that we needn't bother to take any food of our own. If there isn't, then we'll come armed with sufficient grub to see us through. If there's a restaurant car but we didn't know and we've brought our own, then we'll feel like fools, as well as being encumbered by additional stuff to carry for no good reason. If we expected provision on board but there isn't any, then we face starvation and dehydration and a thoroughly uncomfortable experience. Knowing whether or not there's on board provision for food and drink, and at what level, is not a luxury but an absolute necessity, especially if you're going to be on the train for a lengthy period, perhaps all night and half the following day.

We were travelling along the shore with the lake on our right.

'How do we get back to our car?', I asked. Mike was otherwise occupied, peering through the windows at the intersection, watching out for suitable scenery to photograph.

'Yuri, our driver, is waiting for us at Listvyanka. We get there on the ferry from Mysovaya on the east coast on the opposite side of the lake. It takes 25 minutes.'

'I rather fancy a boat trip across Baikal! But there's a problem,' I suggested.

'Mysovaya is north-east of Slyudyanka, where we boarded the train. If we're going in that direction, the lake would be on our left.'

'Yes.'

'But if you look out of the window, you can see it's actually on our right.'

'Oh.' Ira's voice dropped to a whisper.

'So we must be travelling in precisely the opposite direction. Explain, please.'

Ira turned round in her seat to check out what I'd just said. She realised that I was right.

'We're not heading north-east up the side of Lake Baikal towards Mysovaya, but north-*west* back towards Listvyanka,' she admitted. 'The ferry we're due to catch doesn't leave from Mysovaya but from Port Baikal on the opposite side of the Angara from Listvyanka. It only takes ten minutes.'

Ira may be the guide, but she doesn't seem to have much of a sense of direction! But there's no harm done. We can relax. Because we know she has a sense of humour, we can josh her gently about her discomfiture. The passengers may be in two, or even more, minds about which way the train's going, but we can rest assured that the man who matters knows – the driver! The railway track only goes one way. To Port Baikal.

The final stop was for an hour-and-a-half, and we spent much of the time having tea and I took the opportunity to have my customary mid-afternoon nap. Arriving at Port Baikal, Ira had to use her powers of persuasion to get us on the crowded ferry to Listvyanka, only a ten-minute crossing, where Yuri, our driver, was waiting to drive us back to our hotel.

On the ferry I was accosted by the chap sitting next to me, who heard us speaking English.

'Are you English? I learned a bit at school, but that was ten years ago. I haven't used it since.'

'Oh? Yes.' I murmured, feigning interest. Little did I expect what was coming next.

He pointed at Mike, who was sitting on Ira's other side. 'Your friend over there, what football team does he support?'

I can't think of a more stupid question to ask. You meet a foreigner, you want to air your language skills, and the first question you ask him is not which football team he supports to possibly start a discussion of the relative merits of his team and yours, but which team does *his mate* support. What does it matter to him what football team my friend supports?

'None. He's not interested in football and doesn't support any team any more than I do.'

The conversation came to a rather abrupt end.

As a matter of fact, I was way off. Mike is a keen Arsenal supporter, but I was totally unaware of that. In all the years I've known him he'd never mentioned it, as he knew it wouldn't be of any interest to me.

We repeated the long drive we had taken yesterday from Listvyanka to Irkutsk. Attractive countryside, undulating hills, woodland and small villages and the occasional very modern petrol station. I didn't mind doing it for a second time, bearing in mind that it was also the last time. I kept thinking to myself, 'Look closely at everything. You're never going to be here again.'

We originally planned to have a light dinner in the bar, but . . .

'We've got so much food left after buying all that stuff for the train, I think our best bet is to eat some of it now in our room, then go down to the bar for coffee.'

'OK. It'll also mean you don't have to carry so much.'

Next morning, packed and ready, at 09h30 we set off with Yuri again for the six hour drive to our next destination, the island of Olkhon* in the middle of Lake Baikal.

'We must remember to pay the laundry bill before leaving,' I said to Mike.

'Got enough roubles, or are you going to use your credit card?'

'Not sure yet. Depends how much it is.'

'Maybe I'm getting shirts washed more often than necessary, but I prefer that to carrying dirty linen around infecting all the clean stuff.'

'Right, Yuri. We're off.'

'Oh. We've got a new guide!'

Nizneangarsk

Severobaikalsk · Iarki island

Baikalo-Lenskii reserve

Baikalskii range

Barguzinski Nature Reserve

Barguzinskii range

Taza

Kurumkan

Sarankhur

Ushkanii
Islands

Cape
Khoboi

Barguzin

Zalari

Kutulik

Uzuri

Cheremkhovo

Maloye More

Khuzir
-1637

Sakhurta

Olkhon Island

Usolie-Sibirskoe

Ustordinski

Angarsk

Shelekhov

Irkutsk

Port Baikal

Selenginsk

Ulan Ude

Angasolka

Listvianka

Kultuk

Mar'itui

Sliudianka

Babushkin

Ivolginsk

Utulik

Baikalsk

Tankhoi

Vidrino

Tarbagatay

Khamar-Dabanrange

Gusinoozersk

Gusinoe Ozero

Navushki

LAKE BAIKAL
REGION

| 1 cm | = 16 miles

LAKE BAIKAL: OLKHON ISLAND

Sunday 16th September
Meet a shaman and drive to Lake Baikal to catch the ferry to Olkhon Island

We left at 09h30 for our four-day visit to Olkhon, a large island in Lake Baikal, with yet another guide, another Olga, who turned out not be a trained guide but a professional translator who specialised in French. This didn't matter, as there was nothing on Olkhon which she would need to explain. All we really needed her for was to do the talking when required, for example, if we stopped for lunch *en route*.

She told us she was familiar with Olkhon.

'I go there every summer for a couple of weeks' holiday with my family. It has lovely beaches. It's very quiet. In summer the water is warm enough for swimming. We usually camp on a beach and go into town for groceries and bottled water.'

I was mildly relieved to know that she knew how to get there and what to do when we arrived. That was all that mattered.

'We're not going straight there, are we? Aren't we supposed to be meeting a shaman on the way?'

'Yes. He lives at Ust Ordinsky*. It's only a small town but it's the capital of an autonomous Buryat enclave in the province centred on Irkutsk province ('*oblast*'* in Russian).

Shamanism is the original belief system of the indigenous Buryats. Essentially they believe that there are spirits in the air, the sky, water, stones and trees and that they should be honoured.

'If you see a post with brightly coloured ribbons tied to it, it's a shaman shrine. If you go up close, you'll find the ground scattered with small denomination coins and offerings of sweets and cigarettes.'

'The spirits have a sweet tooth, then? And they like a fag?'

Olga just smiled. 'I don't know. You'll have to ask the shaman.'

Orthodox christianity came to the Buryats with the arrival of Russian colonisers. From Mongolia, a century later, came Buddhism. Like all religions during the Communist period, shamanism was persecuted. Many of its priests were sent to gulags or executed but it still survived in rural areas. The Buryat Republic, or

Buryatia, is rural. Most of it is located on the eastern side of Lake Baikal.

At Ust Ordinsky, we began by visiting the museum.

'There's only one staff member on duty,' I whispered to Mike. 'If she takes us round, there'll be no one on the desk.'

She stayed at her post. We were left to go round unaccompanied.

The first exhibit to attract our notice was a Tofalar hut, rather like a Native American tepee, with a high step at the entrance, an open fire in the centre and hardly room inside to move as it's circular and only about seven or eight metres across. Primitive isn't the word.

The Tofalar hut.

'Believe it or not,' says Olga, 'there are still some families living like this. They absolutely refuse to change their traditional lifestyle, despite its obvious lack of comfort.'

The rooms were designed to represent traditional Buryat houses, with displays of Buryat and Evenk costume and household utensils and hunting implements. The Buryats, Olga told us, nowadays wear ordinary clothes and live in ordinary houses.

'They're completely assimilated. Most speak Russian as their everyday language as well as for official communications. They have distinctive oriental facial features, compared to Russians of European descent. That's about the only difference.'

Traditional one-room Buryat hut.

The shaman, Aleksei*, was waiting for us outside his traditional one-room hut.

He was a big man, dressed in a long blue coat and wearing a large fur hat. He spoke extremely good, clear Russian. Russian, a Slavonic language not related in any way to Buryat, which belongs to the group of languages known as Turkic, was just as foreign a language to him as it is to us.

He explained the traditional way of greeting, and asked: '*Are you willing for me to invoke the spirits on your behalf and ask them to bless you?*'

'*Of course.*'

He then dressed us in Buryat costume, consisting of a brightly-coloured tunic and belt and gave us each a fur-trimmed hat to wear. He then sat us on the guest bench behind a table covered in a plastic cloth, ready for the ceremony.

'*The top of the door into a Buryat house,*' he explained, '*is deliberately kept low so that when you enter, you are forced to bow your head and show respect to the owner. When you leave you will have to bow again and that means you are showing respect to the sky, home of the spirits.'*

He went on. *'When I pray to the spirits I have to remember my ancestors back for nineteen generations. It's very hard!'* He smiled. *'Now look up at the sky through the smoke-hole in the roof. Some of the words I'm going to use will be in the Buryat language but afterwards I'll translate.'*

'Olga can earn her corn by translating yet again for us into English,' Mike muttered to me out of the side of his mouth.

The author dons Buryat costume.

The ceremony consisted of lighting some coloured paper in a saucer and carrying it round the room, beating a small hand-held drum and then pouring a white liquid, which resembled milk, from one wooden bowl into another.

Dressed in Buryat costume with Aleksei, the shaman.

Interior of the Buryat hut.

He explained further: '*I'm seated in the men's half of the house opposite the women's half, but you are seated in the middle facing the door, which is the place for guests.*'

We questioned him. 'How does one becomes a shaman? Is there a course of study, does one have to qualify in some way?'

Apparently not. '*A shaman either has the gift of being able to communicate with the spirits or he doesn't. Often being a shaman runs in the family. But if you are not a member of a shaman family, you can become a shaman through being struck by lightning and surviving, or being clinically dead but recovering.*'

Mike and I considered our ethical positions.

'The whole set of ideas behind shamanism may seem primitive to Westerners,' I said. 'We've been brought up in a society heavily influenced by Christianity, including those who, like me, went from being in the choir of a High Anglican church in my late teens to becoming an atheist in my early twenties. Your take may be slightly different, as you're still a practising Christian.'

Mike nodded in agreement. 'I'm still a Methodist, of course, as you well know. But I take your point about what he's demonstrating being a form of primitive animism. It's very revealing to have it explained by a practitioner and to see a ceremony.'

Aleksei was obviously totally sincere. He was trying to bring good into the world in his chosen way. His beliefs didn't threaten anyone else. He wasn't saying that his way is the only way and that those who don't follow him are condemned to retribution in the life to come. He was putting on a good show for his visitors, whom he was treating as guests. He wasn't trying to bamboozle us or to profit from our visit other than, I presume, payment for his time, rather like a consultation fee. He wasn't seeking to get rich or rule the world. He came across as a thoroughly decent bloke making an honest living, and I felt spiritually enriched by having met him.

We posed for photos, shook hands and embraced and he gave us each a parting gift of a small stone with a sun emblem scratched on it, symbolising good fortune. Mine sits on my mantelpiece in the front room, along with other souvenirs of my travels.

The shamanic stone.

Finally Aleksei gave us each a brightly coloured ribbon to tie on his votive stand, making a wish at the same time. He gave Olga some more ribbons.

Prayer flags tied onto a tree.

'There will be prayer stands tied with ribbons along the roadside. Please remember to give a wave of the hand as a mark of respect to the spirits. When you come across one and are able to stop, tie some ribbons onto it.'

Cattle appearing in the fields.

The wide valley after crossing the boundary of the Irkutsk oblast.

As a guest in the land of the shamans, it seemed to me to be common courtesy.

We continued on our way, travelling through undulating, well-wooded countryside. Cattle, which we had scarcely seen since we arrived in Russia, began to appear in fields as we crossed the boundary of the Irkutsk *oblast* and entered a wide valley with low hills and brown grass.

'It's the end of the summer,' said Olga. 'Earlier in the year it was green.' To my surprise, we were driving on an excellent tarmacked road. We stopped at a wayside café at midday for a spot of lunch, which took an hour because I'd ordered *pozy*, which take a long time to cook.

The café's toilet.

The café's toilet was a disaster area: 'squat and grunt', no paper and a pile of human dung visible through the hole. Judging by its dimensions, it had been there for weeks instead of being removed at proper intervals. Do they have public health inspectors in Buryatia?, I mused. When did they last visit this particular café?

The land continued to be bare and to all appearances barren, while occasionally a cow wandered across the road without looking, just as ponies do in the New Forest. There were no signs warning about them. It was just assumed that a driver knows to expect them and take avoidance action if he comes across one. There won't be many, indeed any, foreign tourists on the roads around here driving their own cars. Only locals.

The bare earth road.

The countryside as we drew nearer to Baikal became increasingly barren, with no signs whatever of habitation or human activity outside the very few villages we passed through, other than the fact that there was a road. Then it ran out. We suddenly found ourselves driving on bare earth. It stayed like this for the next ten kilometres. And without any warning.

The car rumbled over rough stones. We then came to a gang of men laying new tarmac. As the existing road was being re-laid, of course it was closed. Diversion? One-way, with a chap at each end with a pivoted 'STOP/GO' sign? Neither. You simply drove alongside the road regardless and created your own new road, until the tarmac work was completed and you could get back onto the old road with its new surface.

At last Olkhon came into view.

On either side of the landing stage low hills sloped steeply down into the lake. The island appeared to be totally devoid of trees. According to the guidebooks, it's 72kms long and 14kms wide and is the third largest island in the world which is in a lake. It supports a population of only 1800, of whom 1500 live in the main settlement, Khuzhir*, which was where we were headed.

At the ferry terminal we found a few cafés and the usual souvenir stalls.

On either side of the landing stage low hills sloped steeply down into the lake.

Souvenir stalls at the ferry terminal.

The free ferry.

'The island may be only 3kms distant,' said Olga, 'but at the height of the season, if you haven't booked your passage, you can wait 24 hours to get across.'

We were last in a queue of five. The tiny ferry was already approaching. The length of time we had to wait was negligible. This was the benefit of visiting out of season.

'Do we have to buy a ticket to get across?'

'No. It's free. It's deemed to be part of the national highway network.'

We crossed in about fifteen minutes, on a boat which took only eight or nine cars.

'If we climb the companionway above the car deck,' I said to Mike, 'we'll be able to enjoy wonderfully uninterrupted views of the coast, both of the island and behind us on the mainland, on a perfect afternoon and not a tree in sight.'

Mike was having an absolute field day with his camera. He was able to choose from a whole range of possibilities: shots of the ferry itself, the passengers, the approaching shore in front or the receding shore behind. In addition, in the distance he had an unimpeded view of the long line of low cliffs which form the western shore of Baikal.

On Olkhon. The 'O' in front is the abbreviation for the Russian word 'ostroff', meaning 'island'.

Driving off the ferry at the other end, we found that there was no longer any tarmac, only a dirt road and a very long line of cars hoping to cross to the mainland before the ferry stopped for the night.

'How long are the cars on the end of *that* queue going to have to wait?', we all wondered.

I'll come to that later.

There didn't appear to be any domestic dwellings at the ferry head, either on the mainland or across on Olkhon. On the mainland side the handful of buildings were all souvenir stalls. On the opposite shore, they were all single-storey cafés. Presumably everyone working here must live somewhere else. When the ferry stops, they shut up shop and go home.

Where that would be was problematical, as on the island, the distance from the ferry to Khuzhir is 37km. The last place we passed on the way to the ferry on the mainland side was called Eliantsy* and that was a similar distance. When the ferry stops, both ferry-heads must be completely deserted, including the boats. It's evident that they have no crew accommodation on board. If anyone is required to keep watch at night, it must be a very lonely job.

The traffic queue for the last scheduled ferry of the day.

Once we'd disembarked, we naturally expected the first cars in the queue going the other way to start their engines and be waved on board by a crew member. This is what happens on the car ferry in Dartmouth, where for twenty years, I owned a flat. The ferry operates a shuttle service. Once the last car's off, the first one in the queue on shore is signalled to drive on.

But no. The Olkhon Island ferry refused to start loading until it was time for the next scheduled crossing.

It was absolutely ridiculous. Dozens of cars were waiting to cross. There was a larger ferry but it was not in service. Why not? It's September. Have they already suspended the summer timetable and reverted to their winter one? I wondered what time the small ferry we'd just used, and which only holds eight cars, would stop for the night. Seven o'clock, perhaps? If that was the case, then everyone in the queue would be stuck there until the following morning.

'No one working on or near the ferries lives on site,' I remarked. 'There are no hotels, nor even hostels or a campsite. They'll have to sleep in their cars. Just about possible for two people, but a family with children? Let's hope they didn't bring the dog as well.'

Coffee break, with Olga, our guide.

'It's been a long drive since lunch. Shall we have coffee before completing the journey up to Khuzhir?', suggested Mike, with a rather pleading resonance in his voice.

'The cafés only serve coffee, tea, soft drinks and snacks. There's no indication that any establishment offers cooked food, Certainly, there's no restaurant.'

'Lack of entrepreneurial sense?' I added, darkly. 'Amongst all these waiting cars, there will be some travellers who'd like a decent meal. If they end up being stranded overnight, they'd pay serious money for a shower and a bed, unless Russian tourists and weekenders are a totally different species to us Westerners, and are content to sleep in or perhaps even under their vehicles and make do with a sandwich and a bottle of water.'

Needing to relieve myself, I proceeded to the public toilet block. My access was partially obstructed by a grazing cow, which ignored me and showed no inclination to move out of the way.

I found once again that there was only one cubicle, and that it was of the 'squat and grunt' variety. It was hardly a surprise. Equally unsurprising was that it stank to high heaven, rather reminiscent of our experience at lunchtime.

Cow grazing by the toilet.

Out in the wilds, main drainage and a sewerage system may be uneconomic or impractical, but haven't they even heard of cesspits?, I thought to myself.

Looking down through the seat hole, the pile of human dung was at least a metre high, and as before at the café, there was no paper. On this toilet there wasn't even a door, just a brick wall beside the access path, partly obscuring the occupant from curious onlookers with or without mobile phones broadcasting them to 'You've Been Framed!' on TV. I can think of no circumstances in which I would voluntarily use such a facility, other than to pass water, which was all I intended to do, with or without the cow's co-operation.

This is a major holiday route throughout the summer and autumn, with literally hundreds of visitors using the ferry. Kyrle's Second Law of Public Bogs states: remove the necessity of using them by using the toilets in your hotel before you leave. As the cliché goes: 'Avoid them like the plague.' I say 'Avoid them, or you'll probably *get* the plague.'

Faced at the ferry with lavatories like these, those gently reared or of a nervous disposition might, if taken short, consider the option of just tucking their trousers into their socks.

It was now half-past four. Time for us to complete the last part of our journey.

'We *must* count the queue of the waiting cars as we drive past!'

We all tried to count, but Yuri seemed to be the most confident. Maybe, being the driver, he had the best view. The upshot was that as we reached the end of the line of traffic facing in the opposite direction, he announced triumphantly, '*There are 87 vehicles lined up.*'

At maybe four crossings an hour and room for only eight cars per crossing and with the service shutting down at 19h00 for the night, some of these people would be lucky if they reached the mainland by midday tomorrow.

What state that they, and the inside of their cars, would be in by that time, I leave to your imagination. Try giving marks out of ten for the importance or the likelihood of the following items: dinner, breakfast, toilet, wash, sleep, lunch, divorce. Factoring in potentially serious issues of public health may give you a follow-up nightmare.

The road to Khuzhir was through an almost empty landscape. All we saw was a couple of farms, presumably keeping livestock as there was no sign of any crops. The land was open, covered in dry grass and on the right it rolled away into the distance. On the left it sloped away gently to a series of sandy beaches on the shore of the lake.

The coastline on the far side of the lake consisted of low cliffs falling more or less straight down into the water, not unlike some of the fjords in North Norway. We saw no sign of habitation on that side, as the shore is inaccessible except by abseilers. It was no surprise to learn that it was a nature reserve. What else could it be used for?

Khuzhir would be our home for the next four days. The accommodation in which we were staying didn't describe itself as a hotel or even a hostel, but as a 'homestead'.

It consisted of a complex of wooden buildings decorated outside with often intricate wooden carvings and the odd antler or two. We were favoured by having an entrance lobby with a table and chairs and the shower and toilet. As we were Room A, obviously we shared them with the occupants renting Room B.

Large padlock on door, a key each.

The Khuzhir homestead.

The nature reserve, on the western shore of Lake Baikal.

The entrance lobby.

Inside our room, showing the round table with Mike's laptop on it.
In the right foreground is the foot of my bed.

Inside, only a small round table. If Mike wanted that to put his laptop on while he edited his pictures, then it was just as well there was another table in the lobby that I could use when writing up my journal which would become this book.

Dinner was served in a communal hall.

Plates of food were laid out on the counter for guests to pick up and take back to a series of long tables with bench seating, three to each side, or possibly four if you knew each other well enough, or wanted to get to know someone. . .

There was no choice. We were served whatever was on tonight's menu. No coffee afterwards. They only served it at breakfast. 'Instant' in a sachet, which you made yourself.

'Why not make this available after dinner, charging for the sachet?' I asked Mike.

He had no more idea than I had.

During our stay the dinner menu fluctuated between a starter of salad and *omul* followed by stewed chicken and mash or stewed beef and rice. Dessert was a sweetened bun which they put on the plate with your starter. If you were not careful, you ate it with the salad and then found to your dismay that you'd buggered up your taste buds as the flavours didn't match.

On the left, the dining hall.

This was yet another instance of the strange Russian custom of serving guests their cold starter and hot main dish both at the same time. It means that if I eat them in the right order, my hot main course is cold by the time I come to it, whereas if I eat the main course while it's hot and then move on to my starter, I end up eating my meal with the courses in the wrong order.

The absence of any coffee after dinner may remind some readers of petty rules during their prep school days, particularly if they attended a very *minor* prep school of the kind where you were not allowed sugar on your porridge for no reason other than that's been the rule since 1876.

'But we're British!' I declared to Mike, striking a mock victor's pose, hand on hip. 'Are we going to allow some petty rule to deny us our customary after-dinner coffee? Are we hell! We've snaffled a few additional sachets of coffee at breakfast in our hotel in Irkutsk, haven't we?'

'And?'

'As the serving area hosts a samovar with a constant supply of hot water, I can bring our cups, fill them and enjoy a post-prandial intake of caffeine despite the management's attempts to prevent us.'

'Thus scoring one point.' In his student days, Mike was something of a fan of Stephen Potter.

'The choice, then, is either to sit outside and smoke with my coffee or retire to our room. I'll be able to sup it in comfort while reading one of the English newspapers I'm still carrying. Having read them, I can throw them away. That'll be a bit less to carry.'

'It's been a fortnight since we left England, but what a fortnight!'

Mike was in philosophical mood.

'We originally set our hearts of getting to Lake Baikal, and here we are. We've made it!'

Monday 17th September
Guided tour of Olkhon Island

Our transport, a minibus seating eight, was waiting. We were joined by two young French backpackers, who didn't seem keen to talk to us.

We headed out of the village, which has no roads as I would understand the term. Just dirt, no pavement for pedestrians, no kerb or kerbstones. It was so wide, 60m in fact, widening to 80m for the main north-south through road, that when standing at the crossroads in the village centre the scene looked like something out a Western. I half-expected to see Wells Fargo hurtling towards me in a cloud of Apache arrows and John Wayne riding shotgun. The ground was pitted with ruts. The only road sign was one denoting a pedestrian crossing, on a dirt road 60m wide with no markings.

The dirt road out of the village. Note the pedestrian crossing sign on the right.

The site of the abandoned fish factory.

One or two buildings had 'Café' or 'Souvenirs' painted above their doorways in Cyrillic, but there were no shops laid out with fruit and veg as we'd expect at home. Everything was inside. Moreover, the doors of all the premises, regardless of what they purported to sell, were shut. Were they open for business, or not?

We were soon well clear of the village. The land was once again very barren and wide open, with, on the left, clear views of the lake and the far shore. Mile after mile there were no signs of habitation. We passed through the small settlement of Kharantsi* and headed for the site of an abandoned fish factory which afforded fine views of the lake.

'This'll suit me fine,' said Mike. 'There are rather nice beaches at the bottom of the slope.'

I was rather surprised when a few minutes later I saw that he was lying on the ground on his side to improve the angle for his photos. I think he was trying to capture the undulations of the beach.

Olga chipped in with an observation from her time spent here on summer holidays.

'The water here is the warmest because it's the shallowest part of the lake. In summer we swim here.'

For readers who don't know, but may wish to, at 31,720kms^2 (12,200 sq.mls.) Baikal is the eighth largest lake in the world and the deepest, at its lowest point 1640m (5380ft). It contains one-fifth of the world's unfrozen fresh water and is so pure that you can see for a depth of 30m. The water is safe to drink untreated. I dipped my hands in and drank some. It was excellent. In winter, it freezes to a depth of a metre and a half.

'There are a couple of houses at the site of the abandoned factory where, apparently, a handful of people continue to live,' Olga told us. 'When the factory closed and all the workers had moved away, there was just one woman left, who refused to move. When her family forcibly collected her and took her to Irkutsk, she ran away and came back to live here alone and miles from anywhere.'

Make of that what you will. Wait for the film.

The road so far had been pretty bumpy, being just a track. There was a choice of tracks across open country where you chose whether to go to the right where the ruts were half a metre deep or to the left where the depth was only two feet. In other words, they were appalling whichever way you went. There were no road signs or

The lake, showing the cliffs along the western shore and a beach on the island.

The rough, bumpy road through the forest.

Yes, it's a road!

sign posts. It was probably safe to assume that the only people driving here are island residents who know their way.

'You've seen nothing yet!' Olga said. 'In the forest they're even worse.'

We didn't think that was possible.

We were wrong.

When we entered a small area of forest, we were tossed about like a roller-coaster ride even though we were in four-by-four vehicle. What it would be like in a private car, I can't imagine. No private car could manage it because it wouldn't have sufficient clearance under the chassis and would be grounded, if it didn't overturn first.

Our driver, another Aleksei, had been doing this drive on a more or less daily basis for visitors for the summer, and for who knows how many summers since his first one? He knew which side of each rut to steer, even though in the back we passengers were bouncing about without seat-belts and without any hand grips to hold on to.

Aleksei showed us three rocks and recounted the following Buryat legend.

Once upon a time a girl wanted to marry a boy from another tribe, but her father refused his permission, insisting she marry someone from her own. But she and her lover ran away. Her father sent her three brothers to find her and bring her back. When they found her they wanted her to be happy. They let her escape and agreed that when they went back to their father they would say that they'd failed to find her. But their father was a shaman and knew the truth, He decided to punish them by turning them into stone.

As a result there are three great rocks and the cape has its name: The Three Brothers.

Then on to the northernmost point on the island, Cape Khoboi*. Aleksei dropped us off at a parking area as close as he could get.

'*Walk the rest of the way,*' he said, pointing to a path leading to the headland. '*I'll go into the pinewoods and prepare our picnic lunch.*'

He pointed out where he intended to park. The path onto the cape was narrow and steep. We decided not to risk it, and settled for just admiring the view from a safe distance. The lake was flat calm. This is also its widest point, 79.5kms, or just short of fifty miles.

By the time we'd walked back to where the van was parked, Aleksei had a fire burning and a cauldron simmering on a tripod as if he was setting the scene for Act 1, Scene 1 of *Macbeth*.

Alongside was a fixed table seating eight to ten picnickers, laid with plates, cutlery, bread and salads to go with his soup of potatoes, tomatoes and *omul*. He served us each two or three pieces of fish, according to our preference.

A number of other tables were set up at intervals in the woods for the benefit of visitors. We found we had an extra

Lunch is on its way!

guest. A fearless and strikingly-coloured bird was perched sideways on the trunk of a nearby tree. Judging it was safe, he hopped down onto the table and, with one eye cocked on me, proceeded to help himself to some of my bread only inches away from my elbow.

Lunch is served!.

The sinitsa.

'Hey, look at this! I've got help! What's he called?'

'*He's a sinitsa.*'

This translates as 'blue and small'. Months later back home, the Hampshire Wildlife Trust confirmed he was a rock nuthatch. He was obviously used to picnickers and the food they brought and knew that they wouldn't do him any harm. Which is just as well, as he was perched on my plate helping himself to my bread while I was eating from it!

We didn't have knives or forks. I'd have to learn how to eat boiled fish with a spoon.

Second helpings were followed by black tea poured from a kettle. There was sugar available, but no milk. Dessert was a sweet bun with a little icing on top.

I was sitting opposite the French girl and decided to try to break the ice.

'Which part of France do you come from?'

'Paris.'

'And him?' I asked, pointing to her companion.

'Him, too. We're brother and sister.'

This was the first time we'd managed to get a word out of either of them throughout the entire morning. Possibly the only reason she spoke now was because I'd addressed her in French.

All morning we'd been preceded by two buses carrying a large party of Chinese tourists.

Mike was thoroughly fed up.

'I keep lining the tripod up for a shot. Then, yet again, a group of these bloody Chinese turn up and spoil it by standing in the way!'

What particularly infuriated him was that most of the time they were not taking photos of the scenery, simply of each other.

We reached Cape Shunte* – 'Cape Left' – which is heart-shaped, to hear yet another Buryat legend.

> *A childless couple wanting a child should sleep for three nights on the rock. If they want a boy, then sleep on the right side of the rock, if a girl, then on the left. Sleep in the middle if they want twins. If after a year they still remain childless, the man should throw the woman into the lake off the rock.*

I wonder what Women's Lib would say about that!

Off after lunch to Uzuri*, the only settlement on the island's east coast.

'It's only there because it has a meteorological station,' Olga explained. 'The resident population is fifteen.'

The settlement of Uzuri, on the island's east coast.

There was a shingle beach, a pond immediately inland and a few wandering cattle. It was two hours by heavily-rutted track to anywhere else. One wonders what the people who live here do to pass the time, living on a bare hillside looking out onto the lake. No matter how splendid the view, they can't spend all their waking hours gazing at it in rapture. Or maybe they . . .

We left the patch of forest with the UNESCO Heritage-standard ruts and proceeded in the general direction of our homestead. We were still in the middle of nowhere when our French couple asked to get off.

Aleksei pointed to a path between two patches of woodland over to the right.

'*Down through there there's a good beach.*'

Off they went, to camp.

'When they want to leave,' I murmured to Mike, 'how are they going to get back to civilization?'

'Let's hope their mobile phones work out here and they speak enough Russian. Otherwise it's going to be one hell of a long walk.'

The reason there are no other settlements on this side of the island is that it consists of mile after mile of low cliffs, like the terrain across the bay on the western side of the lake. As a consequence, it's inaccessible and has no beaches.

Most of Olkhon is, in fact, uninhabited. We drove for miles and saw nothing but low rolling hills covered with patches of dry grass with the deep blue of the lake as a backdrop, then perhaps two or three cows or horses but no houses. North of Khuzhir the island hasn't yet been electrified and relies on solar power or other forms of domestic generation.

Our day clocked up 100km, most of it over bone-shattering rutted tracks across barren, open country or through a pine forest where there were transverse ruts a foot deep crossing others of the same depth, the track sometimes 7-8m wide and the driver constantly having to decide which way to swerve to avoid the worst holes and keep his vehicle upright. Were it not for our minibus having good springs and good upholstery, we'd have been black and blue.

Tuesday 18th September
Free in Khuzhir, the main village on Olkhon

'This shouldn't take long!', I remarked to Mike.

Olga wasn't at all well last night, but didn't tell us until we pressed her.

'I think it was the chilly wind and all that bouncing about in the minibus.'

We were quite worried, and were unsure what to do. She didn't show up for breakfast until 10h15. By that time we'd finished ours. It consisted of semolina porridge with a dollop of jam to sweeten it and two fried eggs which gradually went cold while we were eating the porridge.

I just can't get over this strange custom of serving both courses at once. I tried eating my eggs on *blini* (tiny Russian pancakes) instead of bread. That worked quite well.

Back in the room, Mike set about photographing it for posterity.

A bucket of cold water and a large ladle enabled us to fill the electric heater over the sink. To plug in the boiler, we had to disconnect the light as there was only one socket. This meant that while the water was heating up we had no light in that part of the room. The liquid soap dispenser on the wall was easy to find even in the dark, because we only needed to look for the shiny elongated icicle of solidified spillage on the wall underneath it and follow it back to its source. I was glad that I'd brought my own soap.

Our sink.

A notice in English asked guests not to waste water, yet there was no plug in the sink. We therefore had no option but to wash under a running tap. It was essential that we didn't overheat the water in the heater and scald ourselves. With no plug in the sink, we couldn't put some cold water in first to reduce the temperature.

It was hardly surprising that we were back to grey, elastic lavatory paper without perforations except where you don't want them, by which I mean with holes in the texture as opposed to perforations between pieces. I noted that in hotels the paper was white and similar to English toilet paper, except that the perforated sections are perhaps half as long again as the length that we use. Here, the rolls weren't rolled round a central cardboard core, but simply rolled tightly with just enough room for the arm of the holder to be pushed through.

Our room had two beds, but no bedside stand between them on which I could put my glasses. We put one of our cases there as a substitute. No cupboards or bedside lights were provided, only the one main light suspended in the middle of the room. The only switch was by the door. This meant we had to turn the light off before getting into bed and grope our way back in the dark.

The rest of the room, showing Mike's bed.

Going for a pee during the night entailed finding my way to the door in the dark, unlocking it, feeling my way to the light switch adjacent to the access door to the shower and toilet, turning on the light and then, in reverse order, turning off the light and making my way back, locking the door in the dark and stumbling back to my bed.

Shamanka, or the Shaman's Rock.

Who said the Friends of Nocturnal Diuresis would always be a misunderstood minority?

Olga took us out via the back gate and showed us a line of thirteen wooden stakes festooned with brightly coloured ribbons across the approach to a rocky promontory.

'This is one of the nine most sacred sites in Asia for Buddhists and shamanists. It's called *Shamanka*, or the Shamans' Rock. Only men are allowed to walk out to it, not women or children.

Coins in small denominations lay scattered randomly on the ground. On some stones by the pillars, offerings of sweets and cigarettes had been left for the spirits.

Besides apparently having a sweet tooth and enjoying a fag, the spirits also appear to have need of small change.

Can't think why.

'Do they have shops in the spirit world?', Mike whispered to me out of the corner of his mouth. 'A 10 kopeck coin is worth about ½p.'

'Well, their shops are 'out of this world',' I replied.

The weather being perfect, Mike was in his element with his camera.

Back for lunch, we imbibed hot soup followed by salad and yet more *omul.*

'There's no coffee on offer, post-lunch. I'll go back to our room to get some sachets. Give me the key.'

Pause.

Mike realised that he'd locked the door by snapping the padlock shut but

Offerings to the spirits.

left the key inside on the table. There were two keys on the ribbon, one for each occupant, but we hadn't bothered to separate them and carry one each as we knew we'd always be entering or leaving together.

We reported our predicament to the young chap at Reception.

He grinned at us and said 'Cool!'

So much for our brochure's blunt assertion that English isn't spoken on the island.

'We haven't got a spare. I'll get a hammer.'

Using that and a jemmy, he proceeded to prise the lock off its hinges so that we could go in and get our key to unlock the padlock. He put the nails back in the same holes and banged them in again with his hammer. I got the impression we were not the first guests for whom he'd had to provide this service.

While drinking our coffee we struck up a conversation with a young man who turned out to be from Munich. Then a couple of fifty-something Australian ladies joined us when they heard us speaking English.

Olga turned up and I asked, 'Olga, do you know a shop where I can buy some postcards?'

My intention was to buy them here, but post them next week in Mongolia for the sake of amusing my friends with unusual stamps.

Mike was still talking to the ladies when I got back. I left them discussing Australia.

It was half past three. Time for my mid-afternoon nap.

Mike came in, as the two ladies had gone off for a walk. After detoxing my mind with a few hands of solitaire on the lap-top, I settled down to writing my cards. I had ten, but soon realised I'd need six more, which I'd buy somewhere in Mongolia and post the lot together.

'Arrangements for tomorrow? I suggest we have lunch before leaving. It's going to be a long drive back to Irkutsk.'

Olga agreed.

'Yuri will have to drive up from Irkutsk in the morning. It'll be a good idea if he has a rest before starting the return leg, bearing in mind that it's 300kms or thereabouts each way.'

Mike considered our position.

'We're not going back to the hotel but directly to the railway station. We won't be able to have anything more to eat until late in the evening, depending on what's on offer in the station café at that time of night. Omul, no doubt. We'll also have to find a way of depositing our luggage in a safe place, as our train's not scheduled to leave until half-past three in the morning.'

'Our next stopping-place will be Ulan Ude*, the capital of the Buryat Republic, I added, 'where trains on the Trans-Siberian Railway divert for Mongolia and China.'

The menu at dinner was advertised as peas soup, but in fact was pease soup, made with dried peas, not fresh ones. Then dishes of plain rice, with soy sauce available to give it a bit of flavour.

We got chatting to the Australian ladies again, just to pass the time as there was nothing else to do. They told us that they'd made a previous trip in 1996 all over Siberia and were now well into their second expedition spread over 7½ months. They had lots to talk about, and it was very interesting to listen to their 'travellers' tales'.

I thought it was possibly our turn to brag, if only for the honour of England.

'Back in 1959 when we were young chaps fresh out of university, we went to Norway and hitch-hiked round North Cape,' I told them. 'I've also written a book of travel anecdotes. It's entitled 'Martin Kyrle's *Little Green Nightbook.'*

While I was in full flow explaining what prompted me to write a book in the first place, Mike excused himself to get a photograph that he could entitle 'Sunset over Baikal'.

Wednesday 19th September
Drive back to Irkutsk to catch the train to Ulan Ude

I risked the shower this morning, which functioned satisfactorily once I'd worked out which way to turn the tap to control the water temperature. We packed, ready to leave after lunch. I walked down to the post office, a remarkably modern building, to send a postcard to one of the receptionists I'd met at our hotel in Moscow. She was keen to improve her English. I hoped she'd return the favour by helping me improve my Russian.

The modern post office in Khuzhir.

The only other customer was a short Buryat woman collecting her pension while talking on her mobile phone. She was clearly more plugged into modern life than I am, as I haven't got a mobile phone. She was also wearing perfectly ordinary Western clothes. Ordinary Buryats no longer wear traditional costume, but dress just like the rest of us. The only way that I knew she was a Buryat and not a Russian, or even a tourist, was because of her oriental features.

The clerk took my money and the card, but I didn't see her stick a stamp on it. The sneaky thought crossed my mind that if she just bins the card once I've gone and keeps my 25r. I'll never know. If she does it to all the tourists, it could be quite a nice little earner.

It turned out that my suspicions were quite unfounded, as the card arrived safely in Moscow, although it did take six weeks. I wondered whether or not I should have felt any shame at entertaining such suspicions in the first place, but consoled myself with the thought that if she'd stuck on the stamp in my presence there would never have been any doubts. If I had suspicions they were partly her fault.

I returned to the homestead to collect Mike, ready to take a scenic walk around Khuzhir for the last time and photograph for posterity whatever took our fancy.

We walked past a burnt-out minibus lying on its roof by the roadside, and an abandoned car parked against someone's fence. In the middle of a crossroads there was a huge stagnant pond covered in algae and full of junk. Piles of logs were stacked against many of the garden gates. A water tanker was busy, supplying domestic premises. This told us that Khuzhir doesn't have running water.

The burnt-out minibus.

The prevalence of plastic bags and bits of sheeting, flattened drink cans, broken glass, single discarded flip-flops, old tyres and general detritus lying everywhere gave the village an air of

Rubbish left on the ground.

being thoroughly unloved. No one cares. Maybe they used to, but they've given up and are now past caring. If anyone drops anything, they just walk on and leave it. The next passing car squashes it flat and it becomes part of the scenery.

Whatever happened to civic pride? As a former councillor, I know that long before the area I represented got one-tenth as bad as this, I'd have been getting complaints.

Indeed, things would never have got as bad as this in the first place, because I'd have done something about it myself long before simply as a matter of civic duty.

Olga had gone to the thirteen pillars on *Shamanka* to tie onto them the coloured ribbons given to her by Aleksei, the shaman. We were on our own to wander through what little there was of the village while Mike set about making his photographic record. It was eleven o'clock in the morning on a fine day yet there was hardly a soul to be seen. When we passed the school, there was no sign of any children.

Anyone seen a Pied Piper?

There was almost no traffic. We could wander unconcerned all over the road, which was so rutted no one could drive at more than about 10mph. It was so wide that instead of honking, vehicles could simply drive round us. It made me wonder yet again why they have a post with the sign saying 'pedestrian crossing' when in all other respects the road is totally unmarked. Nothing was painted on the road surface because the road *had* no surface. It was just dirt. Enough civic pride to want a pedestrian crossing sign in the middle of their village, but not enough to employ a bloke with a long-handled litter-picker to collect all the rubbish lying around and dispose of it.

It was difficult to know if the few shops were open or not. The shop I chose to buy my postcards was a single room. The door was not only shut but also locked, with a note by the bell inviting potential customers to ring it, which I did. The owner came out of the house next door, opened the shop, served me, locked up behind me and went back indoors to what was obviously her private house. It made sense, with few customers about at the end of the season, not to spend all day sitting behind the counter doing nothing. It was a sufficiently unusual shopping experience for me to think it worth recounting.

The only buildings of any interest were, in fact, the ones in our homestead, where at least some attempt had been made to build in distinctive, even idiosyncratic, rustic styles and decorate the hut exteriors. I'm sure the guests were charmed. We were certainly taken by it. But it wasn't typically Russian, typically Buryat or indeed typically anything. Nikita, the proprietor, would probably have built it in exactly the same way had he been within sight of Blackpool Tower. Had we ever met him, I might have asked him.

Lunch was as dire as usual: a pleasant but unidentifiable soup, the only certainty being that it wasn't fish, followed by a concoction of chopped tomato and sweet onion, with a piece of cold *omul* and spaghetti, which was also cold and hence inedible. We raided our supply of coffee again, and shared an apple which had survived from Novosibirsk. I recalled that while I was resting in our room in the hotel after my hospital treatment the staff had brought me some fruit.

Time to go. We didn't feel the need to say any goodbyes. Although the staff, mainly young, were perfectly friendly and often remarkably proficient in English, it was all in a day's work. We hadn't established anything remotely approaching a genuine rapport with anyone.

I summed up my feelings to Mike.

'I won't ever be here again. While I've enjoyed exploring Olkhon, we've seen all there is to see except that it may look different in winter when the lake is frozen. Staying in Khuzhir has been fun. You might even perhaps call it 'an experience', but it's not an experience I would ever want to repeat.'

Mike nodded. 'I feel the same way. An eye-opener in many respects, but once is enough.'

One small settlement of half-a-dozen houses and a couple of isolated farms were all we saw on the drive back to the ferry, which took an hour, bouncing about in places where the gravel and large stones gave way to bare earth and the ubiquitous ruts. Half-a-dozen cars were ahead of us in the queue. Meanwhile the small ferry was standing idle, while the crew waited for the next scheduled departure time before letting anyone board.

This time the larger ferry was returning with a load of cars. Once it had disgorged its cargo, it, too, shut down, presumably until the skipper looked at his watch and decided that their next timetabled crossing was now imminent. We ended up waiting half an hour, time enough for a leisurely restorative coffee on a veranda overlooking the strait and to make use of the café facilities. I was not going anywhere near those public bogs again or risking life and limb having to squeeze round a cow.

Mike set off to take yet more photos of the buildings, boats and coastline.

The crossing again lasted fifteen minutes but we were afforded wonderful photo-ops in all directions from our vantage point twenty feet above the car deck.

'We've been fortunate with the weather. We've been in Russia almost three weeks without seeing a drop of rain apart from a brief shower one morning in Moscow. The sun has shone every day.'

'I've had all the natural light I've needed to take photos,' said Mike.

'I'm sure the turbulence in the water halfway across is the *omul* congregating to say a collective goodbye and to thank us for going on our way before we eat them to the point of extinction.'

Once on dry land, Yuri got busy trying to re-inflate his offside rear tyre, which appeared to have split. Considering the road surface on which he had had to drive all the way from Khuzhir, it was hardly to be wondered at.

As we passengers couldn't do anything to help, we wandered off to look at what was on offer on the souvenir stalls. We treated ourselves to another coffee, served in a plastic cup for 40r. by a rather smart and attractive Buryat girl. After half an hour, Yuri informed us that he'd have to go to a garage to get it repaired or replaced as his spare wasn't serviceable (*now he tells us!*). The garage was in the township of Eliantsy. We'd have to drive slowly for an hour to get there. We still had 250kms to go to Irkutsk and the small matter of a train to catch.

Yuri tries to inflate the tyre.

The countryside was, as before, almost entirely empty. A long section of the road was being laid with tarmac to a very high standard, which meant that we couldn't drive along it but had to drive alongside it on the bare earth and associated stones and ruts. All that with a dodgy tyre.

Fingers crossed!

Eliantsy was surrounded by miles and miles of emptiness. We wondered why it was even there. What employment was available for the people? It was open country with low, rolling hills covered in brown grass, with here and there a few cows on the loose, wandering into the road without looking. Only twice all the way from the ferry was there a building, one of which was a roadside café.

The garage that Yuri was looking for in Eliantsy was, you've guessed it, shut.

Sod's Law operates even in Siberia.

'There's a café next door,' said Olga. 'We can have some supper while Yuri goes off in search of another garage.'

I went up to the counter to survey what was on offer. Pork chops. Real ones? Indeed, yes. They were the best grub I'd had in five days. A chocolate bar for afters, with the brand name 'Snickers' in English but everything else on the wrapper in Cyrillic.

Another hour passed. The café gradually filled up with the local 'yoof', for whom I guess this is a local hotspot of warmth, food, drink and company. No one took any notice of two foreigners, sitting at a table, eating, with Mike's massive camera parked on the table in full view.

Yuri turned up. *'Everything is now fixed. We can get going at full speed to Irkutsk.'*

We arrived at the station at Irkutsk at 21h15.

'Is there somewhere we can leave our luggage? We've got a long wait, and we'd prefer to do it without having to cart all our stuff around with us.'

'There's a left luggage room. It'll cost you 650r.'

The left luggage office was conveniently located: in the basement down two flights of steep stairs! Another example of poor planning. Passengers have to lug their cases all the way down the stairs and then all the way back up again. Once again, you couldn't make it up.

Time to say our farewells. I thought Olga, who'd been definitely under the weather since we set off, would be glad to get home and relax. Yuri, too, who must have been exhausted after a round trip of 600kms to Khuzhir and back in one day, added to which he'd had the anxiety of having one of his tyres let him down. Olga pointed us in the direction of a café. We made our way there to see what was on the menu. Our train was due in at 02h50 and left at 03h29. We hoped to get aboard as soon as it arrived and get our heads down even before it departed.

ULAN UDE

Thursday 20th September
Arrive in Ulan Ude. Free.

'We've finished supper. What now?'

'There's nowhere to go, unless you want to sit on the platform for three hours. Why don't we just sit tight, kill time, hope no one twigs?'

'I guess if we order a coffee from time to time, they'll think we're just customers who drink slowly. At least it's warm, we've got a table in a corner and the toilets are clean.'

'OK. Give it another two minutes. Then I'll go and order a second round.'

At around 02h00 we pottered back to retrieve our luggage from the bowels of the station. The attendant was making his all-night shift more bearable by relaxing in a huge armchair. I don't think it was supplied as standard. He'd brought it himself from home.

The electronic board showed no indication yet as to the platform from which our train would depart, but eventually it came up: Platform 1.

We headed off down the stairs which Olga had told us gives access to the platforms, but the numbering seemed to start with 2-4, then there was 5-7. No sign for No 1.

We were still encumbered by our bags.

'You stay here,' I said. 'I'll go back up the stairs and try to find out what we're missing and where Platform 1 has been secreted.'

This is the kind of situation where a knowledge of the language was going to be helpful, as Mike realised when he first suggested that, on his projected journey across Russia, I accompany him.

In the waiting area three porters were lounging in chairs, arms akimbo, legs stretched out at full length in front of them with their feet wide apart. As they were doing nothing, naturally I asked them,

Please, where is Platform 1?

One of them clipped on a silly grin and said, in English, 'Can I help you?'

'*Yes,*' I repeated, still in Russian. '*Where is Platform 1?*'

'Can I help you?' he replied, silly grin still in place, friends either side smirking.

The one on the right muttered something about *outside on the left*, from which I deduced that I had to go out through the main door, turn left. It would be somewhere there.

None of them got up from his chair or made any attempt to give me the practical help which they purported, in English, to offer. They had the Russian word for porter, *nosilshchik**, in fluorescent lettering across their jackets. Helping us with our bags was their job. A foreign tourist was in need of that help. What was the point of silly grins and 'Can I help you?', bum still firmly bolted to a chair? Yes, you bloody well could, if you weren't three idle layabouts with the combined IQ of an *omul*.

Returning to Mike to rejoin him as he lugged our bags up the stairs again, I saw a girl in uniform.

'Excuse me, please. Can you tell me where to find Platform1?'

'Go out through the station entrance. Then turn left and you'll come to the gate for Platform 1.'

The point I want to make is that we could see no signs in the waiting area informing passengers that Platform 1 is not down the stairs and through the tunnel. That tunnel takes you *under* Platform 1 to all the other platforms. Platform 1 is accessed via a gateway on the *outside* of the station building. Passengers get onto it directly from the street outside, without going into the station building or its waiting area.

All aboard for Ulan Ude!

It's logical enough when you analyse it, but totally confusing to a stranger who assumes when there's a tunnel to the platforms, then it's to all of them. I was only able to find this out because I was able to ask for directions in Russian and understand the answers. Anyone without some knowledge of the language would find themselves in a bit of a spot. This was happening, remember, at two o'clock in the morning, when few of us are at our most alert.

On the platform the train was just arriving.

We found our wagon and showed our documents, for the first time, to a male attendant.

He was rather young and seemingly short on confidence.

'*I must go and consult . . .*'

I missed the next bit, presumably the Russian word for 'supervisor' or the supervisor's actual name, which would account for me not recognising the word.

What he meant was that there were two of us but we had *four* tickets. He couldn't make the mental leap to figure out that this was because we'd paid for the extra seats to have a compartment to ourselves, with the additional privacy and comfort. In his mind, there are four tickets, there must be four people. Where are the other two?

We were shown to our compartment, but the beds were not made up. Any thought of getting our heads down before the train departed had gone up in smoke. The attendant was standing on the platform waiting for the rest of his first class passengers to turn up. He wouldn't be handing out bedding until everyone else was on board, which clearly told us that he wouldn't start doing it before the train moved off.

Luckily no one was late. Following his simple logic, to match our four tickets, he gave us four sets of sheets and pillows.

'Does he think we're each going to sleep in two beds at once?'

A politically-incorrect thought crossed my mind. 'It might be an attractive prospect for a schizophrenic with a split personality.' I thought better of saying it aloud.

'I'm going to sleep on the lower bunk and put my cases on the upper one.'

'Good idea. Me, too.'

Woke up at 08h10.

'There's no time for breakfast! Even if we knew how far down – or is it up? – the train the restaurant car was. We're due in Ulan Ude at 09h54.'

At approximately 6½ hours duration, this was by far the briefest of our train journeys at any time during the trip. I sought some free hot water from the attendant, who overnight had morphed from a callow youth into a diminutive girl. We still had some of the well-travelled cakes Tatiana had given us in Moscow. With a cup of tea, that would have to do.

We were at this point travelling along the southern shore of Lake Baikal. It seemed that we were as yet nowhere near Ulan Ude, which is inland and well away from the lake. As we progressed through another station, I read its name. It slowly dawned on us that we were not due at our destination at 09h54 local time but at 10h54. There'd been another change in time zone to confuse us. We could have had breakfast after all. Now it was gone ten o'clock. There wasn't enough time.

The scenery was quite interesting. Leaving Baikal, its shoreline turns north-east and the train proceeds straight on due east. We began to follow the course of the River Selenga, whose delta, when it falls into Baikal, is a vast (680km^2) wetland and nature reserve, important to wildlife.

The scenery following the river Selenga.

The hills in the distance were higher, no longer *steppe* and the river was dotted with large villages. Smoke was funnelling from some of the factory chimneys. Clearly, they were operational.

Our next guide was waiting for us on the platform.

'Hello! I'm Alina. Call me Ala*'.

By looking at her I could see that she was a Buryat, not a Russian. By way of introductory small-talk, I asked her, *'Where did you study?'*

This threw her completely. I think I was the first Western tourist she'd ever met who knew any Russian.

Her qualifications were surprising.

'I studied in Cambridge and Edinburgh.'

That's one hell of a long way for a teenage girl student to go alone from Ulan Ude!, I thought to myself. Intrepid, one might say.

'We missed breakfast. We really want coffee and a snack before doing anything else.'

Once we'd arrived at Hotel Gesir and dumped our stuff in our room, No 205, we headed for the café. No food available as it was now nearly eleven o'clock, but we could get a coffee.

'I note,' said Mike, 'that lunch is served from 11-1. By the time we've unpacked it'll be nicely timed to come back down again and enjoy an early lunch.'

We tried *bookhler*,* a Buryat soup. To follow, I ordered two pork chops, which were listed in

Our guide Ala.

English on the menu as coming with onions, aubergines, olives and red peppers, liberally doused in tomato ketchup. Mike ordered another dish, without either of us having any idea what it was. While waiting for our soup, the waiter directed us to the cold buffet where I settled for a little coleslaw to nibble to clean the palate. I no longer have the moderately gargantuan appetite for which I had quite a reputation in my younger days.

However, I also took a couple of very ripe plums, while they were there and before other guests helped themselves and they all disappeared.

By the time we'd eaten our starter, the *bookhler* had arrived: potatoes in a broth containing pieces of mutton on the bone and quite delicious. Mike's exploratory order arrived, and turned out to consist of about a pound-and-half of fried liver and onions. The waiter, a young Buryat, had quite passable English, and – joy of joys! – was able to serve us each a glass of wine without us having to buy the whole bottle.

Much refreshed after our interrupted night and tedious journey, we were now ready to tackle an afternoon walkabout in the middle of Ulan Ude. Even though about 80% of its population are Russians, it is, after all, the capital of the Buryat Republic. We were certain it would have government buildings to admire and for Mike to photograph.

We didn't have the services of a guide today but the hotel was easy walking distance from the city centre via a series of backways. Ala offered to pop back, lead us there and leave us to walk around, then find our own way back. We politely declined. We had no intention of venturing out beyond the main square, and wouldn't be in any danger of getting lost. It was a lovely day. Mike was looking forward to exploring the city centre.

'Before we go, I'm going to have a shower and wash my hair for the first time since my accident in Novosibirsk ten days ago. I've been wary of the risk of re-opening the wound.'

'It looks as though it's now healed. But don't go mad. Avoid vigorously scratching it with your fingernails,' said Mike.

I ought at least to be able to try to wash out my green streak.

Wedding photo in front of Lenin.

The city centre of Ulan Ude is laid out on a grand scale and is dominated by a plinth topped by a huge head of Lenin, reputedly the largest anywhere in the former Soviet Union. A bride and groom with all their family members were posing in front of it. Across the square, out of shot, were lines of cars of other wedding parties waiting their turn to line up in front of it.

The government buildings nearby are designed in the flamboyant style that one would expect in a country which at the time was looking forward to its future with supreme optimism. They are very impressive and show no signs of grime or weathering. The sun was so hot we had to carry our coats. The music being played at moderate volume over the public address system was Vivaldi! Very pleasant, relaxing and civilised. Top marks to the Buryats.

The city centre in Ulan Ude is something worth seeing. We looked for souvenirs at the side of the main square that Ala pointed out to us. After an hour of fruitless searching, we gave up. We returned to the hotel to catch up on some sleep.

Government buildings.

Our hotel.

Friday 21st September
Guided visit to Ivolginsk*, centre of Buddhism in Russia

Buddhist monastery at Ivolginsk.

It was a drive of 35kms south-west to Ivolginsk. We'd been joined by a couple of ladies from London. We visited the Buddhist monastery and seminary, known in Russian as a *datsan*. It was very exotic, with many statues and images painted in very bright, not to say garish, colours. We all went into a temple to look at the idols. When Ala stopped in front of one of them to pray and leave offerings, it immediately became apparent that she was herself a Buddhist.

We turned every prayer wheel as we passed, on the basis of 'when in Rome.' We noted that in front of a *stupa**, containing relics or ashes of the departed, the offering often included rice.

Prayer wheels.

The footpaths between the buildings were scattered with small denomination coins, as we had encountered on Olkhon.

'It feels very strange actually walking on money,' I said to Ala. 'Does anyone ever pick up any of the coins? It seems to me to be such a waste, as the people dropping them clearly intend them to be an offering. If the authorities picked them up and used the money to further the education of novices, embellish the *datsan* or indeed anything they like, this would be a completely legitimate use of money freely given by believers.'

'I don't know,' Ala had to admit.

In another temple a young monk was chanting from a book open in front of him, turning the pages rapidly and ringing a small

A stupa, with offerings of rice.

bell held between two fingers and cradled in the palm of his hand.

'What language is it?', I asked, as clearly it was not Russian.

I was expecting Ala to answer, 'Buryat'.

To my surprise, she replied, 'Tibetan.'

It's from Tibet, of course, that Buddhism found its way to the nomadic tribes in this part of Asia three centuries ago but I was surprised to discover that they still chant in the original language.

On the other hand, Latin is still used in Christian churches, even in Protestant England. I sang plenty of introits in Latin in my days as a choir member in my late teens and early twenties, simply because they were traditional and originally written in Latin. Few in the congregation, or amongst us in the choir, had any idea what the words meant, but they enjoyed hearing the singing. Tibetan can at least claim to be a living language, even if it's living a long way from Buryatia.

Leaving Ivolginsk our journey was another hour's drive before we were scheduled to stop for lunch. We were joined by a second car, with a second guide, to conduct us to the village of Desyatnikovo*, and then through various back streets to wherever it was that we were expected.

Dressed in traditional peasant costumes, three middle-aged ladies were lined up outside the garden gate to welcome us. It appeared that we had a reception committee!

The shortest one introduced herself.

'I'm Galina.'

She had a weather-beaten peasant's face but spoke very clear, educated Russian. Despite being dressed as a peasant she clearly wasn't one, nor anything like one. Her costume was the uniform for the job in hand: making a living or at least a bit of one, entertaining tourists with demonstrations of what life was like in the old days. The message was: this is how the people living in these parts used to do things. We don't live like this now, but we can show you what it was like.

We stood outside the farmhouse.

'Does anyone want use of the toilet? It's just over there, a few yards up the garden through the gate.'

Some took the opportunity. While the rest of us were waiting, Galina asked

'Can anyone speak Russian?'

'Yes, I can speak a bit,' I said.

'Where are you from?'

'England. And you?'

'I come from another province to the east. I came here when I got married.'

Invited inside, the low door opened directly onto some stairs. We went up and across the landing into a room laid for a traditional peasant feast.

Traditional peasant feast laid out for us.

First, a soup of meat and vegetables. It wasn't *bookhler*. Then a glass of cranberry juice, followed by another of what they told us was home-made wine but was in fact distilled and tasted rather like brandy. We sampled slices of cold *omul* tasting rather like herring, slices of pork fat, tomatoes, sweet cakes and a puff pastry version of bread along with ordinary bread. Then some cream and honey, which mixed very well, with glasses of tea.

I slipped outside to wash my hands and caught Galina in animated conversation on her mobile phone. Even in the back of nowhere in Buryatia, the locals are up to date with modern technology!

After lunch the ladies, now joined by a fourth, conducted us to the barn, where, unaccompanied, they sang a cheerful song of welcome, then a religious song.

'*We want to show you how weddings were conducted in the old days,*' said Galina, who appeared to be the spokesman for the group.

Mike was grabbed and dressed in a yellow *rubashka**, a Russian peasant shirt, and a cloth cap with a yellow plastic sunflower on the peak. One of the London ladies was decked out in bridal costume to the accompaniment of an appropriate folk song. All good fun until Ala disappeared to consult the other guide and our driver while the demonstration with explanations was going on, leaving me desperately struggling to translate.

The bride and groom are serenaded by the women of the village as in Tsarist times.

The 'wedding photo'. Front row from the left: Galina, the 'bride' and 'groom'.

Our next port of call was to a group of Old Believers, who lived in the village of Tarbagatai*. Our host was a young man named Alexander, who showed us what he called his museum. It was full to bursting point with old household utensils such as saucepans, flatirons, beds, photos, posters, old farm implements and ploughs, old horse-drawn carriages and even some very old books. Most of the objects were covered in dust or simply dirty and were not laid out in any particular order. There were few labels. The ones that I could see were almost indecipherable. Rather than a museum, to my mind, it was a junk yard with a roof.

Across the road was their newly-restored cathedral.

It was tiny. Inside, the icons looked to us as much the same as those in Orthodox churches. Even though there was only room for a couple of dozen worshippers, their small souvenir stall was set up in a corner of the cathedral itself, rather than in the entrance lobby, as one might expect.

We pressed Ala. 'What distinguishes the Old Believers from the rest of the Orthodox communion? Why do they have their own Patriarch in Moscow?'

She struggled to explain but was clearly out of her depth. It was hardly surprising, when she was a Buddhist and not a follower of Orthodoxy, either Old or New.

The split came about in the 1650's when the Patriarch Nikon introduced a number of reforms in the liturgy and practices of the Russian Orthodox Church: for example, how many fingers believers should use when crossing themselves, the correct order for the pieces of music in a sung service and what style of singing.

The newly restored cathedral.

This raised a fundamental question: should the Russian Church stick to its own traditions or accept the practices of the Greek Orthodox, whence it originally came, back in the ninth century?

Some clergy and worshippers refused to accept any of these reforms and were nicknamed Old Believers. They stuck to their guns through centuries of persecution and still persist, for example, in adhering to the pre-Reform practice

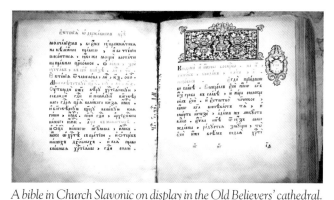

A bible in Church Slavonic on display in the Old Believers' cathedral.

of crossing themselves with two fingers and not three, representing God the Father and God the Son but not including God the Holy Spirit.

There are a number of other differences in ritual which seem comparatively minor to a non-Orthodox person, who can't understand why it matters so much. Perhaps belief, with the accompanying ritual, is an end in itself. Whether or not it makes any sense is not a consideration.

Back at our hotel, we were once again excluded from the dining room because of a wedding party! We sat in the foyer, observing a succession of very smartly dressed young men and women arriving for the bun-fight, a mixture of Russians and Buryats.

Reception tried to reassure us. 'The café is going to be open and will offer the full menu.'

When we arrived, we met up again with the two ladies from London.

'The kitchen lights have blown and the only dish on offer is *pozy*,' they told us. 'Take it or leave it. Drinks are alright, as they don't require any cooking. Desserts are available, provided they're ice cream-based, for the same reason.'

The ladies were passing the time playing scrabble on a miniature board, which clearly they carried on their travels.

Before going to dinner, I had a discussion with Ala about arrangements for our departure the next morning. We were scheduled to leave the hotel at six for our train at 07h26.

'But it's only ten minutes by taxi at the most. Why on earth are we leaving so early just to hang about on the platform for an hour?'

She agreed. 'I'll book a taxi for 7 o'clock. I'll get the restaurant to lay on something for breakfast at 06h20 especially for you, as you've already paid for it but are leaving before the time it's normally served.'

When Ala was gone, I went to Reception to speak to the girl on duty in her own language. She was wearing her name on her uniform badge: Viktoria.

'*I want a call tomorrow morning, please, at a quarter to six,*' and gave our room number.

Viktoria wrote this down.

After dinner, as we came through the foyer, I gave Mike a nudge with my elbow. 'Go over and check with the receptionist *in English* that she's got our call down for tomorrow at 05h45.'

'She confirms that she has,' said Mike, on his return.

INTO MONGOLIA

Saturday 22nd September
On the train to Ulan Bator

Disaster!

I was awake and idly thinking that I might as well pick up my watch from the bedside table and look at it to see how long it was before our booked wake-up call comes at a quarter to six. Fortunately I did. And got the most almighty shock.

It was five to seven!

Reception had failed to make the wake-up call!

Our taxi is due at 7 and the train leaves at 07h26.

We had less than half an hour to be out of bed and on the train. We'd miss the breakfast specially laid on for us.

'There will be *very* serious repercussions when I get back to England,' I muttered grimly under my breath.

Luckily, we'd packed the night before. All we had to do was pick up our toilet bags from the bathroom, dress, lock our cases and head for the lift. I'd even taken the precaution of getting my morning array of pills out of their containers and putting them on my bedside table, so that all I would have to do in the morning would be to put water in a glass and swallow them.

There was no time to wash. Because of this I overlooked my soap dish, which had several tablets of soap in it, filched from hotels on the way. It was left behind, along with one of my freshly-laundered shirts. The taxi was waiting. We were at the station by 07h15.

Our train was not listed on the electronic arrivals / departures board. I went over to the desk marked *Information* and showed our tickets to the young lady on duty.

'*Which platform, please?*'

'*Your train departs from Platform 5 but not at 07h26 but 07h40.*'

As our agency hadn't been in error before, I was surprised at this.

If she's manning the Information Desk, surely she must know?

I went back to Mike, who checked Platform 5 against the departures board, which had been updated while I'd been at the Information Desk. Sure enough, there was a train at 07h40. But it wasn't going from Moscow to Ulan Bator but Ulan Bator to Moscow, in precisely the opposite direction to the train that we wanted. The Information Desk girl had misdirected me.

I went back.

'Will you please to look again at our tickets and read them. We're going <u>to</u> Ulan Bator, not <u>from</u> it. Now which platform?'

'Oh.'

She looked flustered, mumbled something I didn't catch and took me through an archway to another kiosk in the next hall to ask the woman on duty there.

'Oh yes,' she said, firmly. *'It goes at 07h26. It leaves from Platform 3.'*

'Where's that?', I asked.

'Up those stairs.'

She pointed to two steep flights each of a dozen or so steps. It was now twenty-past seven. We'd got six minutes to lug our cases up those stairs, down again onto the platform and make it to our wagon.

'All aboard for Mongolia!'

Sod's Law dictated that it would be at the far end. It was. The attendant knew that he had two passengers not yet accounted for. The moment that he saw us, he started waving vigorously. We clambered on board and were standing in our compartment with our cases at our feet while trying to catch our breath when the train moved off.

We'd done it with two minutes to spare.

Phew!

Had we failed, the next stage of our trip would have fallen apart. The person meeting us would not have found us, how would we get another train and when would it

East Siberian Railway.

be? Would it be tomorrow, or dare we even think it, not till next week? Would our tickets be valid, would there be a first class compartment available? I daren't go on.

As one disaster was averted, only just, another hove into view. No one had warned us that this train, despite taking a day-and-a-half to reach its destination and crossing an international frontier, didn't have a restaurant car.

The attendant had a small stock of snacks, bars of chocolate and cartons of fruit juice for sale. I still had a couple of packets of biscuits from the airport lounge at Heathrow. We'd have to make do with that. There was no possibility of a proper meal. I fetched hot water to make some coffee, then got into conversation with a Dutch lady in the next compartment, travelling with two friends.

'Have you any food?', she asked.

'No. No one told us there wouldn't be a restaurant car.'

She obviously relayed this to her friends, because a few minutes later, one of them knocked on our door.

'We've brought you a food parcel. Here's two packets of cup-a-soup, a muesli bar each and two packets of biscuits.'

We thanked her profusely.

I called Mike over.

'Have you noticed that these bars have Dutch labels? We aren't the only tourists bringing stuff long distances. They've been carrying these all the way from Holland!'

We'd now left the Trans-Siberian Railway and were travelling on the Trans-Mongolian line, which opened in 1949. Including the stops, the journey time to

Mike has a thing about trains. He wants to show you this one.

Ulan Bator is in excess of 24 hours. I hesitate to be exact because the changes in time zone make calculation fraught. I don't think it's unreasonable to expect that a train crossing an international frontier and taking such a long time to deliver its passengers while travelling throughout the night, would have some facility for feeding them. If only for the profits it could generate, as well as some additional employment.

The agency in Russia working for my agency in England ought to have told them that this is the case. After all, we're not the first tourists for whom they've booked seats on this line. They must know that it doesn't cater for passengers in the literal sense. It should pass this information to foreign travel agencies as a matter of routine.

We stopped at every station, because this was not an express train but a working lifeline for local people. Using a timetable screwed to the wall in the corridor, we could monitor exactly where we were and also know in advance how long we'd be stopping at each station. It varied between a couple of minutes and as long as twenty. Funnily enough, when you needed them, there were no vendors on the platforms. A regional variation of Sod's Law?

For no apparent reason, we were scheduled to stop at one little station for 20 minutes. Directly in front of me as I looked out of the corridor window was a building on the far side of the tracks with the Russian word for shop, *magazin**, over the door. Below it was the proprietor's name for it: Beryozka* – 'Little Birch Tree'.

'Wait here,' I said to Mike, 'I'm going to investigate.'

As these words were both in Cyrillic, they meant nothing to the foreign tourists in my wagon, who would like nothing better than to do some emergency shopping if only they could find a shop. The fact that the front door was shut was an added disincentive.

Time for me as the International Brigade's duty speaker of the local lingo to take the initiative. Sound the trumpet! *For-WARD!*

Lacking my charger and sabre, all I actually did was go over to the shop door and ask the old boy lounging on a chair outside in the sun,

'*Is the shop open?*'

'*Yes,*' he muttered. '*Go on in.*'

The local shop, Beryozka, meaning 'Little Birch Tree'.

I opened the door. The staff were all in position, expecting, I suppose, an influx of customers from the train. Those who could read Cyrillic, that is. The rest of the Foreign Legion were wandering about aimlessly up and down the platform, some chatting, some smoking, some cleaning their fingernails. When I stepped outside I was able to convey in impromptu semaphore that this is a shop, come on over with your money in your hot little hand. You've got ten minutes left before the train leaves. I conveyed all this silently, simply by waving one arm madly above my head while with the other making exaggerated pointing motions in the general direction of the shop door.

What followed was a scrimmage worthy of a rugby international with the scores even and three minutes to go for the final whistle. Everyone tried to barge their way to one of the three counters, all shouting at once and all in English, regardless of what their own national language was. As was only to be expected, none of the staff spoke English. At the back, I was sizing up what was for sale and what I would like. I settled for a bar of chocolate, a bottle of fizzy orange, a couple of packets of biscuits and some fruit.

As the scrum subsided and the mass of foreign customers squeezed and shoved their way out through the shop door, I moved to the counter in a cloud of serenity and asked in a quiet voice for the items I'd chosen. The assistant's face indicated total consternation when she realised that after ten frantic minutes being shouted at in English, this traveller was speaking to her quietly in Russian.

Seeing some small round items that looked like pastry balls next to a basket containing rolls, I asked,

'What are these? Some sort of bread?'

' No,' she said. 'They're sweet.'

'I'll take seven,' I said.

She served me, told me the price, was relieved when I understood the numbers, then as I turned to go said, 'You speak very good Russian.'

'Thank you,' I replied. 'You're very kind.'

I only wish it were true. I think after the tourist mêlée and all the shouting and frantic pointing, she was overcome with relief that at least one of this horde of locusts had had the courtesy to speak to her in her own tongue.

Back on the train, I popped next door to the Dutch ladies and offered them each one of my sweet round cakes. I'd deliberately chosen to buy seven: one for each of them, leaving two each for me and Mike. I felt a debt of honour at being subbed out earlier. I'd managed to even the score a bit or at least I'd shown willing.

Our next stop was the main one where we officially crossed the frontier with Mongolia at the town of Nayushki*.

Nayushki, on the Russian border with Mongolia.

'The timetable says we'll be there for 297 minutes, five-and-a-half hours! Does it take that long to go through customs and passport control?' I wondered aloud to Mike.

When we arrived, the attendant told us all that we had 2½ hours to go to the town. Three hours of our scheduled stop had mysteriously disappeared.

Everyone was turfed off the train. The locals disappeared home or about their business, leaving the contingent of bemused, disoriented foreign passengers to mill about on the platform wondering what to do.

Mike and I went through the gates, to examine our predicament.

'Which way's the town, then?'

'Search me. Are you sure there even *is* a town?'

'Well, you saw the name 'Nayushki' over the station building. There must be a town of that name somewhere here. It can't be just a station.'

'There aren't even any taxis. What's wrong with these people? Can't they see a golden opportunity to pick up some fares?'

'They must know the international train's schedule. They also must know that the passengers all get turfed off and have over two hours to hang about. In addition, most of them are hungry.'

Much to our amazement, the station was deserted so far as staff were concerned, or rather, staff *weren't* concerned. Passengers waiting to continue their journey to

Mongolia were left entirely to their own devices. There wasn't even a signpost pointing to where the town itself was or how far.

By sheer chance, a couple of young lads on bikes were riding around in circles in the station forecourt. They accosted me with the only three words of English they knew: 'Hello!' and 'Good morning!'.

I responded with a question: *'Is there a restaurant somewhere here?'*

'Follow me,' replied one of the boys and led me a full thirty yards to my right and pointed to a doorway leading back into the station building. Above it was the word 'Café' in Cyrillic.

The station café at Nayushki.

Leaving the station to go into the car park outside, the first thing a passenger would see would be a road leading straight ahead. Naturally he'd assume this led to the town. Why would he instead turn right and walk along the side of the station buildings? He wouldn't see the café because it doesn't have such a thing as a sandwich board with an arrow. The fact that it's a café is only evident when standing directly in front of it.

'This station boasts its own café,' I said to Mike, 'but doesn't have anything at the exit to indicate that fact.'

'Seems to be another example of the lack of entrepreneurial spirit,' he remarked. 'Every day there's an international train stopping here for 2½ hours with hungry passengers who have cash in their pockets.'

We went into the café. The menu was double-sided in Russian and English. What was on offer was perfectly adequate.

'Well, they've got *solyanka*. Let's have some of that for a start. Then I'll have pork with mashed potato and a fruit juice. What about you?'

'I'll try the dish made of sausage and mashed potato with two fried eggs,' responded Mike. 'I'll wash it down with a beer.'

'As usual. Trying all the local beers, aren't you, as we progress through the country. Are you going to write a rival book: 'Roberts' Complete Guide to Siberian Breweries'?'

He grinned. 'Don't give me ideas!' he said.

To get a bottle, the serving girl pointed to a chill cabinet for Mike to open. When he did, it went 'ping'. Even here in the sticks they use anti-theft devices. He took out his choice and showed her the top so that she could see the price, which was written on it in marker pen.

'*Go and sit down. I'll bring it to your table,*' she said, having taken the order and the money.

The three Dutch ladies from our next compartment showed up. Maybe they'd seen where we were going, guessed we knew something they didn't and followed us.

With time on our hands and nothing to do, we wandered outside to a park with benches lining the path and awash with litter.

'There's a rather imposing building at the end of the path. May as well walk up and see what it is.'

'Club,' I said, when we got there. 'It's written over the door.'

That was all. What sort of club was left unsaid.

'There's no sign of any town centre, let alone in which direction it might be. Maybe Nayushki doesn't have a centre?'

In a desultory fashion we strolled back, passing *en route* a moth-eaten statue of a moose, with nothing to indicate what it was supposed to signify or who put it up or when. We ended up back at the station to kick our heels and talk to other passengers to pass the time. Mike met a girl who went to school in Monmouth, which is where he lives. They exchanged reminiscences about members of staff at the local school. Nayushki is where it's at!

Back on the train, customs and passport control were thorough but pleasant. We were asked to lift the seats in our compartment to make sure they were empty. They then lifted the padded headrests. We hadn't even realised that they moved, let alone had storage room behind them. As it took hardly any time, the time we'd

'Pekin – Ulan Bator – Moskva' in Russian, Chinese and Mongolian. [NB the Russians still use the former name: Pekin.]

spent twiddling our thumbs in Nayushki seemed all the more inexplicable, coupled with the total failure of the locals to show any commercial enterprise in offering marooned passengers something to do.

For example, a local restaurant, assuming there is such an establishment, could send a small fleet of taxis to meet the train and give the drivers multilingual cards which say 'This free taxi will take you to my restaurant where you can have a delicious three-course meal with wine and coffee. We guarantee to get you back to the station in time for the train.' They'd make a fortune.

If not that, then at least the on-site place where we had lunch could have a sandwich board outside the main exit with an arrow with the word 'CAFÉ' in Latin script to direct hungry travellers to their well-hidden premises just thirty yards away.

We came to the first stop on the Mongolian side of the border, by which time darkness had fallen. We had to endure a further delay. Once again, it was thumb-twiddle time. We had half an hour, time enough for me to go out onto the platform and light up a cigar.

I was accosted by a mildly aggressive local who muttered something unintelligible in Mongolian and pointed. What he was apparently trying to tell me was that I can't smoke here but should move along to the far end of the platform. At the same time, he made it clear that he'd very much like one of my cigars! Re-arrange the following words to make a well-known phrase that says: cake, having, eating, your, it, and. Discuss.

In the interests of international goodwill I offered him one of the small cigars in my case, but he tried to take one of the larger ones. Another well-known phrase came to mind, which includes the words 'gift horses' and 'mouths'. No way! Be satisfied! You've got a free cigar, moosh, whatever size it is.

At the end of the platform by the WC was a sign in Mongolian, Russian and English saying 'Smoke Area'. Here, smokers could indulge their habit. But there weren't any ashtrays anywhere. Only an overflowing refuse bin and some concrete seats against a wall.

Our carriage had been removed from the train and all the remaining coaches were third class and crammed full of locals.

'Look's like our carriage has been shunted off into the darkness of a Mongolian night.'

'Yes, but in which direction?'

'No idea. They have to re-attach our carriage to the end of the train but we don't know which end.'

By now we foreigners had become a sort of ragged multi-national Foreign Legion or impromptu militia, hanging together because we'd been thrown together, muttering against the authorities who seemed determined to do whatever it was that they had to do but without giving us any information.

The platform's designated smoking area.

There was only one first class wagon. We were all in it, albeit in separate compartments. The result was that one self-selected group of the foreign passengers wandered up to the far end to see if our wagon was on the front, while another group went in the opposite direction to see if it had been attached to the rear. Each group sent back semaphore signals by waving their arms above their heads, indicating 'No Luck. It's not here', to the scouting party at the other end. Others remained in the middle of the platform, waiting in exhausted despair for someone to come up with answers.

All this was taking place in the middle of the night on a flood-lit station platform.

'Boring' and 'tedious' don't do our situation anything approaching justice.

When eventually our carriage appeared, the ones who'd located it shouted to the others. We all grabbed our hand luggage and headed for the right end, ready to re-embark.

I'd been having an interesting conversation with a young Dutch girl from

Amstelveen, a suburb of Amsterdam, who was a social worker travelling alone. She told me about the trials and tribulations of travelling *platskart* (open carriage, the cheapest seats) to Tobolsk with a bunch of drunken Russians and no common language. It was specifically to avoid this sort of situation that Mike and I had no hesitation when planning our trip to make the decision to travel first class.

Back on the train we are confined to our compartments while the very smartly uniformed Mongolian border officials, male and female, did their job. The only minor inconvenience was that the toilets were locked for the duration.

'We'd better sort out something to eat. What have we got?', Mike enquired.

'Some chocolate. Those sausages we bought on the way back to Irkutsk from Listvyanka a week ago. Good job they're vacuum-packed. We can eat them cold.'

'Yes, there's some processed cheese which we can spread on biscuits and wash down with fizzy orange drinks and the last of our supply of coffee.'

'When we get back home we can regale our friends with stories about the luxuries of fine dining on the Mongolian Express!'

'We'd better make up the beds and get some sleep while we can.'

With the constant muddle over time zones, we found it well nigh impossible to know for certain what the local time actually was. We never did get the hang of it.

As dawn broke we saw the country becoming rugged, with frequent sightings of a huge river, still the Selenga, which we first crossed on the way from Irkutsk to Ulan Ude and which flows into Lake Baikal. We crossed it several times because the railway line goes in a straight line but the river meanders.

We'd only just left the border when, to our immense surprise, we observed a huge banner hung out on railings alongside the track, saying, in English, 'Welcome to Mongolia'.

This confirmed that we really *had* left Russia.

It still strikes me as idiosyncratic, even though perfectly explicable, that on the Russo-Mongolian frontier the 'welcome' sign is not in the language of either country, but in that of a rather small country 5000 miles away.

However, given the fearsome reputation of the Mongols in past ages, it's reassuring to be shown in such an unequivocal manner on an unequivocal banner that these days they're friendly and are pleased to have us come to their country.

Another hoarding at a small station welcoming visitors to Mongolia.

TERELJ* NATIONAL PARK

Sunday 23rd
Guided stay in Terelj National Park

'Change money?'

We'd made the briefest of stops in Mongolia, but a small, fat lady had come on board, clutching a fist-full of local banknotes, offering to exchange roubles. She didn't say what exchange rate she was offering. The railway authorities didn't provide any leaflets with advice to travellers crossing the frontier.

I'd retained a single 500r. note (about £10), knowing that I would need some Mongolian currency when I found a post office and wanted to buy stamps for the postcards of Baikal that I'd bought in Khuzhir. On the basis that I didn't know when I'd next get a chance to change it, I reasoned that I might as well do so now and take a chance.

'Yes. I've got 500 roubles.'

She gave me 20,000 *tugriks**, the Mongolian unit of currency, but whether that was a fair exchange rate or I'd been short-changed, I had no way of knowing.

Some time after this transaction, several other itinerant money-changers came along, offering the same service but again not carrying anything informative, such as a board with the exchange rate written with chalk. They might have been offering better rates, but having exchanged the only Russian money we had left, we were done anyway – in both senses. We wouldn't hinder them as they passed along the carriage to try their luck with other travellers.

We arrived on schedule in Ulan Bator at 06h10 and were last off the train. We'd mixed up the time again. Fortunately this was the terminus. We weren't in any danger of being carried off bag and baggage to Ulan Nowheresville in the middle of the Gobi Desert.

As we emerged into the car park, a young man carrying a placard with our names on it rushed up to apologise for being late.

'My agency gave me the wrong time! I'm Joey, your guide.'

He put us in his waiting taxi. We headed out of town north-east to our destination: Terelj National Park. It took an hour and a quarter over roads of ever-increasing undulation with potholes everywhere. Our driver wove his way from side to side trying, with varying degrees of success, to avoid them. Luckily there wasn't much other traffic.

The city's limits are extensive. One-third of Mongolia's population lives in the capital, which they refer to as 'UB' for short. When we finally left the sprawling city behind us, the land was virtually empty, as is most of Mongolia. It's the size of Western Europe, but has only three million people.

Once out of the capital the countryside became hilly. Mountains were visible on the horizon. The road was not tarmac but simply earth, and of the same standard that we'd encountered on Olkhon. Drivers habitually had driven off the edge in order to avoid a particularly spectacular rut. In the process they had widened the 'road'. No edge was marked. The edge was where the last vehicle had driven and left tyre marks.

Our accommodation was to be a traditional Mongolian round tent, known as a *ger (pron. grrrrr)*. This is made of white felt and has a central iron chimney stack. The nomadic herders, who invented them, dismantled them when they moved on, loading everything onto carts and pack animals.

Our Mongolian ger.

We passed a number of country clubs and holiday resorts with rows of *gers* laid out in lines to accommodate tourists, looking for all the world like an Army camp in the nineteenth century, familiar to anyone who's watched *Sharpe* on TV.

Most establishments had wooden fences with carved gateposts with a crossbar adorned by a set of horns at the entrance, rather like the ones pictured in Westerns. It was clear that the Mongolians go for tourism in a big way. On offer were camping, horse-riding, trekking and wildlife-watching. For less physically active visitors, they offered a taste of what traditional life was like in a traditional dwelling, though with some contemporary comforts such as modern food, plumbing and lighting.

Our encampment was on a hillside with a picturesque view over a valley towards several small forested areas and boasted several rows of *gers*, about eight in each line.

Joey led us to the *ger* at the end of a gravel path. 'This one is yours.' he said. He pointed to a modern building at the other end of the path. 'That's the restaurant and toilet block. I'll see you there for breakfast when you're ready.'

Five uneven concrete steps led from the path to the door of our *ger*, with no handrail.

I immediately noticed something out of keeping.

Our accommodation in Terelj. The restaurant and toilet block are on the left.

'It's got a padlock! Very traditional, I don't think.'

Mike chipped in. 'By the doorposts at ground level are gaps in the felt, where the men who erected it didn't do it properly. I foresee the wind whistling in tonight when we're trying to keep warm and sleep. It doesn't look too promising.'

Once inside, we found our initial misgivings were more than prescient. The door, when closed, didn't stay closed because the catch was broken. We had to find a piece of rope and create a makeshift loop to tie it shut.

Stepping inside, the left-hand side is the men's side, the right hand for women and children.

'Remember,' I said to Mike, 'what Aleksei, the shaman, explained to us about the traditions in a Buryat house with regard to which part is for women, which for men, which for guests. I suppose much the same applies to a Mongolian *ger*.'

'I'll take the bed on the right,' he said, firmly.

'That leaves me the bed on the left, but then that's always what happens when we share a hotel room. Try not to talk with your voice up an octave.'

'I've always managed before.'

I estimate the *ger* was about 10m across. There were no curtains or screens: no privacy. Each side had a large bed with a low headrest. Traditionally, there were drawers underneath or attached to the ends, where the family would store their clothing and bedding and other household furnishings. Strangely, though, ours didn't have these.

The centre was dominated by the central supporting poles and the closed iron stove, absolutely essential in a country where in January the temperature can drop to -40°C with the wind roaring across the treeless *steppe*.

The author writing his diary in the dimly-lit ger.

The chimney poked up through the roof. The men who erected the *ger* had to make the hole watertight by wrapping additional felt round the stack. In the middle of the roof next to the stack was a small section of transparent plastic sheeting which admitted daylight. There are no windows in a traditional *ger*, therefore no natural light when the door is shut. Even when, in the course of time, glass windows became available, they would hardly have been practical, as *gers* were dismantled and carted away each time that the nomads moved to find new pasture for their livestock, mainly sheep, goats, horses or camels.

The beds were already made. We were provided with a table and three small stools, which meant that we had nothing to sit on which had a back to it. Electricity was produced by generators somewhere on site and brought to each individual *ger* by an overhead cable supported by 3m-high street lamps erected at intervals along the path. An energy-saving electric bulb, without a shade, was dangling above the table and another over my bed. A candle-end and some matches had been left on the table in case of emergency.

A young man came in with wood and lit the stove, which very soon threw out so much heat that it was actually too hot! We had to open the door to reduce the temperature to a more comfortable level. Stoves in *gers* aren't fitted with thermostats!

'I think our first priority is breakfast,' said Mike.

'Indeed. We need time to catch our breath after yet another day-and-a-half train journey. Joey told us where to go. I presume he's waiting to show us the ropes. We'll tell him to meet us at 12h30 for lunch and our first trip.'

'We're feeling knackered because of all that hanging about yesterday in Nayushki. In the late evening when we should have been sleeping, we were up and about crossing the border and being buggered about by customs and passport formalities.'

'And without a break, we've followed all that with a pretty bumpy ride here from Ulan Bator, which was, if I remember rightly from my brochure, 75 miles. For me, living near Southampton, that's like travelling home from London!'

Joey conducted us to breakfast.

'I learned my English,' he volunteered, 'by watching American TV shows and cartoons.'

'It's pretty good, with a slight American accent,' I replied, nodding in agreement.

'I've travelled in China, the US, where I got mugged, Canada, Mexico and Malaysia.'

How a man still in his early twenties could afford this amount of world-wide travel he never made clear, nor did he make clear how old he was when he went, nor precisely what he was doing apart from 'taking the road'. Conveniently lost in translation, I suspect.

The weather was again warm and sunny. I sat smoking a small cigar after my coffee. We had a bucolic view through our front door as it swung on its hinges emitting a grinding noise. Mongolia may have no oil, but this was ridiculous.

The proprietors of the club had obviously realised that Western tourists put much store by having western standards of washing facilities. We were delighted to discover the WCs in the toilet block were a proper flush and not a 'squat and grunt'.

However, the adjacent wash basins in the ablutions were unisex and communal.

'It's 50m along the concrete path back to our *ger*.'

'Hope it's not raining tomorrow morning when we wish to ablute.'

One of my word games with my wife was taking nouns and making up what the verbs ought to be. From the noun 'ablutions' the verb must be 'to ablute'. One of the pleasures of being with someone you know well is that you can talk nonsense and be perfectly understood.

'And that there's paper in all the toilet cubicles.'

Which there wasn't. Only in one.

'I see they've cosied up to Western preferences by providing normal food for breakfast. The menu says muesli, cornflakes and fried eggs. There's bread, butter and what looks like marmalade.'

It turned out to be a jam with a taste rather like apricot, presumably a mixture, but quite palatable. Our eggs, though, when they arrived had hard yolks and were served with a frankfurter sausage sliced lengthways. Seemed a strange combination.

After lunch, we moved off in the car along switch-back roads into the hills, which are extremely scenic, similar to the foothills of the Pyrenées or the Massif Central. That the terrain was sub-alpine was not surprising when one considers that we were 1500m above sea level.

'I'm taking you to see a Buddhist shrine and some amazing natural rock formations,' Joey told us.

Mike was excited by their intrinsic beauty. The play of light and shade gave him the opportunity to vary his shots and even to wait patiently for a passing cloud to cast its shadow and then take the same angle again, only with different light.

On the way we passed a solitary Bactrian camel, the kind with two humps, and a few ponies with their owners, waiting patiently for customers to stop their cars and buy a ride for their children. It was Sunday and schools were closed. Teachers with hordes of youngsters were on excursions and dozens of families were out for the day from UB.

Next, please!

219

The different play of light on the rock formations.

'Let's hope the owners of the animals do well before the season ends in a couple of weeks and their income with it,' I commented to Mike as we drove past.

'Wow! Aren't they absolutely astounding!' Mike exclaimed when we caught sight of the Buddhist temples. They were at the end of the valley, built at the top of precipitous slopes under the lee of the summits. At even greater height and away to the right were multi-coloured inscriptions painted directly onto the mountainside.

'They're in such difficult positions that you can't imagine how those who put them up there did it, short of abseiling from ropes from the summits.'

Buddhist inscriptions painted directly onto the mountainside.

'They look as though they're defying the laws of gravity.'

It was a long walk uphill. Then we were confronted by a one-in-four flight of a couple of hundred steps leading up to the shrine itself.

At intervals along both sides of this path were large signboards on posts, bearing Buddhist exhortations and proverbs, all with English translations underneath. I stopped to read some of them and was struck by how banal, superficial or commonplace they were, often calling on people to embrace faith for its own sake and claiming that someone who has faith is superior to someone who hasn't. Well, I thought to myself, those who believe in religions would say that, wouldn't they.

The Buddhist Temple.

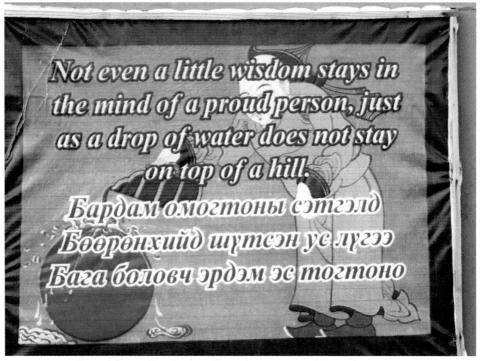

One of the signboards along the path carrying Buddhist exhortations.

The view back down the valley from this vantage point was reward enough for the struggle to reach it.

By half past three, we'd completed the visit. It had been rather a short trip, as we hadn't set out until after lunch. In fact we were quite glad. After the privations of the journey from Ulan Ude and then from Ulan Bator, we were both in need of a proper rest.

When we spotted the *ger* directly in front of us being dismantled, we felt like the last customers in a restaurant when the waiters start stacking the chairs. Being able to observe the process being carried out in front of us gave us the chance to understand how *gers* are put together in the first place.

'We're here right at the end of the season. As there won't be anyone on site all winter, the *gers* have to be taken down and stored.'

'Seems that the minute a tourist moves out, their *ger* is demolished, loaded onto a trailer and driven away. '

I noted that the wind was rising.

'We're on an exposed hillside,' I said to Mike, with an element of anxiety in my voice.

'Bearing in mind the holes in our *ger* wall were due to inefficient erection, I wonder whether we're going to need that stove tonight.'

We enjoyed a very pleasant dinner, but were the only clients. At least they sold wine by the glass. I was allowed to sit and smoke afterwards. There was no lounge, just the restaurant.

A ger being dismantled.

Monday 24th September
Horse-riding, an archery lesson and being introduced to traditional nomadic life in Mongolia

I woke at 02h15 to the sound of falling rain, three feet above my head as the *ger* had a sloping roof. As the beds were against the wall, the slope of the roof brought it down to just above my prone figure. I reached up two feet to the light switch dangling loose just above my head, then slipped on my shoes, anorak and cap intending to nip outside for a surreptitious pee. I was not going to traipse fifty yards to the toilet block in the rain in the middle of the night, when we were the last *ger* in the row. There wasn't likely to be anyone else around to see me. If there was, they'd be having a pee, too. *Snap!*

The floor was shining in the glare of the bare electric light bulb. The minute I put my foot on it I realised why. The rain had been coming in through the hole for the chimney stack as the erectors, as with the gaps by our doorposts, hadn't done their job properly. We were leaking. The floor was covered with water!

I couldn't do anything about it. In any case I was being driven by a greater need, the pressure on my bladder. To go outside, I had to unloop the piece of rope holding the door shut in case a gust of wind blew it open. As we were on the side of a hill, that was quite likely. And to endeavour to do this without waking Mike.

Outside the lamps on their posts were all alight. Despite the hour, I navigated my way with some trepidation down the uneven steps from our doorway to *terra firma* and walked round to the far side of the *ger* away from the toilet block, just in case there was anyone about. A night security guard, perhaps? Beyond our *ger* there was no one to see me. It was open country.

There I was, feet well apart to avoid pissing on my shoes, wearing my cap to keep my hair dry and my anorak to keep the gentle rain off my body, in full flow, when without any warning, the lights went out! A fuse had blown in one of the lamps, which also meant my own dim bedside light inside the *ger* would also have gone out.

Because the rain clouds completely obscured the moon and stars, there was no natural light. Not only did I have to finish the business in hand in the pitch black of a Mongolian night, I also had to grope my way back up the five uneven concrete steps, creep inside, try to shut the door and loop the rope, disrobe and hang my coat back on the coat-rack, wriggle out of my wet shoes and wriggle back to bed, all without waking my *ger*-mate.

Not a chance! Mike was by now wide awake, and pissing himself – with laughter. He could picture my predicament. I was relieved that he hadn't got his flash and his camera handy.

We woke up again at 06h00, to find to our relief that the rain had stopped and that the water on our floor seemed to have drained away. The weather would be clear for our next excursion.

At 07h00 I woke up again, to espy the dim outline of Mike lighting the fire. Looking over to the far side of the *ger* to his bed, I saw in the daylight from our roof panel that he was still in bed. Either he'd overcome a major law of terrestrial physics and was in two places at once, or it was someone else lurking in our *ger*. One of the staff had come in silently to warm it up for us sybaritic Europeans. As he turned to go, I reached up to my light bulb and caught his attention to indicate, by signs, that it was not working. He acknowledged and left. Hopefully someone would now mend the fuses.

Mike and I chatted for an hour. There was no reason to get out of bed. With no chairs and a damp floor we were more comfortable *in situ*.

'It's eight o'clock. Time to head for the ablutions.'

Without electricity, of course, there was no power to operate the water pumps or the heating system. All we got from the wash basin taps was a dribble of whatever cold water was left in the pipes. All we could do was to wipe our faces as best we could and hope for better times to come.

To be fair, we were in the wilds on the Mongolian *steppe*, a semi-desert. We couldn't reasonably expect to have all mod. cons. On the other hand, if these resorts have been set up specifically for tourists and a promise

The doorway into our ger.

of these 'cons', then at least they ought to work. What's the point of installing them otherwise? If we'd wanted a camping or trekking holiday and all the 'roughing it' that that entails, we'd have booked one. We hadn't.

The rain had cleared, leaving a fine mist hanging in the silent trees in the valley. It was very picturesque. I mused that Grieg or Sibelius would have found inspiration.

'I must try to work out how to photograph that mist effectively,' said Mike. 'I wish I'd brought a wide-angle lens with me.'

By now it was so warm that he'd stripped to the waist. Thankfully the fire in the stove had gone out, otherwise the inside of our *ger* would have become unbearably hot.

Morning mist on the steppe.

According to our schedule, we were to see a demonstration of traditional Mongolian archery and to have a lesson. In our minds we envisaged a professional archer, probably employed by the Mongolian Tourist Board and in his other life a member of the Olympic team, dressed up in traditional costume for the benefit of visitors with cameras. He would be an expert marksman, able to demonstrate how the Mongols in the Middle Ages became so proficient in mounted warfare that they were able to create the largest land empire the world has ever seen using only bows and arrows fired from horseback. He'd have a traditional bow and would show how it differs from those used in the modern Olympics. He'd describe how it was made and probably require our guide to translate. He'd demonstrate his skill by shooting off a few arrows at a target. Then he'd offer us a chance to try our hands, under his guidance.

No such luck.

What happened at this juncture was that Joey went into the restaurant and picked up a bow and three arrows kept behind the bar, led us a couple of hundred yards across a field, took up his stance fifty yards from a target, fired off the arrows and then handed me the bow to have a go.

The target itself was an animal skin stretched out between two uprights and two horizontal branches, with slightly rising ground behind. I hadn't fired an arrow since my childhood when, like every other little boy in my rural village, I made my own bow and arrows out of new hazel branches, strung it with ordinary string and took aim to hit a tin can on a stick from twenty paces in my own garden at a safe distance from the house. If the cat was around, he'd probably get shot at

Should Genghis Khan attack,
he has nothing to fear.

just for the fun of watching him demonstrate his capacity for transmogrifying into a cheetah and breaking the land speed record for *felis felis*. I am therefore no expert.

More to the point, nor was Joey.

When my first three arrows missed, he ran to the hillock behind the target, picked them up and handed them back for me to try again. It took me eight shots to work out the angle to fire at from this distance. Then I hit the target twice in succession to demonstrate that the first direct hit wasn't a fluke.

Mike had a go, with similar results. Half an hour passed. What now? Our brochure said 'An archery lesson'? Is that it?

Indeed, that *was* it. We'd paid good money for this farce. Perhaps it was a good job that the arrows were blunt.

We were left with another two hours before lunch and the next item on the programme. Once again it was thumb-twiddle time. What's more, we were actually paying for it. This afternoon our programme promised us horse-riding, which once again one expected would consist of a demonstration of horsemanship, for which the Mongols are world famous. Tourists who can ride might be given a chance to go for a canter on a Mongolian horse with the expert. If we had equestrian skills, it might well have been the high spot of our trip.

I must confess that I've only twice in my life ever sat on a horse. The first time was on a horse belonging to my next door neighbours when I was about twelve. They were taking him from the field to his stable. They let me sit on him bareback while he was led. The second time was half a century later when I was Mayor of Eastleigh. I was asked to sit on a horse wearing my chain of office (me, not the horse) to pose for photographs to promote an equestrian charity. Despite this, I would have liked to see an expert demonstrate his skills even though at my age it would not be sensible to risk life and limb.

Mike and I had a confab.

'This 'archery lesson' is a con.'

'It certainly isn't Joey's fault,' I replied. 'It's his employers who are exploiting us. The proprietors of the tourist agency who sold us the package have swindled us by promising 'an archery lesson' which consists of letting the guide shove a bow into our hands and show us how to notch an arrow.'

'That's about as elementary as you can get. It certainly doesn't qualify for the description 'archery lesson'.'

'What do you suppose this afternoon's horse riding will consist of?'

'Based on this morning's débâcle, I reckon it'll be a bloke in trainers and a tee-shirt with a horse on a lead, who'll say, 'This is a horse. You can sit on it if you want to.' And he'll have charged us fifty quid for the privilege, no doubt.'

'Who needs it? We have horses in England, even if not Mongolian ones, but horses nonetheless. They're hardly exotic. What's more, I have a good friend back home who runs her own stables. I see plenty of horses whenever I visit her. If I wanted to mount one, I'm sure she'd supervise me while I did it, provided I wore a helmet and appropriate footwear.'

The outcome of our debate was a decision.

'We'll abort the horse riding,' said Mike. 'We'll make the scheduled visit to a nomad family, then leave this afternoon for UB and spend an extra night there in a hotel, where we can hope to have comfortable chairs to sit on and guaranteed power for my laptop.'

'And the roof probably won't leak.'

Kyrle's Third Law of Tourist Guides states that if the programme that you were promised falls below expectations, you don't have to go through with it.

'When Joey comes back, we'll ask him to make the new arrangements. '

On our return to the *ger* after our triumph with the bow, one of the staff brought us a thermos of hot water. I had our two cups and two tea bags. Presumably that was what it was for. But no sugar and no spoon. Luckily my ditty bag would provide, including the plastic spoons which we'd bought in Listvyanka. It was a nice thought, a mid-morning tea-break, even if not properly managed. Like providing four flush toilets in cubicles, but neglecting to ensure that each one has toilet paper.

After lunch, we were looking out of the restaurant window when a couple of dozen horses ran past, being moved by their owner to some new grazing. Will we now see a Mongolian herdsman in traditional dress, riding his own trusty steed?

To our delight, sure enough the owner of the horses hove into view, wearing jeans, a baseball cap and a tee-shirt and riding a small motorbike. His assistant was running along twenty yards to one side, shooing a horse lagging behind the rest. When it had caught up with the others, he nipped over to his boss and hopped onto the pillion seat.

Mongolians have embraced the twenty-first century. They don't hang onto traditional ways when modern ways are more convenient.

It was now time for our promised introduction to nomadic life, which turned out to be a short walk over the brow of the hill behind us to a solitary *ger* outside of which was a young woman making something. Joey told us it was cheese. This was supposed to be our introduction to Mongolian tradition, so it didn't augur too well that she was wearing a jumper, brown corduroy slacks and knee-length black leather boots.

Her *ger* was furnished inside in traditional style, except for a TV covered by a tea towel clearly emblazoned 'New Zealand' and with a map of the islands. Outside a wired-up solar panel was leaning against the side of the *ger*. A satellite dish was positioned on the roof.

Making cheese.

A small child with a pony-tail was running around. We assumed it was the woman's little girl.

'No,' said Joey. 'It's Mongolian custom not to cut a child's hair until it's two years old. Then there's a big family ceremony. All the relatives are given a lock as a keepsake. He's actually a little boy.'

We sat down at the central table. Without uttering a word, the woman put bowls of fermented mare's milk in front of us. It was white and thick and had a rather acid taste. Out of politeness I drank some, but didn't care for it enough to want to finish the bowl. A bit like my first glass of beer when I was 18. Once was enough, never again.

The owner's little boy.

We were then offered a traditional Mongolian sweet, looking a bit like popcorn, in a large bowl from which you helped yourself.

On the bed facing us all this time lay the prone figure of large young man, apparently a cousin, who was fast asleep and appeared to be sucking his thumb. He remained there throughout our visit without waking up. I noted that he was asleep on the bed in the side of the *ger* we'd been told is reserved for women. So much for tradition!

Joey called our attention to the display of family medals.

'These were won in horse races.' He pointed. 'There's a traditional saddle. It's not very comfortable to sit on.' He continued. 'The family move in the autumn to a more sheltered spot to look after their horses.'

'Are there any other children?'

'Yes. They're weekly boarders at a school in UB.'

Trying fermented mare's milk.

Young man asleep on the bed in the ger.

Display of family medals won in horse races.

Traditional saddle.

'Where do they sleep when they come home? There are only two beds.'

'On the floor. They also own a flat in UB.'

Or was it more than one? I wasn't quite sure.

Moving house in the winter, I thought, doesn't make them nomads. It merely demonstrates that they reside in different places according to the season. My late second step-father used to shut up his house in Cornwall for most of January and February and decamp to the south of Spain with his wife. That didn't make him a nomad. Merely a seasonal migrant.

I voiced my irritation to Mike.

'This whole episode strikes me as a charade laid on for gullible foreigners to make a few bob for someone with a *ger* conveniently located walking distance from our resort. They've got some sort of arrangement: 'We'll bring our clients over to you. You give 'em some mare's milk and sweets and go back to your chores while we give 'em the tourist pitch. Afterwards, we'll slip you a wad of *tugriks*.' We're being had – again.'

I remember back in the '70's taking a school party to Holland and visiting a house on Marken, an island in the IJsselmeer, previously known as the Zuyder Zee, where an old lady kept a fisherman's cottage in traditional style and dressed up as a seventeenth century fisherman's wife and gave a wonderful explanation in English describing how the people on the island lived in those days. She did it as a show for tourists. She didn't pretend that off-duty she dressed like this or lived in a house furnished in this way or that in her own private life she lived without modern conveniences.

That experience was very instructive and interesting, with no attempt being made to fool the visitor into thinking they were seeing a way of life which still existed. In fact, Marken was by that time no longer an island, as a causeway had been built linking it to the mainland which provided a road for vehicles to cross. Thinking back on our visit to a traditional nomad family, I am reminded of my grandmother's phrase for describing people who pretended to be what they're not : 'About as genuine as a two-pound note.'

Ten minutes later we were back at our *ger*. We'd already packed our bags. We could take them down to the car park, get in the car and head for UB without wasting any more time in this rip-off joint. Potholes all the way, our new chauffeur driving as if being pursued by a starving wolf pack, but simultaneously exhibiting the fact that he was a very skilful driver.

At the entrance to the city we had to pass vehicle control and pay a fee of 500 *tugriks* (about 20p).

With this money extracted from every vehicle, one might have expected the road surface to improve. But no, it was still ruts and no kerbs until we got close to the city centre. There, the problem was no longer ruts, but congestion. From all sides, weaving and changing lanes and bumper-to-bumper traffic, it was just like Moscow a month ago on our taxi ride from the airport to our hotel.

Traffic police were doing their best to exert some sort of control, with the word 'POLICE' in English emblazoned across the shoulders of their fluorescent jackets. As Mongolian is written in an adaptation of Cyrillic script, I questioned Joey.

'Why is this? Is it expected that all Mongolians can read Latin script? Isn't there a Mongolian word for police?'

He didn't explain.

The Hotel Bayangol, where we were booked for the rest of our stay, had made our room available for an extra night. We were comfortably provided with proper beds and a bathroom, reliable electric power and no fear of rain coming in during the night. Since we were on the ninth floor, we had a panoramic view across the city and a balcony for Mike to position his tripod to take some more photos.

Joey tried his best to put a brave face on the fact that his two tourists were not best pleased by what had been going on.

'I've chosen a restaurant for dinner,' he said. 'The agents will pay for it, in lieu of the meal you would have had back at Terelj.'

'I suspect he's chosen one where the company will get a discount ,' I murmured to Mike as an aside.

'I'll bet you're right,' said Mike, 'but what the hell!'

To reach this restaurant we had to drive a few hundred yards to the city centre. We were stuck in traffic for the whole of the journey.

The food was nothing special, certainly not worth sitting for three-quarters of an hour in a virtually motionless traffic jam. I've no doubt that it would have been quicker to walk.

A traffic cop does his best to control congestion in Ulan Bator. [Note that the word 'Police' on his tabard is in Latin script, even though in Mongolia the language is written in a version of Cyrillic.]

ULAN BATOR

Tuesday 25th September
Guided tour of Ulan Bator

*The main square, Ulan Bator, with the parliament building
and a statue of Genghis Khan seated on his throne.*

We started the day with a cup of black tea and a hearty European-style breakfast of bacon and fried egg, followed by bread and marmalade. There was no facility for making toast.

It was a quarter to ten. First thing, I needed to go to the post office and get some stamps and post my cards.

'Me, too,' Mike added. 'I want to send one to my little granddaughter with some exotic stamps on it. She's only three. She won't be able to read it, but she'll like the pretty stamps which she can keep as a souvenir.'

'Then Joey can take us to the main square to see the parliament buildings, where I want to have my picture taken with the statue of a certain famous person.'

Guess who!

Mention Mongolia to most people and they have only one thought: Genghis Khan.

Genghis Khan.

Yes. They vaguely remember that in the Middle Ages he led the Mongols on a rampage across Central Asia and reached the frontiers of Europe, destroying everything in his way and on his way.

Modern Mongolians take a different view. The huge statue says it all.

'I notice, by the way,' said Mike, 'that they spell it as '*Chinggis Khaan*'.'

I went on to explain. 'He's seen as a national hero, the father of the nation, who first united the nomadic Mongols to create a vast empire. And, note, he only destroyed those who opposed him. Those who submitted were allowed to keep their own customs and religion.'

'Indeed?'

'Yes. That was a degree of toleration which was certainly not found in contemporary Christian Europe in the early thirteenth century, when Jews were persecuted and heretics routinely put to death often in particularly nasty ways.'

Our tour of the city began with paying our respects to Chinggis Khaan and visiting the museum devoted to his times. The exhibition area was large and well lit, with display cases arranged in the centre and others against the walls.

I called Mike over. 'Look. This case has some interesting coins from the Early Middle Ages.'

'And this one's displaying the banners carried by armies when they approached a town to show whether they came in peace or war. It says a white banner meant they came in peace. If it was war, they carried a black one.

The banners carried by armies approaching a town.

237

'I wonder if that's got anything to do with our custom of using a white flag?'

Part of the museum was closed to the public, due to a foreign delegation visiting Ulan Bator. We moved off to our next venue.

This was the Gandan monastery, which was thronged with devotees buying bags of nuts from street vendors to feed the hundreds of pigeons who knew that despite strenuous denials from nay-sayers there *is* such a thing as a free lunch.

Pigeons in the Gandan monastery.

Joey explained about the government's future intentions.

'There are plans to re-locate the monastery to a new site about 50km away and to erect a statue of the Buddha which will be taller than the Statue of Liberty. A model of his foot is displayed on a plinth, giving some idea of just how colossal that statue will be.'

We had lunch in a Mongolian barbecue, where the dexterity of the cooks amazed us. The customer filled a bowl with whatever it was he or she fancied and gave it to one of the cooks. Two of them worked simultaneously, cooking for separate customers on a circular hotplate about three metres in diameter. They used very long spatulas to toss the food sideways to ensure that it was all properly cooked, then

The size of Buddha's feet indicate the scale of the rest of the statue when it's constructed.

scooped it all up and with a theatrical flourish deposited it back in the customer's bowl.

'I'm now going to take you to the memorial to Russian-Mongolian friendship

Mongolian barbeque lunch being cooked on the round hotplate.

and to those who died during the Second World War,' said Joey. 'It's at the top of Zaisan Hill.'

We arrived to be faced by 300 steep steps. At the top was a round display area, with the walls painted with patriotic scenes. It was very obvious that the architects and painters were strongly influenced by the concept of socialist realism. For once, it had worked incredibly well, even when allowing for the element of propaganda contained in a succession of portraits depicting sturdy, good-looking men and women dressed in a variety of uniforms, smart and ready for a ceremonial parade.

The Memorial to Russian-Mongolian friendship.

We had an interesting encounter there with a young Chinese couple when we overheard them talking to each other in English. When questioned, they explained that they'd met on the train.

'I'm from Hong Kong', the young man explained, 'so I don't speak very good Mandarin.'

'I come from south-west China,' chimed in the girl, 'and I can't understand his Cantonese! We decided that as we'd both studied in Britain, it was easier to talk to each other in English than struggle to communicate using two different versions of Chinese.'

Mike and I both smiled. It was an interesting vignette of the dominance of English as the world's *lingua franca* that two educated Chinese opted to use it as the easiest way to talk to each other.

The Mongols were conquered by the Chinese in 1691, but when the Manchu Dynasty fell in 1911 they declared their independence and turned to their religious leader, the Tibetan-born lama, the Bogd Khan. Until the twentieth century they remained a largely nomadic people, even moving their capital, known at that time as Urga, with them.

The Bogd Khan's palace, built between 1893 and 1903, was open to tourists. The interiors of the pavilions were well kept and full of sublime examples of Buddhist art, calligraphy and especially *thangkas*. While the skill and devotion of the artists is not to be doubted, the fact is that the displays are largely meaningless to a viewer unfamiliar with the intricacies and symbolism of Buddhist religious art. The buildings themselves needed a lick of paint and the open spaces between them were surprisingly unkempt.

The Bogd Khan agreed to become king. Despite, as a lama, being committed to celibacy he even agreed to take a wife so that the people could have a queen. His throne was on display in the audience chamber, replete with 28 thin cushions representing the 28 provinces of Mongolia. Also on show were the Queen's throne, various ceremonial costumes and the seats where religious and lay officials sat during an audience.

Ten years later the Bogd Khan accepted constitutional limitations to his power. When he died in 1924, the communists took over and set up a dictatorship in imitation of what was happening at that time in their vast northern neighbour, Russia. Mongolia became, to all intents and purposes, a Soviet satellite.

As we all know, the Soviet Union broke up in the early 1990's. Belarus, Ukraine, the Baltic States, Trans-Caucasia and much of Soviet Central Asia became independent. It is less well known that at the same time the Mongolians threw off the communist yoke and set about building a functioning democracy.

'At six o'clock I'm going to take you to a performance of traditional Mongolian music and dance,' Joey informed us.

It turned out to be the cultural highlight of our visit. A small, predominantly young, professional troupe, dressed in elaborate costumes and quick-changing between acts, amazed us with their dexterity. The traditional Mongolian violin has a square box and is held between the knees. A girl played a dulcimer at supersonic speed, another played an enormous zither and exotic dances were performed by other artistes.

In due course, we heard the world-renowned local eccentricity, throat singing, *hoomii* in Mongolian. The sounds emanating from the performer were almost

Musicians in traditional Mongolian costume.

unearthly, at enormous volume and pitched either below bass or above soprano. The singer's face showed no signs of strain, yet it is reputedly extremely difficult both to learn and to perform and requires many years of training.

Joey elaborated. 'The show is staged between six and seven every night and is essentially for tourists.'

Who can forget a contortionist who starts her act by standing on her right leg with her left leg at 180° with her knee against her ear and then for her finale, sticks a peg in the floor, grips the top in her teeth and proceeds to perform a slow-motion head-stand!

'I actually know her,' Joey claimed. 'She's 23 and has been preparing for her career since the age of seven.'

Dinner was in a Korean restaurant. I was disappointed not to find 'dog' on the menu. Whether or not I'd have chosen it, if it was offered, is another matter.

Back at the hotel we took the laptop down to the IT suite. I wanted to send an e-mail to my son, Rupert, as we hadn't been in contact for a week, to reassure him that we'd left Siberia, were now in Mongolia, that I was alright and to give my apologies for missing Eastleigh Liberal Democrats' constituency dinner: 'Dad sends his apologies. He's in Ulan Bator.' (Pause while the laughter subsides).

Joey, our guide, appears surprised that a Westerner is competent with a pair of chopsticks.

Wednesday 26th September
Free

I'd been in touch with the Civil Will-Green Party of Mongolia, asking if they'd like to meet me during my stay and exchange ideas with a fellow Liberal. Their representative, a mining engineer who had trained in Canada and therefore spoke excellent English, duly rang me, and took us for lunch in an Irish pub. In Ulan Bator? They get everywhere! I gave him some publications as gifts and we posed for a photo.

The author meets Gana Zunduiseren, a member of the Steering Committee of the Civil Will-Green Party.

For the first time since we left Moscow a month ago, it was raining, though not hard. We set off again to the post office to post the rest of my cards.

'If you want souvenirs,' Joey said, 'they're cheaper there. There's also more variety.'

The souvenirs didn't have any prices marked on them. We had constantly to get an assistant to get off her mobile phone and take the item out of the display cabinet and tell us the price, while she stood waiting while we made up our minds whether or not we wanted it.

To my amazement, they refused credit cards. This in the main post office and souvenir shop for foreigners seeking mementoes. Some want to choose from the enormous range of special stamps which Mongolia prints each year purely for collectors and for the foreign market. They can't possibly need them for pre-paying postage.

The next part of the process was to tot up the total for multiple purchases and mentally convert the price from *tugriks* into sterling at 2200 to the £, which is not the easiest of calculations to make in your head. While we were doing the mental arithmetic and debating the merits of this item or that, the assistant stood, holding the various items, eyes glazing over in boredom as she gazed into the middle distance.

Because they insisted on cash, we had to go to the cash point, draw out the money, go back to the counter, pay and take the goods. No wrapping paper or bags were offered. Although unsaid, the implication was clear: 'You've bought it. Here it is. It's yours now. Take it away.' If I decided that I'd like to make another purchase, I would have to go back through the whole rigmarole again and draw out more money.

I left Mike in charge of my second tranche of purchases while I went to the machine to get the cash. It would be much more difficult for a customer who was alone. One of the additional items I'd bought cost 2000 *tugriks*. When I received my credit card statement back in England a month later it showed I'd been charged 92p for the currency and a £2 handling fee for withdrawing it!

Mike only wanted some stamps costing a few hundred *tugriks*. He found the machines only paid out in multiples of a thousand. There were two machines. One didn't work.

Back at the hotel the restaurant was closed to us as it was hosting…

Guess what? A wedding!

We opted for the bar on the 3rd floor. The waitresses knew hardly any English, even though this was a hotel much used by foreigners and the menu was in both Mongolian and English. I ordered a glass of wine. When the waitress brought it, she muttered something to Mike, not to me, which he took to mean that it wasn't the wine I'd ordered but another one at the same price.

What she'd actually said, in Mongolian, was that the main course he'd ordered was not available, but without inviting him to choose something else. His first course of soup arrived, followed by my order of a pork chop. When he'd finished, he watched me eating while he waited for his second course to arrive.

Of course, it didn't and was not going to – but neither of us was aware of that.

'I'll call her over and ask her in Russian,' I said to Mike. 'If she doesn't know any English, maybe she'll understand that.'

Sadly, she didn't.

'I'll go to the bar and find someone who speaks more English,' Mike growled, beginning to lose his patience.

Eventually the manager, who understood sufficient English, intervened and the situation was resolved. Mike asked what *was* available and made a choice.

'I fancy a dessert,' I said. 'What's the betting we get anything?'

A new waitress came over. She, too, was unable to understand either English or Russian.

When I said 'ice cream' she understood, but couldn't explain the varieties they stocked. There was no dessert menu to show us.

Having seen someone behind the bar filling a glass with ice cream and chocolate, I asked for one of those. Eventually it was brought to our table.

'The point here is,' I said to Mike, thinking about how I'd write up this saga in my diary, 'the waitress didn't ask me if I wanted dessert, I had to ask *her*. I had to *ask* for coffee. Again she couldn't understand enough to take my order, only saying 'cappucino' which I indicated very clearly I did *not* want but just a plain black coffee. When it came, it was in a large cup. I didn't *want* a large cup, only a small one after my meal. There was no sugar. I had to *ask* for some. She brought sugar but with lumps and a pair of tongs but no spoon. Which finger am I supposed to stir it with?'

Mike was in total agreement. 'The bar is geared up to provide coffee and sugar, but the waiting staff are not geared up to offering these to their clients without being asked directly. What sort of service is that?'

'In a suburban café I wouldn't mind if the staff weren't proficient in foreign languages, but this is a city centre hotel catering for foreigners where the staff would expect most guests to speak English, even if that's not their first language. Do they really expect foreign visitors to have a working knowledge of Mongolian?'

Ulan Bator.

Ulan Bator today is a thoroughly modern city. Its traffic jams bear comparison with the rush hour in any large conurbation, except that it has them all day long! From our hotel room on the 9th floor we could see a dozen cranes and as many half-built tower blocks, a clear indication of the influx of people into the capital and the need to accommodate them.

The city may not be beautiful, lacking as it does anything resembling an 'old quarter' of the kind so keenly sought out by Western visitors to towns in foreign countries. But vibrant it surely is, and the smile on the face of Chinggis Khaan's statue doubtless indicates satisfaction with the modern Mongolia created by his descendants.

Thursday 27th September
Take the train to Beijing

Despite having an alarm call booked, I didn't sleep soundly. Probably because of the fiasco at Ulan Ude, I was afraid of a re-run. Missing the train this time would not be an inconvenience but a disaster, as there was only one each week. I was up at 05h45 making tea to take my pills. We were both more or less ready when the phone rang at the pre-arranged time with the wake-up call. According to our programme the train left at 08h26, but Joey said that should have been 07h15. At precisely that time we moved off.

'So much for programmes,' I said to Mike, with a feigned sigh of relief.

The weekly Ulan Bator-Beijing train.

An attendant.

246

'Thank heavens Joey was on the ball,' he replied.

It was once more a cloudless day. After half an hour of travelling remarkably slowly and stopping now and then for no apparent reason, we were still in UB, which seemed to spread itself forever across the *steppe*. Viewed from the train, many suburban single-storey houses in largish plots had a *ger* as well, in lieu of the garden shed that we in England would have. Even more incongruous to a Western eye were plots of land with a *ger* and a car parked alongside. A marriage of convenience of the old and the new.

Suburban view from the train.

Our compartment was two-berth but had a single armchair. We had a shower and toilet, shared with the compartment next door and with a lock which automatically worked on both sides so that there was no danger of an embarrassing intrusion.

Our neighbours were a recently retired English couple.

'We're taking six months out to travel to Australia to visit our son,' they told us.

'One of mine lives in Melbourne.' They had an immediate rapport with Mike.

Our berth.

247

'What's this on the table?' I asked Mike.

'A free booklet on Mongolia?'

'Written in damned funny English! Why didn't they ask someone in the university's English Department to go through it for them?'

Glancing through it, I came across an article which described an exchange of letters between the third Great Khan, Güyük (1246-48), and Pope Innocent IV (1243-54), each calling on the other to submit and convert. It seems the modern aphorism: 'Compromise. Do it my way' isn't so modern after all.

After leaving UB behind, it was hour after hour of more or less empty landscape. No signs of any kind of farming, bare hills rolling away into the distance and a very thick frost not yet despatched by the morning sun. For the next eight hours we saw just the occasional small herd of horses or cattle. What few trees there were, were 100m apart. If there was more than one, in other words enough to merit the designation of being 'a clump', it was 100m from the next clump.

The only evidence of human activity was the continuous line of fencing separating the track from the open land and the similarly continuous line of telegraph poles. Very occasionally we saw a tiny settlement of half-a-dozen houses with a station and a name, but we seldom stopped. The major evidence of human activity was the train on which we were travelling and the line on which we were running, which is a marvel of engineering in a hostile environment. The Trans-Mongolian Railway wasn't built until 1948.

We had a packed breakfast provided by the hotel for our journey.

'I wonder what they've given us?'

'Looks like three small sandwiches. One's cheese and two of, er, some kind of meat. There's some chopped cucumber and tomato, a tea bag and a sachet of coffee-with-milk, a piece of cake and a round sweet biscuit.'

In the restaurant car, lunch was a starter of grated carrot and cabbage in a piquant sauce, followed by mushroom soup, hot mutton in hot gravy with cold rice and cold chips, a small piece of chocolate Swiss roll for dessert, coffee. Additionally, for Mike a beer and for me an apple juice. The bill was 400 *yuan* (£40). We might still be in Mongolia, but this was a Chinese restaurant car wanting payment in Chinese money. And cash. No credit cards.

We spent the day alternately gazing at the unchanging view, reading, playing solitaire and sleeping. The semi-desert ran into a true desert: the Gobi. But the view

The restaurant car and kitchen.

from the train hardly changed. Sometimes it was immense, but uniformly brown. Sometimes hills were visible on the distant horizon, sometimes not. Later they were whitened by early snow.

Dinner at 18h30 was the same starter, mutton again but cooked slightly differently and with the same rice and vegetables, both again cold and the same dessert. There was no printed menu. If you wanted lunch, that's what you got. Dinner, the same arrangement.

As it happened, we finished our meal just in time, as the staff were preparing to close in anticipation of reaching the border and the attendant customs and passport control procedure. No one had warned us. Had we waited until the more usual time for an evening meal at half past seven, we'd have found the restaurant shut.

The desert view whitened by early snow.

I'm sure that there's a space here for another of Kyrle's Laws, but I can't think what to call it. Probably 'Kyrle's Law of Never Taking Mealtimes for Granted on International Trains'. With a name which doesn't so much trip off the tongue as drop with a thud, somehow I don't think it'll ever catch on.

At 19h10 we reached the Mongolian side of the border at Zamin Uud, where we were relieved of our documents. We were then subjected to much shaking and juddering as coaches were uncoupled and new ones added. We were on our way again at 20h35 and arrived on the Chinese side of the frontier at Erlian. High up above the station entrance, the station name blazed out into the night sky not only in neon-lit Chinese characters but also in English ones. It was 21h35. We were twenty-five minutes late.

We were frightened out of our wits when they started lifting the carriages off their mountings.

'What the hell's going on?'

'They're changing the bogies.'

'The what?'

Mike explained. 'Russian and Mongolian trains work on a gauge of 1520mm, approximately four feet eleven and five-sixths inches. That's different from the gauge used in China and most of the rest of the world. They run on standard gauge: 1435mm or four feet eight-and-a-half inches. When we cross the frontier, they have to change the bogies in order to fit onto the rails.'

Changing the bogies.

With passengers still aboard, every carriage had to be lifted on hydraulic jacks and put onto new bogies of the correct width. This was a slow, noisy process but quite riveting for anyone interested in watching advanced engineering work in progress.

Carriages were uncoupled, lifted, and lowered very slowly and precisely onto their new bogies, then shunted back into position to be re-coupled. For railway *aficionados* the photographic opportunities were immense. You can guess who was in his element!

Carriages being lifted and lowered before re-coupling.

'It says on the time-table that we're not scheduled to leave Erlian until 00h57 and it's now only 23h30,' I said. 'I'm going to sort out my bed. Even if I can't sleep because of the noise, at least I can doze.'

'Go for it!'

In fact, I fell asleep and didn't wake up until 02h00, just as we were moving off.

BEIJING

Friday 28th September
Arrive in Beijing. Free

Searching for the restaurant car for some breakfast, we walked the entire length of the train to the final carriage at the rear. The restaurant car turned out to be in the end carriage, but at the other end.

'At least we've worked up an appetite. What are they offering us?'

'An omelette, bread and jam and two cups of coffee.'

The first cup arrived, black without sugar.

'May we have some sugar, please?' we asked one of the passing waiters.

A waitress brought us some, loose on a saucer with a Chinese spoon, the sort they provide in restaurants if you order soup.

'Where's the spoon to stir it with?' I wondered aloud to Mike..

The second cup of coffee arrived.

'Ah! We're getting there,' said Mike, with mock triumph in his voice. 'This time there's sugar, already in and already stirred. But they've added milk, which we didn't order.'

An ethnic Chinese chap at a neighbouring table leant across. We'd passed some time with him a week before while we were all hanging about at Nayushki on the Russian side of the border with Mongolia. He'd explained the reason for his excellent English. He'd emigrated to Australia and was now living in Brisbane.

'You need to order lunch by 12h30 because they then shut down.'

Again, no one amongst officialdom had told us. There were no public notices informing travellers and certainly there had been no announcements. We were lucky to have got into conversation with a fellow passenger who spoke Mandarin and who had overheard the staff talking amongst themselves.

In the lobby between carriages, smoking was allowed and a small wall-mounted ashtray had thoughtfully been provided.

I was enjoying a cigar, when at twenty past nine, Mike drew me to the opposite window.

'We're passing through the Great Wall!'

He sounded quite excited. But then he'd never seen the Great Wall before, only read about it and seen pictures in books. This was the real thing!

'We are? Where?'

The Ulan Bator-Beijing railway cuts through the Great Wall.

He gesticulated, indicating that I should bend down and look through the window and upwards at a steep angle..

There were low, steep, bare hills and the remains of the Wall clambering along their summits.

'This landscape reminds me vaguely of parts of Lanzarote,' I said, 'where as you know I have a time-share. With the difference that on the plain below them here, there's intensive agriculture.'

By 10h10 we were passing through a wide plain of enormous fields of maize. Most houses in the villages had solar panels on their roofs. The next area we passed through was dominated by acres of polystyrene tunnels being used for cultivation. Suddenly it was back to arid scrubland, without any signs of cultivation.

At eleven-fifteen I finally finished off the sports section of the newspaper I'd picked up at Heathrow. It was still newsworthy. As I hadn't seen an English paper since the armful I'd scooped up in the airport at the very start of our trip, it had kept us supplied with reading matter for a month.

'Breakfast was only 30 *yuan*. For lunch they're trying to charge us 200! Looks suspiciously like a rip-off', I observed to Mike.

He nodded. 'They know they can get away with it because there's no printed menu, therefore no printed prices that we can point to when we get the bill.'

'And you can bet your bottom *yuan* they won't be giving us till receipts, either.'

'No wonder the manager is so cheerful, sitting with his mates enjoying a beer and a smoke and laughing. My guess is that us foreign stooges are paying his mortgage. His official salary is just an extra.'

Lunch consisted of a bowl of rice and spicy chicken followed by scrambled eggs with tomato. Chopsticks wrapped in paper were laid alongside our plates. If you weren't proficient in their use, tough. You're in China now. When in China, do as the . . .

Luckily we were both adept. At home I've been regularly patronising my local Chinese takeaway for forty years. I keep several pairs of chopsticks in a drawer to keep in practice.

'Coffee's come this time in a cup with no saucer and no sugar.'

'I'll ask for some.'

It came, but loose, with a big Chinese spoon for the sugar, but no ordinary spoon to stir.

'I suppose we could use the Chinese spoon, but it's a bit on the chunky side.'

The view outside was gradually becoming more diverse. For half-an-hour either side of the station at Zhu Wo we went through a series of tunnels, some of them several miles long. Some distance away was another series of tunnels and another railway line running in parallel.

Between the tunnels, the scenery was spectacular, with deep gorges, precipitous slopes, sheer rock faces, craggy hillsides and outcrops. Occasionally far below a lonely farmstead was reached by a snaking road. We marvelled at the skill of the railway engineers who built these lines.

A railway bridge indicates the existence of a second line.

We arrived on time at 14h04 in Beijing which, *en passant*, I noted the Russians still call '*Pekin*' on their timetables, using the name we used in English until recently. It's shown quite clearly on the destination boards on the sides of their trains.

We were met by our guide, who made an immediate impression because he was at least 2m tall, about 6ft 7ins.

'Call me Percy,' he said, in a fairly quiet voice but with a strong accent.

We were only too happy to be met efficiently and taken to the hotel where we could settle and have a bath and a rest. There was nothing programmed for today.

The Russians still call the Chinese capital 'Pekin'

With our guide, Percy.

Our room this time was on the twelfth floor, with a view over *hutongs*, the Chinese traditional narrow alleys connecting courtyards where working class people lived. We took stock of our new surroundings.

'We've got no balcony nor any comfortable seating,' I complained. 'There are no armchairs.'

'Look on the bright side,' said Mike, 'after what we had to endure back in Terelj. We've got a good bathroom and the beds are well sprung.'

We had no difficulty in deciding where to go for dinner: the hotel restaurant. This apparently simple exercise proved, when we got there, to be rather more fraught than expected.

Although the menu was illustrated and written in English as well as in Chinese, dishes were not listed as starters, main courses or side dishes. There was no way of knowing how large the portions were.

Twelfth floor view from our hotel.

'Are they sufficient on their own, or do you need an additional dish to fill you up?'

'Search me. Ask the waitress when she comes over.'

The waitresses, when they came to our table, had minimal English, but were very willing and eager to please. We managed. The food, when it came, was excellent.

It was only twenty to nine when

'Not sure what it is, but it's very tasty!'

they indicated that they were about to close the restaurant. We were the only people left in the room. In an international hotel, the main restaurant closes at nine o'clock! We went to the lobby for a smoke and a coffee, for 40y a cup plus 10% VAT, and found easy chairs in which to relax and collect our thoughts.

Saturday 29th September
Guided tour of Tiananmen Square, the Forbidden City and the Summer Palace

Our wake-up call came at 07h00. Breakfast presented us with a vast range of choices, most of them not my idea of breakfast fodder: for example, soup and broccoli. There was the variety of Chinese dishes one wouldn't risk without a local expert to advise you what they tasted like. They pandered to Western taste buds by providing bacon and scrambled eggs, even though both were cold.

Percy, our guide, arrived at 08h30 to take us to Tiananmen Square. Before starting out, he gave us each a small packet of what looked like biscuits.

'This weekend is our National Day. It's the custom to give your family or friends something to mark the occasion. These are special biscuits. We call them 'moon cakes'.'

'That's very kind of you. May we try them now?'

'Of course.'

We opened one of the packets and tried this new confection. They were extremely tasty.

These would make an interesting present to take home next week, not too bulky or heavy to carry, I thought to myself.

Being China's national day and in consequence a public holiday, of course Tiananmen Square was crowded. Many tour guides were holding flags and

Tiananmen Gate on the north side of Tiananmen Square.

shepherding their charges, as well as countless Chinese couples and families endlessly photographing each other, without any regard to the background for their photos.

The square was so big that a mobile litter-picker was on permanent duty, wearing a protective mask.

Mobile litter-picker.

Percy's explanations of Chinese history tended to be on the detailed side. Moreover, they were difficult to understand or to put into perspective, unless you already knew something about the subject and were familiar, even if only minimally, with the symbolism in Chinese culture of certain animals, real or mythical; for example, dragons.

An additional problem related to Percy's height. Mike, with his aural difficulties, couldn't hear. His hearing aid refused to work properly and Percy's mouth was a good six inches above Mike's ear. If Percy bent down to speak to him directly that created a problem for me, as he had now turned his head away and *I* couldn't hear him!

Our next visit was to the Forbidden City.

'This is much as I remember it from when I was here twenty years ago,' I said to Mike. 'The way the Chinese emperors lived and ruled is very difficult for a European to understand. For example, why were they always *carried* everywhere. What was so wrong with walking, if only for the sake of their health?'

'It's a source of amazement to me that they ruled in such total isolation from their subjects, right up to the beginning of the twentieth century.'

'By something of a coincidence, so did the Ottoman Sultans of Turkey, who met a similar fate at about the same time.'

Lunch was taken at a restaurant where presumably the agency had an arrangement, by which I mean the agency had negotiated a discount. There could be no other explanation for driving for forty minutes through constantly recurring traffic jams, passing dozens of other restaurants on the way, any of which would have been acceptable.

With Percy's help we chose three dishes. Instead of joining us at our table, he abandoned us to sit at another one some distance away. He offered no explanation.

'Why's he done that?'

'Company rules?'

'Who knows?'

After ten minutes the waitress returned with Percy to tell us that the dishes we'd chosen were not available.

'Why did it take her ten minutes to find that out?', I asked.

No explanation was offered.

'When we made our choices with you helping us,' I said to Percy, 'surely they could have told you then that they didn't have them.'

Again, no explanation.

Percy helped us wrestle with the menu again, doing his best to explain what various items were.

When my choice finally arrived, it was half-cold. The vegetable dish that we'd ordered turned out to be so green, glutinous and unappealing that we left it untouched. No wine was available by the glass.

'At least I know the rice will be O.K.'

As a good guide doing his job, Percy asked at the end of the meal if everything was OK.

'Frankly, no. The food from my local Chinese takeaway at home is better.'

'I must admit my own meal wasn't very good, either,' Percy added, glumly. 'I'll tell the agency. Maybe they won't use this restaurant again.'

'And it certainly wasn't worth driving for forty minutes in heavy traffic to get here,' Mike added, reinforcing my expressions of dissatisfaction.

'It's very simple, Percy.' I said. 'When I order a hot dish, I expect it be hot when it reaches me at the table and not half-cold before I even start. I expect a restaurant to be able to serve me a normal order such as a glass of orange squash, not to tell me they only have fizzy orange and only sell it in bottles. And litre bottles at that. If they want Western customers, they should be geared up to serving them properly.'

We drove on to the Summer Palace, three-quarters of an hour in a traffic jam. Such was the constant jolting, I dozed off for much of the journey. Again, Percy tried to explain everything, but the cultural gap and differences in mind-set between 21st century Europeans and 19th century Chinese was, most of the time, too great.

'Protect the railings!!'

I always thought railings did the protecting.

The lake in the grounds of the Summer Palace was exquisite as the surface shimmered in the sun. Quite different from the last time I saw it. Then it was at the end of December. The lake was frozen.

An unusual request to the public.

'All aboard for a trip on the lake.' A dragon boat.

We took a trip on a dragon boat (15y each) and enjoyed the views. Mike was having a wonderful time with his camera.

The car back to the hotel took an hour and three-quarters because of the traffic. Our next day was free, but we decided not to go anywhere on our own as we were both too exhausted by all the sitting in traffic, walking everywhere and having to concentrate very hard both to catch and at the same time to understand Percy's explanations. He was a very nice chap and trying really, *really* hard, but it got a bit wearing when you had to give your full attention all the time to both hear what he was saying and to wrestle with his accent.

Dinner. The hotel restaurant where we ate last night, *Tian Qiao Yuan*, was closed to other residents for – *aaaargh!* – a wedding party! We would have to go to the other one, *Huai Yang Cun*.

Here the menu was bi-lingual, with illustrations. We would be able to get what we wanted by pointing.

'Now's the chance for something exotic.'

'How about the three abalone in garlic?'

'Sounds weird, I'll have it. I'll follow it with the stewed donkey meat, Hunan-style, whatever that means. I've no idea what to expect, but at least it'll be new and hopefully memorable.'

'I'll go for a soup. Then goose in a stone pot, whatever *that* means,' said Mike, echoing my pursuit of the gastronomically unknown.

Problems arose when we attempted to ask for rice, which request they had great difficulty in understanding but eventually cottoned on. *'You're in China, and having trouble getting a portion of rice?'* anyone would react, incredulously.

Drinks, however, prove impossible, apart from Mike's customary local beer.

The saga unfolded as follows.

'I fancy some white wine,' I murmured to Mike. 'Any ideas?'

'The wine list is only in Chinese. None of the waiting staff know any English.'

Mike went to the bar. They showed him a bottle of red, but they couldn't understand that he wanted white.

'I think maybe I'll settle for tea, which I regularly drink at home when I have a Chinese takeaway. I'll try calling it by its Chinese name, *'chai'*, which happens to be the same in Russian. In English we have our slang word *'char'*.'

Despite all my linguistic contortions, they couldn't understand. I suppose I must have been saying it in the wrong tone.

In desperation I pointed to my cup.

The waitress went away, came back and filled it.

With hot water!

Our table was laid without serviettes. In Mike's place they'd forgotten to lay any chopsticks. As none of the waitresses seemed to have noticed our predicament, when no one was looking Mike leant across and pinched a set from the next table.

The food itself was good, even if we had little idea what it really was that we were eating. However, that didn't compensate for our feelings, a mixture of frustration and humiliation. This was a restaurant in a hotel which specialised in entertaining foreign tourists. We were being served by waitresses who couldn't understand a word of the principal language most of those tourists were likely to speak. They spent their time standing at the bar in a group, giggling.

To my mind it was unprofessional on the part of management and deeply embarrassing for the clients.

We were not asking that every one of the waiting staff should be fluent, only that at least one person on duty should be able to come to the rescue of foreign diners who can neither read nor speak Chinese. Such a staffing regime would surely be good for business.

To cap it all, when we attempted to pay by credit card, this was examined in awe as something from a recent TV programme entitled *The World of the Future* which they were seeing for the first time. It was an excuse for another outbreak of giggling. They only accepted cash.

After this heroic struggle to get fed and watered, we decamped to the lobby for coffee.

'At least here they know what we want. No fits of the giggles when we try to order,' Mike remarked.

However, the sole waiter on duty was being hassled by a group of Caucasians on another table, who were apparently trying to get him to clear their table and bring them something to drink. We sat at our table expectantly for half an hour without receiving any service.

Fortunately for us, eventually the manager came over to ask what was wrong.

'We've been sitting here for half an hour. The waiter has spent all of his time dealing with that other table and hasn't come near us to ask us what we'd like,' said Mike.

The manager took immediate steps. The waiter promptly disengaged himself from the other group and took our order.

Did he then bring it?

No.

Once again, he was waylaid by the other table, demanding his services and to hell with any other guests. They were tourists of the worst sort, talking loudly and shouting their orders and generally throwing their weight about, bullying the poor waiter. I was relieved that they were not English, even though that was the language they were speaking.

Eventually a waitress we hadn't seen before arrived with our coffee and my additional orange juice. A quiet smoke and the end of a memorable day!

Sunday 30th September: free

Not going to do much today. Maybe take a walk in the immediate vicinity.

'You can snap some ordinary street scenes. We'll see if we can find a shop that sells genuine Chinese tea.'

Breakfast.

We were sent away, as they were preparing for yet another wedding party!

We went downstairs to the *Simple & Taste Café (sic)* where we were the last clients. It was ten to nine. They, too, were laying the room up for a wedding. They carried on doing this around us while quietly ignoring our presence. Meanwhile, we posed as a small island of placid calm in the midst of frenzied activity of laying tables and rigging up the dais at the end of the restaurant for the ceremony.

The interior of the hotel restaurant.

The containers for the various hot dishes on offer were all closed, each with an extravagant bow tied on the lid to enable clients to lift it without burning their fingers. Nonetheless, as usual, all the allegedly hot dishes, such as scrambled eggs, sausages and bacon, were half-cold. There wasn't even any proper toast. The toaster only slightly browned the bread without making it hard and crisp as we would make it at home.

The tea that I was served on our first night was so good that I wanted to find some to take back to England. I went to the restaurant and found the drinks menu, showed it to one of the staff and asked her to write it down for me in Chinese so that I could take it to a shop and show an assistant. The waitress was very obliging. I was struck by the speed and dexterity with which she could copy Chinese characters.

At Reception the staff gave me the name of the two in-house restaurants so that I could be sure to praise the right one in my diary and criticise the other, not the wrong way round. They also gave us a map and showed us where to find a supermarket selling tea.

As we left the hotel a large crowd of people was gathering, obviously connected with the wedding. Some were loitering in the hotel foyer and others were hanging about outside, in expectation of the wedding car or cars drawing up.

We decided to stop where we were and watch the fun. Other nationalities' wedding customs are always interesting to a stranger.

Lying in wait for the newly-weds.

The welcoming party were all carrying long rolls of what looked like coloured wrapping paper. We were intrigued. What were they going to be used for? Is the groom to be ritually belaboured about the head and shoulders?

When the bride arrived in a white car, followed by four red ones, the rolls turned out to be confetti bombs, which exploded with a loud bang and projected their contents of red paper hearts and yellow butterflies all over the couple who then, smothered in confetti and sporting broad smiles, posed for photos.

It was about a fifteen minute walk to the supermarket. The first item I spotted on the way into the shop were some moon cakes, similar to the ones Percy had given us to mark the public holiday associated with China's National Day, 1st October. When I showed interest, the shop assistant turned up, insisting on explaining the prices to me even though they were clearly marked as, in Chinese, they use Arabic numerals just as we do. When I started to serve myself, she intervened, indicating in no uncertain manner that it was *her* job to pick them for me. I must then pay for them at *her* till and no one else's. Evidently this counter was not part of the supermarket, but a separate concession. Maybe something to do with franchising or perhaps sales bonuses.

Proceeding into the main supermarket we experienced yet another breakdown in comprehension. I was not supposed to take my purchases inside, even though I'd paid for them and had the till receipt. I must leave them in a locker and collect them when I left. I'd never come across such an arrangement as this before. I was at a total loss! These premises were very efficiently organised, as long as you understood the system.

The day was saved by a passing shopper who spoke English and who came to our assistance. She ushered me to the special counter where they gave out printed and numbered tickets for electronically lockable lockers where I could deposit my moon cakes safely. An assistant demonstrated to me how to access the goods on return. I would have to scan the ticket, whereupon the locker door would fly open: *ping!* Security, without any keys being required. And also without charge.

Now minus the moon cakes and also my coat, as there was room in the locker for that as well, we explained to our new-found guide what we'd come to buy.

'All I want is some genuine Chinese tea. Do you know where the specialist department is?'

She asked, then led us up the escalator to the tea counter, where the assistants had about fifty jars to choose from. They didn't sell tea in packets, but instead made the packets up by weighing them out for each customer individually after they'd made their selection. Customers were offered the chance to sniff each and any jar. When, after a few tries, I'd decided which one I preferred, I explained that I wanted ten packets of the same size to give as presents to friends back home. This took some time, as each tinfoil packet was vacuum-sealed.

At the end of this process they charged me 500y (£50), but also asked me to wait. I watched uncomprehendingly as they proceeded to wrap up a small china pot with little legs and a lid and solemnly presented it to me as a gift for being such a good customer. They also fixed a label on it to say that it was a gift, so that I didn't get my collar felt at the exit for trying to sneak out stolen goods.

I couldn't imagine what it was for, but when I showed it to one of the reception staff back at our hotel, they confirmed that it was for burning either incense or joss sticks.

I am still looking for the supermarket in England where, if I shell out fifty quid at one counter, they would wrap me up a free gift as a 'thank you' present.

During this time Mike had been engaged in conversation with the Chinese lady who was helping us.

'I've lived in Jamaica,' she told him, 'and I'm a Catholic.'

As Mike is a Methodist, they started discussing the state of religion in China, where being a Christian, and especially a Catholic, can be a problem. He was planning to be back in Beijing a month later on a private holiday *en route* to Hong Kong to stay with an old friend, and then on to Australia for Christmas with his eldest son. An idea struck him.

'Can I meet up with you during my stay? Perhaps you could show me parts of Beijing away from the tourist high spots?'

They exchanged e-mail addresses. It should be very helpful when Mike returned to Beijing, if he had a local contact who perhaps would be willing to show him something of what life is like for ordinary Chinese.

We parted company so that she could get on with her own shopping. We wandered around. We were not planning to buy anything, but merely to compare the way a Chinese supermarket is laid out compared to an English one. Were there any methods of displaying goods which were markedly different from ours, allowing for the season and local tastes?

The most obvious difference was that potential customers were permitted to handle, and even to sniff, loose items. Fresh fish were displayed in a tank, alive and swimming. You can't get any fresher than that! In contrast, crabs were trussed up in coloured string, ready for the table, and not, as is our custom, kept alive in a tank of water to ensure absolute freshness and safety, always an important consideration when buying shellfish.

Our next problem was how to leave. The word 'EXIT' (*sic*) was prominently displayed, but it turned out that this meant in emergencies only. The real way out was via a cashier. It took some time to find a notice indicating where this was. An unexpected complication was that although the Chinese lady had assured us that they took credit cards, when we tried this, the cashier refused to accept them.

A simple explanation might be that our Chinese friend didn't realise that yes, the store accepts credit cards, but only Chinese ones. Our total bill was 507y. By pooling our resources, we managed to rustle up that sum in cash with just 3y to spare. It would have been highly embarrassing if, after all the time spent choosing tea and a few extra items of food, we'd been unable to come up with the cost in cash.

A further fear: would I have had to give my free gift back?

We enjoyed a light lunch and a lazy afternoon in our room. I brought my diary up to date. Mike reviewed his pictures on his laptop and rejected the chaff.

We'd ordered Peking Duck for dinner. We'd settle for that and then do our final packing.

After five weeks almost continually on the move, we were finally going home!

Monday 1st October
Fly home

Breakfast on our last day didn't fail to yield yet another priceless example of mis-translation on a menu, even in a major hotel in the capital which takes in planeloads of foreigners. A cauldron with some round, white objects bubbling in a sort of soup, was obviously intended as a breakfast delicacy and clearly labelled. Unfortunately the person doing the labelling was not familiar with the English alphabet. While what he meant was clear enough, what he

An unusual breakfast dish. Some might say it's the absolute end.

actually wrote is not for the faint-hearted. It is therefore not shown on this page but on the next. Unless you are confident of remaining totally unfazed by challenges and are possessed of a strong stomach, avert your gaze when you turn over.

Percy arrived to conduct us to the airport, which entailed another lengthy drive through clogged streets. The journey enabled us to see most of China's capital city's modern architecture, which is entirely comparable to other modern cities with grand designs and skyscraper buildings.

At last, we arrived at the airport.

'Time to say our farewells,' I said.

'Yes,' Percy replied. 'Before you go, would you be kind enough to fill in my assessment form for my agency?'

'With pleasure.'

When, with Mike looking over my shoulder, I'd completed the form and ticked the various boxes, I turned to face Percy for the last time.

'You have the potential to be an excellent guide. You have absolutely the right temperament. But you really should seek out a teacher who can help you to improve your accent. You know all the words, but often you can't pronounce them in a way that is immediately recognisable to the English ear.'

As a small parting gift I gave him the carton with my remaining tea bags and instructed him on how to enjoy them with his family. I was secretly amused by the idea of teaching a Chinese how to make tea!

Onto the plane, and the luxury of first class.

Beijing to London, seventeen hours.

Over and out.

Thanks to Mike's swift return to our room to fetch his camera before they discovered their error and corrected it, this unforgettable image is preserved for posterior.

CONCLUSIONS

KYRLE'S LAWS

Kyrle's Laws are meant to be read as a bit of tongue-in-cheek advice for other travellers, particularly any contemplating following in our footsteps. Our adventures show how some of our plans worked, others didn't. Being forewarned, you may be better able to make choices and avoid some of the deleterious occurrences.

Kyrle's First Law of What to Pack is to think about any needs you might have which you cannot meet on the journey. A simple example is your morning tea. It sounds prosaic, because it is. You have to be aware that the British drink tea in a different way from the continentals. Put simply, we take milk and sometimes also sugar; they, in general, favour lemon. The type of tea is different and may not agree with your digestion if you're accustomed to one particular brand. Solution? Take your own. Ultimately the most prescient 'Eureka moment' I had was at the very last minute while packing, when, on a whim, I abruptly stopped counting out teabags enough for two people for 30 days and just bunged the whole carton into my case. It gave us enough tea to enjoy most mornings particularly when we were travelling on the train. A couple of teabags made a handy little 'fun' tip to offer carriage attendants or even guides, as a sort of souvenir to try at home and to experience 'a taste of English life'.

You have to think long and hard about clothing, especially footwear. Find out what sort of weather can be expected, especially as regards temperatures, both day and night, the likelihood of rain and how heavy, how blustery or would it be only passing showers. As regards clothes, especially underwear, hotels offer a laundry service. Using this extensively enabled us to economise on the number of changes of clothing we needed to take. Our plans worked out splendidly. In other words, 'as planned'.

Are you on any regular medication? Count out the number of pills you're going to need for the entire time you expect to be away from home, then add enough for a couple more days in case of emergencies, such as breaking out a pill from its foil and it rolls down the sink. Prepare a brief written explanation of the medical conditions you are having treatment for, in the languages of the countries that you'll be visiting. Should you need replacements due to loss, or even theft, this precaution may prove to be quite literally a life-saver.

Kyrle's First Law of Tourist Guides is merely to remember that a paid guide is doing a job. It's business. She's not someone doing you a favour and to whom you in consequence have a reciprocal obligation. Let the guide take the strain! After all, you've paid for her services. Let her provide them. You have a contract. Be pleasant, of course, and be interested or even enthusiastic. Ask perceptive questions, make jokes, lavish praise, pay for coffee or treat her to lunch, enquire about her background, her family and where she learned English. Indeed, try to 'make her day' just as she is hopefully making yours. But it's business, not the start of a life-long relationship. You're never going to meet again.

The Second Law is a general warning about not letting an over-enthusiastic guide spoil your visit by exhausting you, either mentally or physically or both. Ensure that you get food, drink and rest at the sort of intervals to which you're accustomed or your health or age require, thus safeguarding both physical and mental wellbeing.

Kyrle's Third Law of Tourist Guides states: if your scheduled excursion, visit or other activity doesn't meet your expectations, you are not obliged to go through with it to the bitter end. 'He who pays the piper'. 'Abort and live' is not the non-sequitur it sounds. If you feel you've had enough, tell the guide and ask to be taken back to your hotel.

Kyrle's First Law of Public Bogs (those amongst you who were gently reared might prefer the more genteel words: lavatories or toilets) is a general warning to expect the worst in Russia. I dare say it's equally applicable in many other parts of the world where I've never been.

In non-urban areas don't expect a flushing system and decent, or even any, toilet paper, other than in a hotel or at a main railway station. And don't be surprised if there is ample evidence of use by previous clients.

Kyrle's Second Law is always to carry your own supply of toilet paper. Pack a roll before leaving home, check out all public lavatories before committing yourself and remember to have your roll with you before you lock the door behind you. Otherwise you may find that when you really, *really* need it it's back in your compartment and a fat lot of good it was bringing it.

A roll of toilet paper showing perforations where you don't want them!

Kyrle's First Law of Hotel Locations is a warning. If, when planning your trip, you factored in some free time for sightseeing on your own or simply wandering round the shops, then your hotel has to be within walking distance. In the vicinity of our hotel in Novosibirsk there was nothing of interest apart from the bridge over the River Ob, with the result that our free day was largely a waste of time.

Choose a hotel which provides an opportunity to wander at leisure, admiring the architecture, quaint streets and alleyways, shop window displays, street musicians and so on, or where you can sit in a café and pass the time 'people watching'. Perhaps ask the waiter a question about the food or drink. If he addresses you in English, ask him where he learned it. Perhaps strike up a conversation with a customer sitting at the next table by patting his dog or commenting on the weather. In Novosibirsk we could walk halfway across the river and admire the view of the shoreline, mix briefly with ordinary Russians ordering their lunch and learn a little about cafés and what people ate at lunchtime in a part of the city unconnected to the tourist industry. That's not much of a tally for a whole day free, planned to be spent sight-seeing.

Kyrle's First Law of Settling the Bill. When travelling with a domestic partner, it doesn't really matter who pays for lunch or dinner or the shopping, as ultimately it all comes out of the same pot: the family income. Travelling with a friend, as was the case with Mike and myself, presented a different situation. Best friends we may be, but neither of us was reckoning on paying for the other's holiday. How did we manage, when it came to settling up after a meal?

Our solution was to carefully keep receipts. At the end of the day or at least the following day, we compared them, keeping a rough running tally. If we took turns at paying, then expenses evened out more or less. If I paid for a coffee in the morning then Mike would buy the drinks in the evening. At the end of each reckoning up, one of us either paid the difference in cash or made a mental note that a certain amount had to be discounted off the next day's total.

The vital thing we had to bear in mind was that we were going to be closeted together for five weeks and relying on each other. We couldn't spend our time bickering about small change or arguing along the lines of 'Your starter cost 300r., mine was only 275r., so you owe me 50p.' Forget it. Keep a sense of proportion. In the next restaurant the rôles will probably be reversed. Stop counting.

Remember: you're not on expenses, this is your own money. You're with your best friend. After all the years you've known each other, he's no more likely to be out to screw you for a couple of quid than you would be out to screw him. Were that not the case, you wouldn't be best friends, would you.

However, if you're travelling in a larger party, perhaps including people you don't know very well or not at all, there may be problems when one individual regularly eats or drinks more or significantly less than anyone else. This invites the invocation of **Kyrle's Second Law**.

If an individual's additional consumption is known in advance, they must expect to pay their own bills while the rest of the party set up a kitty without including them, so as to avoid constantly subsidising them. Their excess may be down to being greedy. On the other hand, they may simply have a bigger appetite and need more food. It could be that one member enjoys spirits, whereas the rest of the group only drink wine. Or the reverse: everyone drinks wine except one person, who only drinks mineral water which is half the price. That person would opt out of contributing to the kitty, to avoid subsidising the rest of the group.

Kyrle's First Law of Changing Money reminds you that when entering a country with whose currency you are unfamiliar, it's vital to have some idea of the exchange rate. Entering Mongolia we'd neglected to do this. We weren't even sure what the local currency was called, let alone how many of them there were to the pound.

This 5 tugrik note is worth approximately ½p. [two-thirds actual size]

The authorities in both Russia and Mongolia should take some responsibility for the itinerant moneychangers who operate on the railway, at least to the extent of requiring them to carry some sort of card displaying the rates they're offering set against the official rate, and the commission that they're charging. I think the exchange rate that we received at the time was reasonably fair, but it could have been a rip-off. By the time we found out, they'd be long gone and we'd be hundreds of miles away. 'Welcome to Mongolia' rings hollow if your first experience when entering the country is the suspicion that you're being taken for a ride.

Kyrle's First Law of Restaurant Cars is a warning. If you're going to be on a train for a long time, you need to know whether or not refreshment is going to be available. If you ask your guide and they say 'I think so', that's not good enough. You need them to find out by ringing the railway office and asking what sort of arrangements, if any, they have in place for providing passengers with food and drink. Moreover, are those facilities open for the whole of the time that you're scheduled to be on the train?

Kyrle's Second Law is a refinement of the first. You need to know what sort of refreshments are on offer. Will you be able to get a proper meal or is there merely a bar where the only sustenance is bars of chocolate and packets of crisps, or the local equivalent. The consequences of being caught without food or drink can make for a very uncomfortable journey.

You may have noticed that references are often made to the weather; that it was almost always sunny and warm. It was not chance that we travelled in September, but a deliberate choice.

When friends first heard that I was planning to go to Siberia, the uniform reaction was, 'Isn't it cold?' My answer was, 'Yes, in winter, devastatingly so. But we're not going in the winter, nor are we going to the outback, trekking in the Far North or across the tundra with a dog team. We're going first class on a railway in the most populated part of the region, where there are proper towns and cities and all the associated facilities (such as the hospital in Novosibirsk, which I had no idea I'd need for emergency treatment). We're not going on an adventure holiday in the sense that we're camping out in the wilderness and looking at wild life and wondering what they live on, while the aforesaid wild life is looking at us and thinking, 'They look tasty. Can I catch one for supper?'

Of course, you could travel in Siberia and do exactly that, but it was never part of our plans, if only because of our advanced ages. However, having read our account of the trip, you might take the view that in many other respects it *was* an adventure holiday since we chose our own itinerary rather than taking a package. Although we engaged guides at various points along the way, we were not fully escorted in the sense of travelling at all times in a bubble, with a guide on hand, insulated from local conditions and the local population.

When events occasionally went belly-up in Russia, how we'd have surmounted them had neither of us known a word of the local language is, however, another matter.

To conclude, having read our account, would you feel tempted to undertake such a trip yourself?

Are we glad we did it? You bet! Wouldn't have missed it for the world. Would we do it all again? No. For a start, we could never again expect to be so lucky with the weather: five weeks virtually without any rain. Under grey skies, many of Mike's pictures illustrating this book would not be as spectacular as they are. Let's face it, it was a fairly strenuous enterprise for men of our age. We'd be even older were we to do such a trip again. Our seventies have now slid into our eighties.

I think we made our trip just in time, we were lucky enough to enjoy it and get back in one piece. Even travelling first class, we still had to carry our own bags, pack a month's medication and remember to take it. We still had to be fit enough to clamber onto a top bunk and be totally confident of the efficiency and adjustability of our digestive systems. We had to be able to cope with disrupted sleeping patterns, with catching a train in the small hours of the morning and staying on it for far longer than is even possible in UK. Remember that 'long distance' in Britain pales into insignificance when set against the vastness of Siberia.

We were a very long way from home. We couldn't turn to the tour guide because there wasn't one. For lengthy periods we were on our own. At some stage the unexpected was going to happen. When it did, we needed to have our wits about us and find our own immediate solution.

If your idea of a holiday is lying on a sunbed waiting for your next jug of chilled orange juice to materialise, courtesy of a watchful waiter, our Siberian journey was a different world and is not for you. But it was for us. I hope you've enjoyed reading about it. Mike hopes you've enjoyed looking at his evocative, often awe-inspiring, pictures.

Spasibo, i do svidanya!

PRACTICAL CONSIDERATIONS

Anyone who is considering following in our footsteps will have picked up a few tips as they've read this book. Let me try to draw a few threads together and offer some practical observations, based on our experiences. What do you need and what do you need to be able to do, in order to undertake an extended and complicated journey such as ours while still being able to relax and enjoy it?

First of all, although it seems obvious, you need to be physically and mentally fit. We travelled first class. So that we could have a compartment to ourselves, we bought four first class rail tickets, even though there were only two of us. Even then, we had to carry our own luggage wherever we went and stow it on racks on trains or in the boots of cars and taxis and carry it up to our hotel rooms, sometimes after a long, tiring journey through the night and much of the previous day. For that reason, I chose to have two medium-size cases, each with wheels and an extending handle, rather than one large suitcase.

A first class compartment contains two long seats which convert into beds and two top bunks. To access these, you have to climb a ladder, then twist into a horizontal position in a confined space just below the ceiling. If you're overweight, exceptionally tall or suffer from a physical disability that affects movement, that may present problems.

You may have noticed that in the photo captioned 'Have I Got Everything I Need for a Month?', as well as my two cases I also carried a shoulder bag. On an aircraft, the two cases went into the hold but my bag was hand luggage and came with me into the cabin. In it were such essentials during a flight or a long car journey as a jumper in case I felt cold, sometimes a pair of shoes in case of rain or if we were likely to be walking on gravel, which is not practical when wearing sandals. In addition, I included my cap and my neck cushion, which I inflate as a headrest on planes or on long car journeys.

I kept our refreshments in the bag, plus any reading matter, such as maps and brochures and anything we bought such as souvenirs or replacement food and drink. Most of the time Mike was carrying his camera and couldn't be expected to be encumbered with a bag. Therefore, my holdall had to be big enough to allow for the requirements of two people. It had a zipped side pocket, in which I kept a folder with the travel agency's papers detailing our hotel reservations. As we left each hotel,

I put that page underneath the pile so that the one with the details of where we'd next be staying was uppermost. This made it easy to present on arrival as evidence of our reservation. As this side pocket was easily accessible, I also kept my passport, travel insurance documents, spare roubles and all our tickets there, not loose, but in a clear plastic zip bag, approximately 28 x 18cms (10 x 7ins) which I could retrieve if I needed to show my passport or get some more cash to replenish my wallet. This bag, too, had a zip side pocket, in which I kept items which I had to carry but which would not be needed on a daily basis; for example, my credit card and receipts for purchases. My English money and my house keys were consigned to the bottom of one of my cases.

In the main bag I kept a smaller one, which I referred to as my 'ditty bag'. When we were walking or with a guide, I dangled it in my hand by its carrying loop. It could be carried as a rucksack if I needed to have both hands free as it had two shoulder straps and two zipped-up compartments. In the larger one I carried my sunglasses in their rather large but very rigid case, and any maps which we were likely to use that day. I also carried reading material and my neck cushion, deflated, in readiness for any plane journey or lengthy car ride. It was also big enough for any shopping, such as a packet of biscuits or some replacement drinks. In the smaller zipped pocket I kept my cigar case and also my lighter, which I had to remember to remove and put in my hold luggage when we took the plane. In short, Mike carried his own passport and money but I carried everything else: hotel reservation papers, tickets, emergency food and drink and any odd items we bought when out and about.

What clothes should you take when you're going to be away for a long period but on the move most of the time? We planned to be away for over a month but that didn't mean four weeks' worth of clean clothes because all of the hotels provided laundry services. By making use of them immediately on arrival, we hardly ever found ourselves carrying dirty washing.

Shoes are important. I carried a pair with perforated uppers for comfort when it was hot and an ordinary pair for evenings or wet weather. On the train or plane I wore sandals. Each pair of shoes was kept in an ordinary plastic shopping bag. When I changed, one set of footwear came out of the bag and the other set went in. In that way, dirty shoes could be stuffed into my shoulder bag without any fear of them contaminating anything else.

What precautions should you take in case of a medical disaster? We each consulted our doctor, took advice on updating injections and ordered adequate supplies of our regular medication. When I was packing, I carefully counted out enough pills to last me for the month and a couple of days to spare to be on the safe side. I checked that I had the right kind of travel insurance. My documents carried telephone numbers for the agency's local contact in each place we stopped. I didn't expect to have to use them and, in point of fact, never did. I took a roll of lavatory paper. I packed a folding umbrella. I needed to use it only once, but on that occasion it was worth its weight in gold!

If you are a UK citizen you need a visa for each of the three countries that we visited. Provided you haven't got a criminal record, visas are granted on demand, but are quite expensive. Obtaining a visa takes time. While you're applying to one embassy, you can't send an application to another until your passport is returned. The most cost-effective and anxiety-free way to obtain the required documents was to employ an agency specialising in obtaining visas.

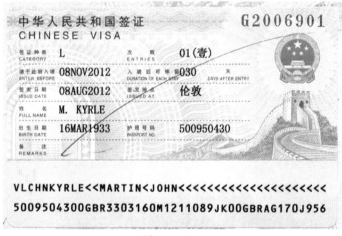

Chinese visa.

There's the question of language. Do ordinary people in Russia speak English? On the whole, no. Your specialist guide will, as will hotel reception staff, though the standard varies. Shopkeepers, ticket collectors and railway, museum, restaurant or medical staff won't. It's the same in Mongolia and China, unless they're young people who, unlike previous generations, have learned English at school. Be prepared!

If you can't speak any Russian, at least try to familiarise yourself with the Cyrillic alphabet enough to be able to read simple signs such as 'Exit' or the name of a station. 'Thank you' is quite easy in Russian: *spasibo*.* 'Please' is a bit more difficult, but this isn't the place for a Russian lesson. If you can read Cyrillic, it's just about possible to read notices in Mongolian because it's written nowadays in an adapted form. Traditional Mongolian script is another matter and is absolutely indecipherable to a layman! However, in Mongolia as well as in China signs are displayed in Latin script in places frequented by foreign tourists, that is, 'in English' in the sense of using our alphabet.

Finally, with whom are you going to travel? You're fit and up for it, but are you absolutely sure your companion is? You're going to be living in each other's pockets for a month. Undressing in a confined space on the train to get to bed is a bit like ballet in a telephone box, taking turns to manoeuvre in the space between the benches, one-third of which is taken up by the table. This table is fixed. It can't be folded down when it's not needed. There you are, standing on one leg trying to take your pants off over your head when the train lurches and you both fall over, at which propitious moment the *provodnitsa* slides the compartment door open and bustles in with the vacuum cleaner nozzle in the 'Charge!' position to give your carpet runner a brisk once-over.

You may find yourself sharing that compartment for 24, 36 even as long as 42 hours between your stops. You may have to cope with catching a train at three o'clock in the morning and arriving at your destination at tea-time the same day. Think what that will do to your circadian rhythm. If travel arrangements mean that you have to have lunch at what your body clock says is 8 a.m., will your digestive system cope? Are you confident of remaining even-tempered despite irritation or extreme fatigue? How about your travelling companion? Is there any danger of having to calm down someone who, on a train halfway across Siberia, finally flips, simply because they're bored stiff with the constant view through the window of nothing but *steppe*?

Mike and I have known each other for over fifty years and travelled together before in out-of-the-way places. We know exactly what the other is like, foibles included. We can rely on each other with absolute confidence. Where I have a weakness, Mike has a compensating strength and vice versa. We operate as a team, often automatically, without the need to say a word. There's no possibility of falling out. Choose to travel with the wrong company and you're doomed to a shared experience you may both thereafter prefer to forget.

Which brings me neatly to the other kind of 'company' and another essential consideration. I studied the map and read up about the places we could visit, made choices and worked out how many days we'd need in each place and obtained Mike's agreement before moving to the next stage. We employed an experienced travel agency to make the bookings. They, in turn, consulted an agency specialising in travel in Russia and the East. Between them, they booked us bed-and-breakfast accommodation in all our hotels, all our travel by rail, taxi or private car, arranged for us to be met at stations where we requested it and booked the guides. We paid for all these in England before we set out. In Moscow, our guide had our train tickets for each section of our forthcoming journey as far as Ulan Bator. There, our guide gave us our tickets to Beijing. If, as described on a couple of occasions the wheels came off, most of the time our arrangements ran like clockwork.

Anyone undertaking a journey of this sort would be well advised to consult professionals.

EPILOGUE

The very name 'Trans-Siberian Railway' may sound exotic to us in the West, but to Russians it's simply the name for the public transport service which runs across Siberia. The special Trans-Siberian trains don't run every day, but ordinary working trains, those not starting from Moscow, use the lines all the time. For anyone wanting to reach a Siberian town on or near the line, it's the cheapest and quickest way to travel. The immense distances make car travel really a non-starter, even assuming there's a road (!). Air travel is much more expensive. In many ways, rail is the *only* way to go. The track is also used intensively by very long freight trains.

To give an inkling of times and costs, from Moscow to Irkutsk takes three days and five hours on the train. With the exchange rate at about 47r. to the £, the fare was about 11,000r. (£220) for *kupé*, a seat in a compartment. First class is about double (but includes a bed), and *platskart*, a seat in an open carriage, not compartmentalised, is about 40% less.

A very long freight train - the raison d'être of the Trans-Siberian Railway.

AUTHOR'S MEMOIR

I visited Moscow for the first time in 1957 when, immediately after graduating, I attended the World Festival of Youth and Students. These festivals were held in alternate years in the capitals of Soviet-bloc countries around Europe. The one immediately before Moscow had been in Warsaw and the next one was planned to take place in Sofia. This was only a year after the Russians had sent their troops to suppress the Hungarian Uprising. The regime was keen to lure as many young people as possible from Western Europe, hoping to make propaganda showing by our presence that we were in some way condoning what they'd done.

Of course, we didn't condone their action nor in fact did we acknowledge any connection whatever between our condemnation of Russian brutality in Hungary in 1956 and our decision to join in a world-wide student gathering the following year, which by chance was being staged in Moscow and being heavily subsidised by the Soviet government.

Having spent many months during my national service in the Royal Navy learning Russian, I wanted to take the first opportunity to go to the country to try out my language skills. Russian visas were virtually impossible to obtain, unless you were a paid-up member of the Communist Party or had friends or contacts in the Soviet Union who had given you an invitation. For the Festival, visa requirements were temporarily waived. It was an opportunity not to be missed.

 Half a century on, I don't remember much about the Kremlin or the numerous different cathedrals that I saw, though attending a service and hearing the Patriarch preach made a lasting impression. After the service, he met his somewhat exotic Western visitors and gave us each a tiny golden cross as a memento. I still have mine, which I keep in a tin in my bedroom.

On one occasion during my stay I found myself in Gorki Park. I was quietly observing the special spaces set up for chess players to play chess, table tennis players to – you get the idea. Sculptors, too, had their own venue. When I hove into view they pounced and insisted that I sat for them as a model. I don't think it was my indisputable personal pulchritude. It was because I had a beard, which was not the fashion in Russia at that time. What they wanted was the challenge of modelling a full set of whiskers in clay. Maybe even now, somewhere in

Russia, cluttering up an attic in some family home, there's a bust of a bearded man Granddad made when he was in Gorki Park back in . . . Now they'll know it wasn't a representation of a Greek god or a Roman emperor, but of a scruffy English student who happened to be passing.

Fountain in Gorki Park.

GLOSSARY OF RUSSIAN WORDS AND GUIDE TO PRONUNCIATION

Doubtless many of the place-names and other Russian words found in these pages will be unfamiliar. This guide may help you to pronounce them correctly, if you wish.

In England off the north coast of Devon we have Lundy Island, stressed on the first syllable: **Lun**-dy. In Scotland the fine city of Dundee carries its stress on the second: Dun-**dee.** If you went to Scotland and asked the way to Dundee and pronounced it to rhyme with Lundy, you'd attract puzzled expressions. Dundy? Sorry, never heard of it. Then after thinking for a moment they'd say, Oh! You mean Dun**dee**!

The Trans-Siberian Railway starts from Moscow, an anglicised version of its Russian name, Moskva: Musk-**va**: stress on the last syllable. It ends at Vladivostok, where again the stress in Russian is on the end: Vlad-ee-va-**stok**. If you ask a greengrocer for a banana, you say it with the stress on the second syllable, but if you ask the assistant in the menswear department for a Panama hat, you'll stress in on the third. Maybe you've never consciously thought about stressing words on the correct syllable. But you do it automatically in your own language every time you speak.

I won't subject you to any more instruction on this subject.

If you've just read that sentence with the correct stress on the word 'subject' each time, without thinking consciously that you stress it on the second syllable when it's a verb but on the first syllable when it's a noun, then I've proved my point!

Ala: **Ay**-lah

Aleksei: Alex-**yay**

Alyonna: Al-**yon**-na

Angara: An-ga-**ra**

Assambleya Nikitskaya: Ass-am-**blay**-a Nee-**keet**-sky-a

Beryozka: B-yair-**yoz**-ka

bookhler: **boo**-hler

Boris Godunov: Ba-**reece** Gudd-oo-**noff**

Borodino: Ba-ra-deen-**o** (o as in 'top')

Buryat: **Boo**-ree-yat

Cape Khoboi: Hub-**boy**

Cape Shunte: **Shoon**-teh

Chita: Chi-**ta**

Derzhavin: D-yair-**zhar**-veen

Desyatnikovo: Dyess-**yat**-nee-ka-va

Domodedovo: Dom-a-**dyedd**-a-va

Ekaterinburg: Yek-**at**-er-in-burg

Eliantsy: Yell-ee-**ant**-see

Ershov: Yair-**shoff**

Evenki: Yev-**yen**-key

Fyodor: F-**yodd**-er

Gerasimov: Gher-**ass**-ee-moff

Grigory Shelekhov: Grig-**or**-ee **Shell**-ee-koff

Irkutsk: *Ear-**kootsk***

Irtysh: *Ear-**tish***

Ivan: *Ee-**van***

Ivolginsk: *Ee-vol-**gheensk***

Kazan: *Ka-**zan***

Kharantsi: *Ha-**rant**-see*

Khuzhir: *Hoo-**zheer***

Kirov: ***Kee**-roff*

Kolchak: *Kol-**chak***

Krasnaya Ploshchad: ***Krass**-nigh-ya **Plosh**-chad*

Ksenia: *K-**sen**-ya*

Kyrle: ***curl***

Lake Baikal: *Buy-**karl***

Lev: *L-**yeff***

Listvyanka: *Leest-**vyan**-ka*

magazin: *ma-ga-**zeen***

Matvei Gagarin: *Mat-**vyay** Gag-**ar**-in*

Mendeleev: *Myen-dyel-**yea**-yeff*

Mikhail Romanov: *Meekh-a-**eel** Ro-**marn**-off*

Muravyov: *Moo-rav-**yoff***

Nayushki: *Nigh-**yoosh**-kee*

Nikita: *Nick-**ee**-ta*

nosilshchik: *na-**seal**-shcheek*

Novii Urengoi: ***Nov**-ee Oo-ren-**goy***

Novosibirsk: *Nov-a-see-**beersk***

oblast: ***ob**-last*

Olga: ***Oil**-ga*

Olkhon Island: *Oil-**khon***

omul: ***om**-ool*

Perm: *P-**yair**-m*

podstakannik: *pod-stack-**can**-eek*

pozy: ***po**-zee*

provodnik / provodnitsa: *pruv-vud-**neek** / pruv-vud-**neet**-sa*

pyelmyeni: *pyel-**myenn**-ee*

Radonezh: ***Ra**-don-yezh*

Rashid: *Ra-**sheed***

rubashka: *roo-**bash**-ka*

St Innokenty: *In-no-**kent**-ee*

sbityen: ***zbee**-tyen*

Sergiev Posad: ***Syer**-ghee-yeff Po-**sad***

Sibir: *Sibb-**ear***

Slyudyanka: *Sl-yoo-**dyan**-ka*

spasibo: *spass-**ee**-ba*

stupa: ***stoo**-pah*

Tarbagatai: *Tar-bag-a-**tie***

Terelj: *Ter-**elzh***

Tobolsk: *Tub-**oilsk***

Trubetskoy: *Troo-bet-**skoy***

Tsar kolokol: *tsar **ko**-le-kol*

tugrik: ***too**-grik*

Tyumen: ***Chew**-myen*

Ulan Bator: *Oo-**lahn Bar**-ter* ('Ulaan Baatar' in Mongolian)

Ulan Ude: *Oo-**lahn** Oo-**deh***

Ust Ordinsky: *Oost Or-**deen**-skee*

Uzuri: *Oo-**zoo**-ree*

Vladimir: *Vlad-**ee**-mere*

Vladivostok: *Vlad-ee-va-**stok***

Yenesei: *Yen-yes-**yay***

Zhukov: ***Zhoo**-koff*

Znamensky: ***Zna**-myen-skee*

BIOGRAPHICAL NOTES

MARTIN KYRLE and MICHAEL ROBERTS were students in the 1950's. They shared a house with two other young men while Martin was preparing his PGCE (Post-Graduate Certificate in Education) and Mike was doing his Finals.

Born in Portsmouth, MARTIN KYRLE is a graduate of Southampton University (BA (Hons) in History, PGCE and CertHE (Mod Langs)) and the University of Sussex (MA in Russian Studies). Before taking early retirement, he was, for twenty years, a pastoral Head in a large comprehensive school.

In addition to teaching, he pursued a parallel career in politics, entirely unpaid, as a parliamentary candidate in the 1970's and 1980's, having joined the Liberal Party shortly after leaving university. Fifty years ago he moved to Chandler's Ford, which lies midway between Southampton and Winchester but is part of the borough of Eastleigh. There he served on the borough council for twenty years, was Mayor in 1993-4 and in 2015 was elected an Honorary Alderman of the Borough of Eastleigh.

Amongst his hobbies he counts travelling with his eyes open and writing about places of interest, amusing things which happen and chance encounters with interesting people. The result is two collections of anecdotes of his travels, spanning sixty years, sometimes with Mike and at other times with his wife or with other companions, or alone. Intended to be read last thing at night before you go to sleep, *Martin Kyrle's Little Green Nightbook* and *Martin Kyrle's Little Blue Nightbook* are each a series of stories arranged alphabetically, with maps, photographs and cartoons. Both are published by Sarsen Press, Winchester, (200pp, £8.95). Further volumes are in preparation.

Encouraged by an MP friend to commit to paper his reminiscences of what politics, especially local politics, were like when he first got involved more than half a century ago, he has put together two brief memoirs. In the first, entitled *The Liberals in Hampshire – a Part(l)y History. Part 1: Southampton 1958-65: object lessons*, he describes, with a light touch, local politics and personalities and analyses his experiences. A shortened version was entered in the Local History competition at the International Winchester Writers' Conference in June 2013, anonymously in accordance with house rules, and was awarded the accolade of *'Highly Commended'*.

The second volume, entitled *Part 2: Eastleigh 1965-72: out in the suburbs something stirred!* describes how his wife, Margaret, became the first Liberal ever to be elected to Eastleigh Borough Council. She sat for thirty years, became Leader of the Council and served twice as Mayor. In 1991 she was appointed OBE and in 2003 made a Freeman of the Borough of Eastleigh. She also served as a magistrate on the Eastleigh Bench and, after amalgamation, on the Southampton Bench for 29 years. She died in 2011.

The contents page of this present book, with three sample pages of text, were submitted in the *Slim Volume, Small Edition* competition at the Winchester Writers' Conference in 2013 and were awarded Third Prize.

MIKE ROBERTS is a graduate of the universities of Southampton (BA General Arts), Sussex (PGCE) and Birmingham (MEd) and was a secondary school teacher, mainly of History and Geography. Between 1959 and 1972, he worked in Sussex, apart from a two-year appointment at Bourne School in Kuala Lumpur. In 1972 he married his wife, Anne, a graduate of Swansea (BA (Hons) in History). In 1973 he moved to a Deputy Headship in Birmingham, where their three sons, Simon, Gareth and Jonathan, were born.

He was appointed Headmaster of Queens School, Newport in 1982 and in 1989 Consultant (IT) to Gwent County Council. He retired from full-time work in 1993, but then embarked on a ten-year part-time career as an Ofsted School Inspector. He finally retired in 2004.

From 1982 he and Anne lived in Monmouth, while travelling extensively in Europe, North America and Israel. As their son, Simon, had settled in Melbourne, they took the opportunity to make several visits to Australia.

Anne died in 2009. Since then Mike has become interested in photography and has continued to travel to many parts of the world, including the Middle East, Sri Lanka and China and frequent visits to Australia in addition to this Trans-Siberian adventure.

ЗОРЧИГЧИЙН ГАЛТ ТЭРЭГНИЙ ХӨДӨЛГӨӨНИЙ ХУВААРЬ

УЛААНБААТАР-БЭЭЖИН

24-р галт тэрэг		Өртөө	23-р галт тэрэг	
ирэх	явах		ирэх	явах
УЛААНБААТАРЫН ЦАГААР				
	7.15	УЛААНБААТАР	13.20	13.50
	7.27	АМГАЛАН		13.08
	7.37	ТУУЛ		13.00
	7.52	ХОНХОР		12.50
	8.05	БУМБАТ		12.40
	8.19	БАЯН		12.30
	8.30	ХАЙРХАН		12.21
	8.41	ХООЛТ		12.11
	8.51	ЦАГААНХЯР		11.57
	9.00	ЧУЛУУТ		11.42
	9.10	ХАНГАЙ		11.30
	9.20	БАГАХАНГАЙ		11.19
	9.32	МААНЬТ		11.08
	9.54	АГУИТ		10.46
10.16	10.26	НАРАН-ЭЛГЭН		10.24
	10.49	ООРЦОГ-ЭНГЭР		10.04
	11.10	ЛҮН		9.42
11.33	11.53	ЧОЙР	9.04	9.19
	12.11	ШИВЭЭ ОВОО		8.44
	12.21	ШИВЭЭГОВЬ		8.34
	12.35	ӨЛЗИЙТ		8.17
	12.45	ОЛОН-ОВОО		8.04
	12.57	ЦОМОГ		7.53
	13.15	АЙРАГ		7.34
	13.41	АЛТГАНЫ ГОЛ		7.09
	14.13	УЛХЫН ОВОО		6.35
	14.36	АГЬСУМБЭТ		6.11
15.06	15.43	САЙНШАНД	5.21	5.41
	16.12	ТҮШЛЭГ	4.50	4.53
	16.38	ӨРГӨН		4.25
	17.01	ДОЛООДЫН ХӨНДИЙ		3.56
	17.21	УЛААН УУЛ		3.38
	17.41	НОМТ		3.24
	17.52	ЦАГААНХАД		3.12
	18.04	СУМАНГИЙН ЗОО		2.57
	18.15	АВГЫН ГОЛ		2.44
	18.32	НАРТЫН ХОШУУ		2.24
	18.52	ШАРГЫН ӨВОО		2.03
	19.05	ЗАМЫН ҮҮД 2		1.45
19.10	20.35	ЗАМЫН ҮҮД	0.25	1.40
БЭЭЖИНГИЙН ЦАГААР				
21.00	0.57	ЭРЛЯНЬ	20,37	23.59
5.47	5.56	ЦЗИНИННАНЬ	16.03	16.09
7.59	8.11	ДАТУН	14.04	14.16
14.04		БЭЭЖИН		8.05

Route-map and timetable (written in Mongolian) displayed in the carriages of the train from Ulan Bator to Beijing.

Two examples of the amazing nature of the decoration of the stations of the Moscow Metro.